Americanos

Americanos
Latin America's Struggle for Independence
John Charles Chasteen

A Most Holy War
The Albigensian Crusade and the Battle for Christendom
Mark Gregory Pegg

AMERICANOS

Latin America's Struggle
for Independence

John Charles Chasteen

OXFORD
UNIVERSITY PRESS

OXFORD
UNIVERSITY PRESS

Oxford University Press, Inc., publishes works that further
Oxford University's objective of excellence
in research, scholarship, and education.

Oxford   New York
Auckland   Cape Town   Dar es Salaam   Hong Kong   Karachi
Kuala Lumpur   Madrid   Melbourne   Mexico City   Nairobi
New Delhi   Shanghai   Taipei   Toronto

With offices in
Argentina   Austria   Brazil   Chile   Czech Republic   France   Greece
Guatemala   Hungary   Italy   Japan   Poland   Portugal   Singapore
South Korea   Switzerland   Thailand   Turkey   Ukraine   Vietnam

Published by Oxford University Press, Inc.
198 Madison Avenue, New York, NY 10016

www.oup.com

First issued as an Oxford University Press paperback, 2009

Oxford is a registered trademark of Oxford University Press

Chasteen, John Charles, 1955–
Americanos : Latin America's struggle for independence / John Charles Chasteen.
p. cm. — (Pivotal moments in world history)
Includes bibliographical references and index.
ISBN 978-0-19-539236-4 (pbk.)
1. Latin America—History—Autonomy and independence movements.
2. Latin America—History—Wars of Independence, 1806–1830.
3. Latin America—History—1830–1898. I. Title.
F1412.C48 2008
980—dc22
2007028595

Maps by Craig Dalton
Gallery designed by Cherie Westmoreland

Printed in the United States of America
on acid-free paper

To América

CONTENTS

Maps may be found on pages 7, 69, 70, 111, 112, 161

DRAMATIS PERSONAE

IN ALPHABETICAL ORDER

LUCAS ALAMÁN, b. 1792—Mexican statesman and historian, Guerrero's
  nemesis

IGNACIO ALLENDE, b. 1769—Hidalgo's second in command

CARLOS DE ALVEAR, b. 1789—an aristocrat of Buenos Aires

JOSÉ BONIFÁCIO DE ANDRADA, b. 1763—a Brazilian founding father;
  brothers are Antônio Carlos and Martim Francisco

JOSÉ ARTIGAS, b. 1764—federalist leader who challenged Buenos Aires

JUANA AZURDUY, b. 1781—leader of patriot guerrillas in Upper Peru

MANUEL BELGRANO, b. 1770—Buenos Aires revolutionary, defeated in
  Upper Peru

ANDRÉS BELLO, b. 1781—Caracas-born man of letters, long resident in
  London

WILLIAM BERESFORD, b. 1768—British officer who fought in Buenos
  Aires and Portugal

SIMÓN BOLÍVAR, b. 1783—the liberator of five countries

TOMÁS BOVES, b. 1782—Spanish leader of llanero lancers, defeated
  Bolívar

FÉLIX MARÍA CALLEJA, b. 1753—nemesis of Hidalgo and Morelos,
  eventually viceroy

CARLOS IV, b. 1748—king of Spain, abdicated in favor of son, Fernando VII

CARLOTA JOAQUINA, b. 1775—Fernando's sister, married to João VI of
  Portugal

JAVIERA CARRERA, b. 1771—woman of a leading Chilean patriot family

JOSÉ MIGUEL CARRERA, b. 1785—Javiera's brother, rival of Bernardo O'Higgins

JUAN JOSÉ CASTELLI, b. 1764—Buenos Aires revolutionary, defeated in Upper Peru

THOMAS ALEXANDER COCHRANE, b. 1775—admiral of the Chilean and Brazilian navies

FERNANDO VII, b. 1784—king of Spain, the "Desired One" during his captivity

GASPAR RODRÍGUEZ DE FRANCIA, b. 1766—dictator who made Paraguay independent

MANUEL GODOY, b. 1767—despised lover of the Spanish queen

VICENTE GUERRERO, b. 1783—third major leader of rebellion in New Spain

MIGUEL HIDALGO, b. 1753—radical priest who began rebellion in New Spain

ALEXANDER VON HUMBOLDT, b. 1769—Prussian scientist, explorer, and expert

AGUSTÍN DE ITURBIDE, b. 1783—americano officer acclaimed Agustín I of Mexico

JOÃO VI, b. 1769—prince regent, later king, of Portugal; fled to Rio de Janeiro

ANTONIO DE LARRAZÁBAL, b. 1769—Guatemalan leader in the Cortes of Cádiz

IGNACIO LÓPEZ RAYÓN, b. 1773—organizer of the Zitácuaro junta

SANTIAGO MARIÑO, b. 1788—Venezuela's "Liberator of the East"

JUAN MARTÍNEZ DE ROZAS, b. 1759—Chilean patriot leader, patron of Bernardo O'Higgins

SERVANDO TERESA DE MIER, b. 1765—dissident intellectual priest of New Spain

FRANCISCO DE MIRANDA, b. 1750—precursor of the cause of América

BERNARDO MONTEAGUDO, b. 1785—Chuquisaca intellectual, collaborator of San Martín

JUAN DOMINGO MONTEVERDE, b. 1772—Spanish general who defeated Miranda

CARLOS MONTÚFAR, b. 1780—companion of Humboldt, son of Juan Pío

JUAN PÍO MONTÚFAR, b. 1759—head of 1809 Quito junta

JOSÉ MARÍA MORELOS, b. 1765—second major leader of rebellion in New Spain

MARIANO MORENO, b. 1778—secretary of first Buenos Aires junta

Pablo Morillo, b. 1778—Spanish general who led reconquest of New Granada

Antonio Nariño, b. 1765—conspirator, then patriot leader of New Granada

Bernardo O'Higgins, b. 1778—liberator of Chile, collaborator of San Martín

Manuel Ascencio Padilla, b. 1775—patriot leader of Upper Peru

José Antonio Páez, b. 1790—Bolívar's *llanero* ally and later his rival

Pedro I, b. 1798—son of João VI and Carlota Joaquina, declared Brazilian independence

Manuel Carlos Piar, b. 1774—pardo general executed by Bolívar

Home Popham, b. 1762—British admiral who attacked Buenos Aires in 1806

Mateo Pumacahua, b. 1740—Indian leader of 1814 Cuzco rebellion

Andrés Quintana Roo, b. 1787—patriot intellectual of New Spain

Bernardino Rivadavia, b. 1780—liberal president of independent Buenos Aires

Simón Rodríguez (aka Samuel Robinson), b. 1771—revolutionary educator

Manuela Sáenz, b. 1797—patriot of Quito, collaborator of Bolívar

Mariquita Sánchez, b. 1786—Buenos Aires revolutionary (later Madame Mendeville)

Francisco de Paula Santander, b. 1792—Bolívar's rival in New Granada

Antonio López de Santa Anna, b. 1794—young *caudillo*, helped topple Agustín I

José de San Martín, b. 1778—liberator who bowed out at Guayaquil

Antonio José de Sucre, b. 1795—Bolívar's right-hand man in the 1820s

Leona Vicario, b. 1789—organizer in Mexico City's patriot underground

Duke of Wellington, b. 1769—Napoleon's British nemesis in Spain

VICEROYS

IN ORDER OF APPEARANCE

New Spain	Peru	Río de la Plata	New Granada
Iturrigaray, 1803–8	Abascal, 1806–16	Sobremonte, 1804–7	Amar y Borbón, 1803–10
Venegas, 1810–13	Pezuela, 1816–21	Liniers, 1807–9	Montalvo, 1816–18
Calleja, 1813–16	La Serna, 1821–24	Cisneros, 1809–10	Sámano, 1818–19
Apodaca, 1816–21		Elío, 1810–11	
O'Donojú, 1821			

GALLERY

OF THE PRINCIPAL DRAMATIS PERSONAE

ARTIGAS

ALAMÁN

AZURDUY

ANDRADA   ALVEAR

BELGRANO   CARLOTA

BOLÍVAR

CALLEJA CASTELLI

FERNANDO VII FRANCIA

JOÃO VI GÜEMES GUERRERO

ITURBIDE HIDALGO HUMBOLDT LARRAZÁBAL

LÓPEZ R

NAPOLEON

L'OVERTURE

O'HIGGINS

MEJÍA

MORELOS

PÁEZ

MIRANDA

MORENO

NARIÑO

PEDRO I

PIAR   RODRÍGUEZ   SÁNCHEZ

SALAVARRIETA   SANTA ANNA

SÁENZ

SANTANDER   SUCRE

SAN MARTÍN   WELLINGTON   VICARIO

CHRONOLOGY

1799 Humboldt begins his travels in América
1806 Renegade invasions at Buenos Aires and Coro
1807 Napoleon's troops enter Iberian Peninsula
    Portuguese crown flees Lisbon for Brazil
1808 Spanish crown falls into Napoleon's hands
    Crisis of the Spanish monarchy begins; *juntas* form in Spain
    Cabildo abierto in Mexico City, Iturrigaray deposed
1809 Central Junta coordinates Spanish resistance to Napoleon
    Napoleon completes conquest of Spain except for Cádiz
    Who should rule in América? Debate proliferates
    Small rebellions in the Andes: Chuquisaca, La Paz, Quito
1810 Cortes and Regency established in Cádiz
    Juntas formed in Caracas, Buenos Aires, Bogotá, and Santiago
    First army sent by Buenos Aires to Upper Peru
    Hidalgo's multitude sweeps through New Spain
1811 Miranda declares an independent republic in Venezuela
    Civil war begins in Venezuela, New Granada, and Chile
    Hidalgo captured and executed; Morelos takes over
    Forces of Buenos Aires defeated in Paraguay, Upper Peru
    Peru becomes base for Spanish reconquest of Andes
    British and Portuguese forces retake Portugal from Napoleon
1812 Napoleon's grip on Spain loosens as well
    The Cortes of Cádiz promulgates a liberal constitution

The first Venezuelan republic collapses
Morelos survives Cuautla, captures Oaxaca
1813 Bolívar declares "War to the Death"
Buenos Aires again defeated in Upper Peru
Morelos loses momentum besieging Acapulco
1814 Fernando VII restored, annuls 1812 constitution, dissolves *cortes*
Spanish forces from Peru reconquer Chile
Defeated by Boves, Bolívar leaves for exile
1815 Major reconquest force arrives from post-Napoleonic Spain
Artigas confederation united against Buenos Aires
João VI's United Kingdom makes Brazil equal to Portugal
Morelos captured and executed
1816 Spanish reconquest of América complete, except for Río de la Plata
1817 San Martín crosses the Andes from Mendoza to Chile
Bolívar's comeback begins in Venezuela
Pernambucan rebellion reveals "liberal contagion" in Brazil
1818 Guerrero renews the spirit of rebellion in New Spain
San Martín prepares his assault on Lima
1819 Bolívar wins at Boyacá Bridge, controls New Granada
1820 Constitutionalist revolutions in Spain and Portugal
Major Spanish reconquest expedition aborted
San Martin's seaborne invasion of Peru begins
1821 Cortes of Lisbon forces João VI's return to Portugal
Iturbide and Guerrero join under the Plan de Iguala, enter Mexico City
Central America joins the Plan de Iguala, declares independence
Bolívar wins at Carabobo, while San Martín bogs down in Peru
1822 Prince Pedro declares Brazil independent, crowned emperor
Iturbide acclaimed emperor Agustín I of independent Mexico
Bolívar and San Martín meet in Guayaquil
1823 Absolutist counterrevolutions seize both Spain and Portugal
Agustín I overthrown, Mexico becomes a republic
Bolívar's Peruvian campaign begins
1824 Pedro I consolidates power in the Brazilian Empire
Battle of Ayacucho, final Spanish defeat in América

Americanos

PROLOGUE: WHY AMERICANOS?

Long live the Sovereign People!
Our time has come at last . . .

—*"Canción americana,"* 1797

WHY *AMERICANOS*, WITHOUT capitalization? Why *América*—as will be written here—with an accent mark? Americanos are, after all, simply the people of América. *América* is the same word in Spanish or Portuguese and English, one could say. And yet it isn't. For Latin Americans, América has never been synonymous with the United States, nor are americanos simply Americans, and the distinction becomes important in the story told here. Therefore, in this book, *América* will be used to mean what we today call, in English, Latin America, including all the lands colonized by Spain and Portugal. The americanos in these pages are speakers of Spanish or Portuguese, not English.

América and *americanos* were key terms in Latin America's independence struggles. Until 1807–8, when Napoleonic invasions of Portugal and Spain unleashed a crisis in América, *americano* was a term generally denoting whites only. But by the time the dust settled in

1825, years of bloodshed had transformed the meaning of *americano*, stretching the term around people of indigenous and African and mixed descent, the large majority of the population. The transformation had happened as patriot generals, poets, and orators described their struggle as "the cause of América" and called all americanos to join it. The lyrics of the "Canción americana" of 1797, anthem of a revolutionary conspiracy in Venezuela, exemplify the new meaning at an early date: "Our homeland calls, americanos, / Together we'll destroy the tyrant."[1]

The patriot language of América only exceptionally applied the terms of identity—*mexicano, venezolano, colombiano, chileno, brasileiro, guatemalteco, peruano*, and so on—associated with today's Latin American nations. From modern Mexico to Argentina and Chile, the patriots of Latin America's struggle for independence constructed a binary divide separating all americanos, on one hand, from *europeos* (Europeans, meaning European-born Spaniards), on the other. This might seem unremarkable at first. After all, what more obvious separation than the one created by the Atlantic Ocean? Had not the United States already established an analogous American identity?

To the contrary, the semantic evolution of the word *americano* marks a pivotal moment in world history, something no less momentous than had occurred in the English colonies of America decades earlier. The most obvious social distinctions in colonial América did not divide americanos from europeos at all. The colonization of América had created starkly hierarchical societies organized by a caste system. Indians, free people of African descent, and various mixed-race castes differed far more from the white americano ruling class than did americanos from europeos. To summarize the process that we are about to trace in detail, the overwhelmingly white patriot leadership embraced the new, broader meaning of *americano* because that maximized their chance of victory against the mother country. If everyone born in América—everyone in the strongly variegated population that had arisen from the mingling of individuals from three continents—was an americano, and if all were on the same side, the tiny minority of European-born Spaniards (less than 1 percent of the population) did not stand a chance of maintaining colonial rule. To define América's rainbow of castes as the americano people recognized the truth on the ground, but it also created a new truth, an airy but potent abstraction. That abstraction was the Sovereign People, who deserved nothing less than a government "of, by, and for the People." And, unlike what had occurred with the independence of the United States in the 1780s, the

Sovereign People of América who emerged in the 1820s included a nonwhite majority.

The more or less simultaneous creation of a dozen independent nations in América was therefore momentous in a manner that U.S. independence was not. Both signaled important future directions in world decolonization. U.S. independence certainly modeled the creation of a new republic in what had been a European colony, and it inspired a number of influential americano patriots. But one event does not constitute a trend, and people of non-European descent were largely excluded from the U.S. republican model. The creation of the United States of America embodied basic claims of self-determination only for people of purely European descent. In contrast, the mass production of aspiring nation-states in América, in the following generation, *did* constitute a trend and clearly established a template for future decolonization.

The americanos followed the U.S. example, embodying popular sovereignty in a written constitution produced by a nationally elected constituent assembly. But the new template departed from the U.S. example by formally including large populations of indigenous, African, and mixed descent as citizens in that process. (Haiti, it must be recognized, had really pioneered this innovation, but it started no trends, being an example much more feared than imitated by upper-class political leaders in América.) The americano version was imperfect, to say the least. Citizenship for everyone remained more theoretical than real for many decades. Nonetheless, the independence of América meant that the Western Hemisphere belonged to republics. So claimed the U.S. Monroe Doctrine in 1823, and over the course of the nineteenth century americanos made that vision a reality. By the time that European colonies in Africa and Asia gave way after World War II, the successful decolonization of Latin America had become an established, if still conflictive, fact of global history. Americano success ensured the currency of the constitutional, republican template in the new African and Asian nations that proliferated in the second half of the twentieth century. The general dissemination of the model had its limits, obviously. Still, it constituted a truly global triumph of the ideas that U.S. parlance these days often calls "Western" political values, ideas that the rest of the world tends to call liberalism.

In fact, the word *liberal* was coined in Spain during the fight against Napoleon, to describe Spanish patriots whose banner was liberty. Liberals were, in their own terms, enemies of servitude. They stood for constitutional government with the guarantee of civil liberties and for a free market of both goods and ideas, which no official truth, no one group or interest or opinion, should ever dominate totally. The starting point of their political thinking—provoked, as we shall see, by the shocking eclipse of the Spanish crown—was popular sovereignty.

In order to theorize popular sovereignty, it was necessary to define the Sovereign People, which meant defining the nation. And the new nations of América were defined from the outset to include people of indigenous, African, and mixed descent. This process of national self-definition involved some tactical denial and self-delusion, and yet it was, if anything, an even more significant americano contribution to world history than the dissemination of liberal republicanism. Benedict Anderson's influential book *Imagined Communities: Reflections on the Origin and Spread of Nationalism* emphasizes the role in that global process of "Creole pioneers"—by which he means the very people whom I call (and who called themselves) americanos. Anderson gives far too little importance to the wars of independence as formative experiences in América, but he has helped a generation of scholars see Latin American independence as a pivotal moment in the global development of nationalism.

Americanos is not the term used, most commonly, by histories of Latin American independence written in English. Instead, they call American-born whites "Creoles"—a translation of the Spanish word *criollo* (hence Anderson's "Creole pioneers" of world nationalism). *Americanos* is a better term because it clarifies the crucial extension of the definition of Sovereign People from whites only to anyone born in América.

Historians of Latin America view the significance of 1808–1825 in widely divergent ways. Patriotic history (*historia patria*) in each country has provided mythic narratives of exemplary heroes and foundational acts, narratives of the sort that configure national identities around the world. Artigas, Andrada, Belgrano, Bolívar, Guerrero, Hidalgo, Miranda, Morelos, O'Higgins, Páez, Pedro I, San Martín, Sucre, and Santander—a sampling of americano leaders—are the protagonists of historia patria. They are the names of cities, parks, states, and avenues, unquestionably names to know for anyone who wants to understand the independence of América. But in the patriotic imagination, these heroes are also great men or women whose superior intelligence, virtue, and bravery are held up for inspiration and imitation. That is not the approach taken here. For me, these heroes are inspiring not because they were perfect but because they weren't.

Current historiography on Latin America asks above all what impact independence had on the colonial hierarchies, particularly on the relationship between the ruling white minority and the subjugated majority of African and indigenous descent. Because colonial hierarchies eroded only slowly in independent América, academic historians have tended to stress the disappointing outcomes of independence. Republics, after all, were supposed to be societies in which the Sovereign People consisted of equal citizens. Slavery and peonage were fundamentally incompatible with republicanism, although the incompatibility could be finessed for decades, as in the United States. The main patriot movements had committed themselves rhetorically to ending the caste stratification so prevalent in América. But rhetorical commitments do not always hold, and after independence republican ideals were sorely tested.

These independence struggles produced unified nations where the rule of law prevailed unerringly, where all enjoyed equal citizenship, where republican governments represented general interests, only in theory. In fact, "Western" political values have had a troubled history in Latin America (as in the rest of the world, including Europe) because they conflicted with deeply held values and habits that preceded them. Indeed, Western political values have been both powerfully championed and stubbornly resisted in América. By demanding their right to self-determination, americanos defined the direction of world history two hundred years ago, but their bids for effective citizenship were usually defeated before the twentieth century. That part of the story is best left for the epilogue.

This book is different from straight patriotic and scholarly tellings of Latin American independence. The purpose here is to weave together patriotic names to know with a balanced assessment of events in a unified narrative covering the whole region colonized by Spain and Portugal. Portuguese América (Brazil) plays a less important part than does Spanish América, which was a more populous place and one in which the process of independence was more complex, producing a score of modern countries. Yet the same general forces were at work everywhere in América. Let us begin with the following ironic and infrequently made point. Overall, americanos were loyal to their king and not especially eager to embrace revolutionary ideas emanating from the United States and France when, in 1799, one of the most remarkable travelers in history landed on their shores. That traveler, a Prussian named Alexander von Humboldt, an outsider of insatiable curiosity, can be our tour guide in late colonial América.

One

DISCOVERING AMÉRICA

1799–1805

In 1799, travel accounts were the basic source of information about América for readers in Europe and the fledgling United States. In that year, Alexander von Humboldt, surely the most influential traveler ever to visit América, began his famous journey through territories that remained little known to the outside world. Humboldt never used the name Latin America, because it did not yet exist and would not, in fact, during the entire period covered by this book. Within a very few years after Humboldt's visit, América would give birth to a dozen new nations in a painful labor. But none of that was evident in 1799.

Humboldt and Bonpland Discover América

Alexander von Humboldt—would-be explorer, all-purpose scientist, guy who liked guys—was twenty-nine years old when he first set foot in the New World in July 1799. You have to love the young Humboldt: the odd boy who liked bugs too much to be a bureaucrat, as his mother wished; the twenty-year-old who went to Paris for the delirious first anniversary of the French Revolution and worked for a few days as a volunteer helping construct the city's Temple of Liberty for the celebration. Imagine him as the dedicated graduate student of geology and botany who wanted above all to explore the world outside of Europe.

Consider him the cocky Berliner whose excellent Spanish convinced the king of Spain to let him into América when few outsiders were allowed to visit there.

Or you may prefer not to like Humboldt, who, after all, reeked of privilege. He was the sort of kid whose family had a castle, the sort who could afford to bankroll his own five-year scientific expedition. This lanky young German whose democratic principles failed to banish his air of superiority was too good-looking by half. And Humboldt was quite definitely a know-it-all. He represents both the bright and dark sides of the European intellectual and scientific quickening called the Enlightenment. The pure, raw joy of comprehending the universe

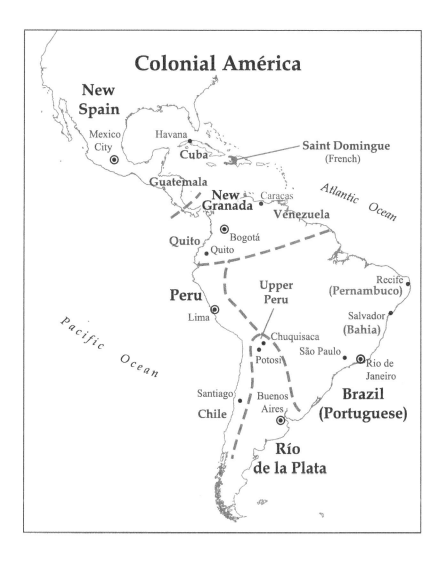

pulsed palpably in the young Humboldt. Darwin said Humboldt's *Personal Narrative* (the journal of the trip that took him to Venezuela and Cuba, the Andes, and Mexico) was his great inspiration. But Humboldt also exemplified the Enlightenment's will to mastery. To "discover" the world was to access it. Classification, one of the Enlightenment's intellectual passions and one of Humboldt's, was a technology of control. Not by accident was Humboldt one of the most famous men in Europe during the great age of European global colonization.

Humboldt received permission from Carlos IV to travel collecting specimens of plants, animals, and minerals, measuring winds and currents, altitudes and latitudes. He would pursue all elements of natural history, a name for the integrated study of the changing earth, most especially the interactive relationship between living things and their environment. Because a French scientist who visited South America in 1735 had heard rumors of a channel connecting the Amazon and Orinoco river systems, Humboldt would canoe for more than a thousand miles through the rain forest searching for the connection. And he would repeatedly satisfy his penchant to climb up any volcano he found and then descend into its crater to investigate choking ash, gurgling lava, and invisible plumes of deadly gases firsthand.

Humboldt and his colleague Aimé de Bonpland were originally headed for Cuba. But typhoid fever broke out aboard their ship off the coast of Venezuela, and Humboldt and Bonpland decided to land at the first opportunity. That opportunity was an ancient and somewhat forgotten Caribbean port called Cumaná, the oldest Spanish settlement on the South American continent—at that time partly in ruins because of a recent earthquake. Fortunately, the Spanish governor of Cumaná was a Francophile intellectual who actively applauded Humboldt and Bonpland and seemed eager to facilitate their explorations in all ways. The earth around Cumaná was alive as only the tropical earth can be, "powerful, exuberant, serene," Humboldt wrote his brother in a deliriously happy letter.[1] Life aboard ship had suited him, he reported, and he had spent much of the time on deck taking astronomical readings and hauling up samples of seawater for analysis. Not mentioning any typhoid fever on his voyage for fear of alarming his brother, the ecstatic twenty-nine-year-old instead raved about tigers, parrots, monkeys, armadillos, birds, and fish in spectacular colors, coconut palms, and "semi-savage Indians, a beautiful and interesting race."[2] The weather in this tropical paradise seemed to suit him, too. Setting foot in the tropics excited Humboldt and Bonpland to the point that they could not carry on a coherent conversation for several days, so rapidly did each marvel supersede the last. Venezuela was rife with species unknown to Western science. And for a few coins, one could rent a house with servants for a whole month. Nearby Caracas, Humboldt assured his brother, had one of the healthiest climates in América. So he was changing his plan. He and Bonpland would spend some months in Venezuela before proceeding to Cuba. The rumored approach of British warships made that plan doubly prudent, because Spain and Britain were at war.

Meanwhile, a daily slave market outside the window of his new house spoiled Humboldt's visions of paradise. Humboldt and Bonpland found the view heart-rending and "odious." Humboldt despised slavery, and he wrote in fury to his brother about seeing buyers force people's "mouths open as we do with horses in the market."[3] The two men would see many, many slaves on the shores of the Caribbean. Only one spot was free of slavery: France's former sugar colony Saint-Domingue, modern Haiti, where the spirit of the French Revolution had helped a slave rebellion become a revolution that destroyed slavery utterly and wiped out the white master class along with it. Cuba, Humboldt's next planned destination, was Spain's great experiment in slave-driven plantation agriculture. And slavery was only one of many social injustices that European colonization had brought in its train.

Yet Humboldt later wrote that during the 1799–1805 trip that made his reputation, he did not anticipate the tempestuous movements for independence that began shortly after his return to Europe. Why not? The British colonies of North America had recently won their independence from Britain. Haiti had won independence from France. Neither Spanish America nor Brazil was strongly garrisoned by European forces. Add to that the resentments of colonial merchants limited by the Spanish monopoly trading system. Factor in the frustration of American-born Spaniards because of the colonial government's constant favoritism toward the European-born. Apply the anger and humiliation of the downtrodden black and brown people who constituted three-quarters of the population, occupying all the lower rungs on the colonial caste system in Spain's América. With all that, a pervasive desire for decolonization might seem a foregone conclusion. Humboldt saw no great love for Spain, and he found a few people who seemed surprisingly proud of being called americanos. But how ripe for revolution was América, really?

In 1800, América as a whole showed few revolutionary inclinations. Humboldt traversed América's major population centers (including three of its four viceregal capitals, Lima, Bogotá, and Mexico City), its

Amazonian lowlands, the Caribbean basin, the Andean highlands, and much of Spain's most important colony, New Spain. Here is the situation he encountered. European-born Spaniards, called *españoles europeos* (*europeos* for short), were less than 1 percent of the population of América. On the other hand, American-born Spaniards, *españoles americanos* (*americanos* for short) accounted for roughly a quarter of the population. Europeos acted far superior to their americano cousins. In addition, the royal government and the church preferred europeos over americanos for employment and office holding—an old and angry grievance of the americanos. Moreover, the richest and best-connected merchants—virtually all those who carried on transatlantic commerce—were invariably europeos. Jealous americanos regarded prosperous europeos as heartless money-grubbers and condescending, would-be aristocrats. Resentment of europeos found voice in unflattering epithets, most notably the names *chapetón* and *gachupín*. Both europeos and americanos felt superior to, and lived by subjugating, the roughly three-quarters of the population whose descent was at least partly African or indigenous American. However much arrogant europeos got on their nerves, americanos anxiously affirmed their shared Spanishness in contrast to the Africans, Indians, and mixed-bloods who occupied the lower rungs of the caste hierarchy. The majority of the population lived in the great frontiers and hinterlands of América, along tropical rivers, in rain forest clearings, on Andean slopes, outside any effective government control, preoccupied with farming or fishing and supplying their own needs in whatever way possible. América's sprawling frontiers could easily provide subsistence for many times the region's population. Only in rare cases was hunger a motive for rebellion.

The 1780s had seen tax rebellions in several parts of América, but only one of them, the Tupac Amaru rebellion of Peru and Upper Peru (today Bolivia), was really threatening. These rebellions generally expressed localized grievances and demanded limited reforms. Their rallying cry was usually something like "Long live the king and death to bad government!" Often they were responses to royal policies that limited economic activities in the colonies. These policies had not gone away. True, some exceptions had been made to the official Spanish trade monopoly, whereby Spanish merchants normally had exclusive rights to buy and sell in the seaports of América, but it had not been abolished. One way or another, however, the moment of colonial rebelliousness had passed by 1800, when Humboldt observed that most people, including (white) americanos, Indians, mixed-bloods, and blacks, expressed overwhelmingly loyalty to the Spanish crown. To a young man imbued with the spirit of revolutionary transformation, the people of América seemed, overall, rather apathetic.

More than internal discontent an external clash between European empires was causing colonial disruption in 1800. Spain and Britain had been often at war in the eighteenth century. Colonial militias had been formed to defend América against British intrusions on land, but the British navy ruled the waves. Colonial goods piled up on the docks and passengers found no passage, as all communications were paralyzed by British warships operating from island bases in the Caribbean. Trinidad, a formerly Spanish island, had become the most recent of these. When Humboldt and Bonpland finally emerged from the rain forest to take ship for Cuba, they found that Spanish ships dared not sail along the Venezuelan coast. Humboldt and Bonpland had to wait four months in Venezuela for a smuggling skiff that served the pent-up Venezuelan demand for British goods by shuttling between Trinidad and the mainland. And no sooner had they put to sea than marauding Nova Scotia privateers (pirates working as military contractors, so to speak, for Britain) swooped down on them. Humboldt and Bonpland found themselves deposited aboard a British naval sloop. Fortunately, the British captain, who had read about their scientific expedition, politely delivered them back to Venezuela, where they continued to wait in vain for a Spanish ship to take them to Cuba. Finally, they had to take passage on a neutral U.S. cargo vessel carrying tons of foul-smelling beef jerky.

Consider a Continent of Frontiers

Beef jerky is made by piling salt-slathered meat in the sun. The salt and heat suck the moisture out of the rapidly decomposing flesh, halting the process before it is too far advanced. Jerky was a product of cattle frontiers all over América. In the era before refrigeration, jerking beef was the only way of more or less preserving it for shipment overseas. High in protein, rich in flavor, jerked beef was principally a ration for sailors and, above all, slaves—the reason that Humboldt's boat full of jerky was bound for Cuba. The shipment that made Humboldt and Bonpland hold their noses may have originated on the Orinoco cattle frontier of Venezuela or much farther south.

Aside from a fringe of coastal settlements, most of South America remained a frontier in 1800. In fact, the population of the whole continent at the time would probably fit into a metropolis such as São Paulo, Buenos Aires, or Mexico City today. Humboldt and Bonpland had a special interest in América's vast frontiers, where they hoped to discover species new to European science. In November 1800, though, the two intrepid explorers were headed to relatively tame and well-known Cuba, so we will visit another frontier without them. Across the continent, on the grassy plains of América's south Atlantic coast, a Spanish officer named Félix de Azara was thinking about the Río de la Plata frontier, land of the fabled cowboys called gauchos.

The Río de la Plata frontier was an endless, mostly treeless plain where hundreds of thousands of half-wild horses and cattle roamed free. This frontier was home to highly mobile indigenous people, comparable to the Apache or Sioux, who had learned to ride and hunted the feral cattle instead of bison. To colonizers such as Azara, this frontier was a resource to be secured for Spain. Though much older than Humboldt and no democrat, Azara resembled the Prussian in his habit of constantly observing, analyzing, and taking notes. He was about to write a famous report to the Spanish crown. Azara, his report, and his assistant, José Artigas, illustrate something about the coming wars of independence. On the eve of those wars, revolt was the last thing on people's minds in América as a whole. When events in Europe involved americanos in international conflict against the French or against the British, they reacted as loyal subjects of their king.

Félix de Azara had first come to América as part of the Spanish team sent to survey and mark a border between Spanish and Portuguese claims. The Río de la Plata frontier was the one part of América where Spanish and Portuguese claims clashed substantially, though, and when negotiations collapsed, Azara stayed to advance the royal project in a different way—by populating the frontier with loyal, armed Spanish subjects. To secure the frontier against the Portuguese, Azara advised the Spanish government to found a string of towns and distribute land for free in ranch-size portions to men who agreed to occupy the ranch with their families, maintain a shotgun, and serve in the militia. The Portuguese had used that model very successfully. Azara recommended that Portuguese settlers willing to live under Spanish rule should be encouraged to set a good example for the Spanish settlers.

The Spanish-speaking population of the Río de la Plata frontier did not impress Azara. Possibly half passed as españoles americanos, he reckoned, but many actually had some Indian ancestry. The others included *pardos* (people of mixed European and African descent), Guaraní Indians from the nearby Jesuit missions, and a few African slaves.

The americanos did not hesitate to work alongside pardos, Guaraní, or even slaves, so long as that work was done on horseback. Few in the Plata countryside owned land, but everyone had horses. Azara made fun of the frontiersmen's dress, including a Guaraní loincloth called a *chiripá*, worn by whites, pardos, and slaves because it was ideal for riding horseback. Grown to manhood on the violent frontier, lamented Azara, these gauchos killed each other "as calmly as one cuts the throat of a cow."[4]

Azara wrote in great disgust that the herds of the Plata frontier had been decimated during the 1700s by the thoughtlessness of Spanish cattle hunters who launched their expeditions in the spring, when many calves died needlessly in the confusion. The Charrúa Indians—who, unlike the Guaraní, had not accepted Christianity–competed for cattle, of course. Cattle were their subsistence. But the Spanish cattle hunters took cattle by the tens and hundreds of thousands, not for subsistence but for their hides, the only part of them that could be profitably exported to Europe. The carcasses of these animals, roughly eight hundred thousand a year in the previous twenty years, were almost all left to rot on the plains. Azara estimated that properly managed herds would grow to almost ninety million cattle in three decades and produce enough beef jerky for all the slaves in Cuba.

Azara was fortunate to have as his assistant a local military officer who knew the Río de la Plata frontier and its people intimately, maybe even a little too intimately for Azara's taste. Captain José Artigas was the sort who went by a nickname, Pepe, and in the presence of gaucho frontiersmen acted very much like them. The europeo Azara was not particularly good at dealing with gauchos, but the americano Artigas had no equal at it, making him helpful indeed. Artigas came from a family well established on the frontier. Both his father and his grandfather had captained the mounted militia of the frontier charged with protecting ranchers and cattle hunters from heathen Indians such as the Charrúa. Artigas had left home to try his luck on the plains at the age of fourteen. He became one of those americanos who joined cattle-hunting expeditions and mingled with gauchos, to Azara's distress. He stayed out on the grasslands for many months at a time, roaming throughout the upper Río de la Plata plains. His home base during this period was an old mission settlement called Soriano, full of Indians and mixed blood mestizos such as plucky Isabel Velásquez, who bore Artigas four children. Pepe and Isabel had not been able to marry, presuming that his family would have allowed it, because she already had a husband in prison.

Young Artigas had been accused of driving contraband herds of two thousand cattle between the Spanish and Portuguese settlements. He was on good terms with both the Portuguese and the Charrúa Indians and had an enthusiastic following among the multihued Spanish-speaking gaucho riffraff of the countryside. In 1795, the governor of Montevideo, Spain's fortified port city on the edge of the Río de la Plata frontier, issued a warrant for the arrest of the accused contraband herdsman. However, the Buenos Aires viceroy, who was the foremost Spanish authority in the Río de la Plata, soon offered Artigas an amnesty and recruited him to head a new mounted police force. Over-night, to the delight of his family, the budding renegade underwent an extreme transformation and became a militia captain like his father and grandfather. Artigas was expected to focus on contraband and on the Charrúa, two subjects that he had evidently mastered. But Artigas proved notably ineffective at killing Charrúas. Other commanders excelled at surprising Charrúa encampments and slaughtering men, women, and children, while Artigas seemed unable or unwilling to attack his former companions.

One day José Artigas would make war on Spain and become the father of his country, the republic of Uruguay. But in 1801 he was a loyal—if "Indian-loving" and, until lately, not particularly well-behaved—military officer of Carlos IV, the king of Spain.

Humboldt's Adventure Continues

Humboldt spent only two months in Cuba. Its position astride major sea routes had made Cuba well known, and it was not a land of uncharted terrain and undiscovered creatures to be classified by genus and spe-cies, as were parts of the Amazon basin. A perpetual target for English raids, Cuba had become, in Humboldt's day, the great economic suc-cess story of América. So Humboldt did no exploring and instead made the collection of statistics on demography, agriculture, trade, and gov-ernment finance his main activity during his two-month stay in Cuba. The primary object of his attention was chattel slavery.

After returning to Europe, he would use the materials he collected to argue that slavery was uneconomical as well as obviously immoral. People in the future, he predicted correctly, would have trouble believ-ing that the routine inhumanity of slavery as then practiced in Havana (or Washington, D.C., or Rio de Janeiro) was once accepted as normal. "Slavery is without doubt the greatest of all evils to have plagued mankind," he wrote in what proved to be one of the most quoted passages of his voluminous travel account.[5] Humboldt's argument was superbly informed. He recorded how the indigenous people of Cuba had been entirely destroyed by the late 1500s, how the island remained a sparsely populated hide-producing frontier zone in the 1600s. Not until the British occupied Havana in 1762, opening the door for British slave traders, did the Cuban economy begin to take off. The spreading cane fields of the 1780s and 1790s made western Cuba an agricultural dynamo. By the time Humboldt and Bonpland arrived, thousands of chained Africans passed through the Havana customs house yearly, with a steady upward trend, and the number for the whole island, including contraband slaves, was much higher. Cuban slave owners imported tons of jerked beef, and many Havana streets stank of it. Slave imports and sugar exports generated millions of dollars annually in tax revenues, and free-spending Havana sugar planters were becoming conspicuous in French, Spanish, and Italian cities.

Fortunately for Spain, Cuba's slave-driven economy made Cuban plantation owners extremely conservative and, in the light of events in nearby Haiti, particularly reluctant to condone rebellious behavior. For that reason—and also because Cuba was fantastically profitable, powerfully garrisoned, and absolutely central to Spanish military strategy in América—Spain's "Ever Faithful Isle," as Cuba came to be called, did not participate in the revolutionary events about to unfold on the mainland.

Their curiosity satisfied, Humboldt and Bonpland returned to the South American mainland at Cartagena and, during June and July 1801, ascended the powerful Magadalena River in what is today Colombia. Their goal was to explore a different face of América, the Andean highlands. Like the highlands of New Spain (modern Mexico) and Guatemala, the lofty plateaus of the Andes mountains had supported relatively dense populations of village-dwelling indigenous farmers for thousands of years before the European invasion. These were not frontiers, but rather the opposite: the core areas of Spanish colonization in América.

Before steam navigation, ascending the Magdalena River was a grueling process. Teams of boatmen, almost always men of African descent, pushed the craft upstream against the strong current using long poles, keeping to the shallows along the bank where the current ran less swiftly (but the tropical sun beat down just as hard). To reach Bogotá from the coast took six weeks on the river and then another three weeks climbing up something that more resembled a mountain streambed than a road. There were no alternative routes. Humboldt took the opportunity to study the several species of alligators, trying to determine their relationship to Nile crocodiles. When the two scientists finally arrived in Santa Fe de Bogotá, capital of the Viceroyalty of New Granada, the scientific and intellectual community gave them a grand welcome. But Bonpland's health had been undermined by the tribulations of the journey. For a European, the chilly mists of Bogotá at eight thousand feet seemed more congenial and inviting than the steaming lowlands of the Caribbean coast. So the two men settled in for a four-month respite, much of which they spent in the library of José Celestino Mutis, one of the first Spanish scientists to apply the Linnaean botanical classification system.

In Bogotá, Humboldt found a city locked inside layers of soaring, steep-sloped mountains where, then as now, roads were hard to construct. New Granada appears to have been, by Humboldt's comparison with Cuba, something of a colonial disappointment. Though populous and enormous, it generated little wealth for Spain. The presence of highland farming Indians (and hoards of gold objects) had drawn the Spanish conquerors to the high plateau of Cundinamarca, the location of Bogotá, but for now, those farms could grow nothing that could be exported profitably to Europe. The jagged geography of the northern Andes made only the most valuable substances, such as gold, worth transporting to the coast. Anything less precious than gold would not pay for itself. This fact made most of New Granada's rural population a subsistence peasantry, sprinkled through jumbled ridges and valleys, clustering around small, widely separated cities, interspersed with small indigenous groups and steep stretches of trackless wilderness. There were some sugar and slaves around Cartagena on the Caribbean coast and along the Cauca River, but nothing to compare with Cuba.

Therefore, the Viceroyalty of New Granada mattered less to the Spanish crown than did its other three American viceroyalties. The Viceroyalty of Peru and the Viceroyalty of New Spain, with their great silver mines, were richer and better established. The Viceroyalty of the Río de la Plata got more royal attention because of the ongoing competition with the Portuguese in the vicinity. But the high Cundinamarca plateau around Bogotá was remarkably lush and beautiful, and the fabulous botanical collection assembled by Mutis made the visit worthwhile in itself. Furthermore, New Granada abounded in something Humboldt especially adored, volcanoes. As soon as Bonpland felt ready to hike, the two were on the road again, traveling south through the Andes toward Lima, climbing every volcano on the way. Ahead, looming over the city of Quito, which Humboldt found lovely but overly solemn with its cold and cloudy skies, stood the great snow-capped volcano called Pichincha. Humboldt climbed Pichincha in the company of an Indian guide. At one point, he and the guide found themselves walking on an ice bridge over part of the yawning crater, its circumference many miles around. Humboldt had such a good time that he convinced Bonpland and Carlos Montúfar, a new friend, son of a local noble, to climb Pichincha with him again two days later. All three then tried their luck on Chimborazo, a volcano that towered over all the others. Humboldt climbed six snow-capped volcanoes around Quito, impressing some highlanders and mystifying others. Scaling Chimborazo, then believed to be the highest mountain in the world, earned him the nineteenth-century equivalent of international stardom. Carlos Montúfar was so exhilarated by the experience that he got his father's blessing to accompany Humboldt and Bonpland for the rest of their journey.

Enter Simón Bolívar

July 1802, the moment of Humboldt's climb to international celebrity on Chimborazo, was also a moment of elation for nineteen-year-old Simón Bolívar, just returning to Venezuela after a three-year stay in Madrid, the capital of the Spanish Empire. Living there with his uncles, the well-heeled young man had acquired a bit of courtly polish, including his first serious attention to spelling as well as private lessons in French and dancing. Young Bolívar strutted around Madrid in a militia uniform (without doing any actual military service), spent a great deal of money, and, in less than a year, fell madly in love with a young woman named María Teresa Rodríguez de Toro. Bolívar was then seventeen. The fact that María Teresa was twenty months older than her beau was a bit odd but no impediment to their marriage. Theirs was a brilliant match, the Bolívar and Rodríguez de Toro families both being *mantuano* families (part of the Venezuelan elite) and longtime allies in Caracas politics. Still, they had to wait a year and a half while the families negotiated careful prenuptial agreements because of the amount of property involved. Immediately after the wedding in Madrid, Simón and María Teresa sailed for Venezuela.

All was right in their world. They were young, rich, and privileged, belonging to the thin upper crust of colonial society—and they really were in love, something of a rarity for people so rich, among whom a marriage alliance was customarily family strategy. Immediately upon arrival at the port of La Guaira, they sent couriers racing up the slopes to Caracas to inform Simón's uncle and María Teresa's aunt. Also in the port of La Guaira, María Teresa met a passenger about to embark for Spain, so she took the opportunity to write her father announcing their safe arrival. "My adored Papá," begins the letter, which is chatty and unremarkable, filled with details of the voyage, news of her cousins who came to meet them in La Guaira, lots of regards, and earnest wishes for her father's good health.[6] The letter would not be worth mentioning were it not, apparently, the last one she ever wrote.

After effusive greetings to friends and relations in Caracas, the happy couple traveled immediately to one of the family's several properties, a sugar plantation just inland from Caracas. They envisioned a life for themselves in the exuberant Venezuelan countryside that Simón had visited often as a boy. María Teresa, born in Madrid, was seeing it all for the first time: the huge trees full of parrots and bromeliads, the cacao orchards on the hillsides, the green carpets of sugarcane in the valleys. There is no record of how she reacted to becoming the mistress of a plantation worked by Africans in bondage. Her family's fortune was, of course, built on slave labor, as were the fortunes of Venezuela's dominant families generally. María Teresa Rodríguez de Toro had always known that. But now she had to see it.

No doubt she simply got used to seeing slaves and began to consider it normal. That was the most common attitude in slave-owning lands. Slavery that is purely a chamber of horrors cannot last, so slave owners mixed discipline with paternalism. In some cases, warm relationships formed between them and their slaves, especially between masters and domestic servants. Simón Bolívar, like so many children of cacao and sugar planters, had been raised by a slave nanny, his black wet nurse Hipólita. Years later, when he was a victorious general leading his army in Caracas, Bolívar spotted Hipólita in the crowd and dismounted to embrace her. He also grew up with slave playmates, the perfect arrangement for a little boy who had to win whenever he competed. Paternalism (and occasionally self-interest) led to the practice of freeing favored slaves or allowing them to buy their freedom, a process called manumission. Humboldt remarked on the frequency of manumission in América.

Over the years, the descendants of manumitted slaves came to constitute a significant portion of the Venezuelan population. These free blacks were normally mixed-descent pardos. Like many of América's mixed-descent populations, the pardos were upwardly mobile. They had no interest in laboring on plantations and refused to do it for any price that the planters were willing to pay. Many were artisans who earned as much as poor whites. But the caste system, designed to keep people in their place, stipulated that pardos, no matter how prosperous, could not do certain things associated with high social rank—such as ride a horse, wear silk, carry a sword, or study at a seminary—reserving those honors for bona fide (white) americanos. These limitations chafed upwardly mobile pardos, and here some resourceful servant of the Spanish monarchy identified a revenue source. In the mid-1790s, royal officials announced the sale of a new item: exemptions that would make pardos legally white, granting them permission to do whatever americanos could do.

The city council of Caracas, called the *cabildo*, where great families exercised quasi-hereditary control, howled with fury. What was the king thinking? The cabildo mobilized the mantuano class to protest this infamy. Simón's uncle and guardian, Carlos Palacios, in whose house the boy lived at the time of the protest, was a ringleader of the protest. The city fathers explained their case with painful clarity in a letter to the king. The pardos were descended from slaves. Some still had slaves in their families. Slaves, of course, were beaten and terrorized as a necessary part of keeping them enslaved. (This they knew well, obviously, being slave owners themselves.) Their point was that slaves had been degraded, stripped of "honor." So how could prosperous pardos be treated as the equals of people such as themselves—people defined by their honorable family histories, by their blood, clean from the stain of non-European mixture? The Marqués de Toro, María Teresa's uncle, also signed this letter of protest to the king. The last thing the titled nobility needed was a challenge to the caste system.

The pardos had recently become insolent, explained the city fathers, crowding into the towns (or out onto the frontiers) instead of laboring on plantations alongside the slaves. The Caracas cabildo mentioned labor needs insistently in the protest. In town, the pardos became blacksmiths, carpenters, silversmiths, tailors, masons, shoemakers, and butchers. Thanks to their easy access to basic subsistence, pardo artisans could charge prices that the city fathers considered outrageous. But worst of all was the participation of thousands of pardos in the new colonial militias. The Caracas cabildo thought that putting pardos in uniform made them uppity. Pardos with a red militia badge in their hats were much too ready to speak up for themselves when appearing before a magistrate.

There was no trace of irony in the cabildo's lament. In the colonial Venezuela where Simón Bolívar grew up surrounded by enslaved servants, the principle of inequality, or rather hierarchy, ruled. Fairness was not an issue. Rulers spoke of inherited honor and privilege without embarrassment. People without honor simply did not deserve the same treatment as honorable people. Only troublemakers tried to work their way up in life. A person stripped of honor should shut up and hang his head in court, believed the cabildo. Moreover, honor, the index of inequality, ran in families. A manumitted slave who did well as a tradesman should know his place, and so should all his children. Finally, puffing themselves up to full "sons of the conquistadors" size, the city fathers warned His Majesty that swarms of "legally white" pardos entering the church, commerce, and public office would drive all honorable people away in understandable disgust. The grim day would arrive, they warned, when Spain would be served only by blacks. Who then would defend the realm and control the slaves?

This last point they considered the critical one. Controlling the slaves had become a major concern in the 1790s because of the ongoing Haitian Revolution. When a massive revolt of plantation slaves had demolished planter control in the French colony formerly called Saint-Domingue, recalled the cabildo, the agitation of free pardos had detonated the explosive charge. Free pardos had hoped that the principles of the Declaration of the Rights of Man and of the Citizen, proclaimed by the revolutionary National Assembly in Paris, might allow them to become equal citizens of the French Republic. The master class of Saint-Domingue had tried to stifle such aspirations in the National Assembly. Robespierre's radicals insisted on declaring the principle of racial equality, but it did not apply to slaves. Unlike the free pardos, the slaves of Saint-Domingue could not stake their hopes on the French National Assembly. Stimulated by talk of the rights of man and denied any hope of enjoying those rights, the slaves rebelled. Their chief leader, Toussaint Loverture, rose to prominence during a decade of bloody fighting and eventually distributed a constitution that abolished slavery and outlawed color discrimination. The Haitian Revolution was the most significant slave rebellion in world history and became, for slave owners, a frightening cautionary tale, told and retold everywhere Africans were held in bondage. For the Caracas cabildo, the conflagration in nearby Saint-Domingue, renamed Haiti, spelled imminent peril.

Simón Bolívar was eleven years old when a slave from Curaçao appeared in Venezuela proclaiming "the law of the French," a clear reference to Haiti. The colonial authorities quickly snuffed out the ill-armed band of would-be liberators who responded to the call. To teach a moral lesson, the authorities severed the head of a free pardo who participated and dangled it in an iron cage on a twenty-foot pole, where passersby could stare at it for months. Another scare came a year later, in 1797, when three European Spaniards, deported from Madrid to the dungeons of La Guaira for their seditious activities, escaped with the help of a few French-influenced local radicals. The radicals' program included abolition of slavery, abolition of the Indian tribute, and free trade. The insignia of this new dawn was to be a multicolored ribbon symbolizing a rainbow coalition of white, black, pardo, and Indian. One of the participants betrayed the conspiracy, however, and it disbanded. Simón's uncle, Carlos Palacios, called it a conspiracy of *la canalla del mulatismo*, roughly "pardo scum." Naturally, the "scum" appealed to "the detestable principle of equality," he wrote to relatives in Madrid. This was just what they had warned the king about.[7]

These anxieties were still in the air in 1802, when Simón Bolívar tried his hand at managing a sugar plantation and María Teresa tried hers at being a plantation mistress. If the young couple feared their slaves, however, they need not have. María Teresa's vulnerability to the unfamiliar environment, not a pardo uprising, was their undoing. María Teresa got a tropical fever that rapidly worsened. Simón frantically transported her to Caracas, where she died in January 1803. Their idyll had lasted for a very few months. Dejected, Bolívar decided to return to Europe immediately.

Humboldt Inspects Peru and New Spain

Humboldt and Bonpland were headed toward New Spain in January 1803, when María Teresa died. To amuse himself on the northward voyage along the Pacific coast of South America, Humboldt did his usual sampling of seawater and currents. In so doing he became the first to measure a major global phenomenon, now called the Humboldt Current, a sort of Gulf Stream in reverse that conveys frigid polar waters toward the equator.

During 1802, Humboldt and Bonpland had investigated Inca history in Peru and become fascinated by the great Andean heartland of indigenous América, with its farming villages where Quechua, the language of the Incas, remained the normal language of conversation. In Peru, Humboldt's imagination was fired by works of Inca engineering, especially the system of paved roads, as many as ten thousand miles of them, still partially in use. The Prussian pronounced them as good as those constructed by the ancient Romans. Examining the bird manure fertilizer called guano, which the indigenous farmers had used since ancient times to maintain the fertility of their garden terraces, Humboldt found it superb and recommended its use in Europe. (When European farmers eventually tried guano years later, they bought twenty million tons of it.)

Resting in Lima, Humboldt wrote one of the rare letters to his brother that actually found its way across the Atlantic. He mentioned highlights of the last few months: the ascents of Pichincha and Chimborazo and his examination of a manuscript in a pre-Incaic language. At this point Humboldt had studied several indigenous languages and argued that they had wrongly been called "primitive." Humboldt was developing an intellectual case in favor of América's indigenous people. During the Peruvian leg of his journey, Humboldt became firmly convinced that "a darker shade of skin color is not a badge of inferiority."[8] It was the Spanish conquest, he affirmed, that had caused the misery in which Indians now lived. Humboldt described Indian porters who earned a pittance carrying travelers on their backs over Andean ridges in New Granada for three or four hours a day. Outraged by the symbolism, he and Bonpland had refused to ride on the backs of these men. But the porters, as it turned out, did not appreciate the moral support, being more concerned about their loss of earnings. Humboldt and Bonpland paid for their gallant gesture in more ways than one, as torrential rains sent water cascading down the rutted, rocky trails, soaking their boots, which eventually tore apart, leaving their feet bare and bloody.

Humboldt heads a long line of European travelers who detested nineteenth-century Lima. Lima mentally faced its seaport and the world beyond, turning its back on the Andes and the Indian majority who spoke Quechua, believed Humboldt. It was a stronghold of Spanish royal and ecclesiastical bureaucracy, not an Andean city at all. He was right. Lima had been one of the first viceregal capitals in América. In the 1600s, the rich silver mines at Potosí made the name Peru synonymous in Europe with fabulous wealth. But Potosí's "mountain of silver" stands (at the highest inhabited altitudes on earth) in Upper Peru (modern Bolivia), and when, in the 1700s, the Spanish crown created two new viceroyalties, Upper Peru (and with it, alas, Potosí) was removed from Lima's jurisdiction. Lima never really recovered from the loss of Potosí. In Humboldt's day, Lima still looked impressive from just outside the city, where one could see its dense clusters of churches and convents, testimony to bygone splendors. The greatest jewel in the Spanish imperial crown now was unquestionably no longer Peru but New Spain, where Humboldt, Bonpland, and Carlos Montúfar landed in March 1803.

Humboldt's first, diplomatic thought upon landing at Acapulco, New Spain's principal Pacific port, was to write a letter to the viceroy announcing his arrival. By this time, he could do so without help in elegant, formal Spanish. He put himself at His Excellency's disposal, offering expressions of profound respect, praising His Excellency's reputation as a protector of utilitarian arts and sciences, and providing His Excellency a full itinerary of the places he had visited in América.

Overall, New Spain struck Humboldt as a far more developed colony than anything south of it. New Spain was the most populous, prosperous, and profitable of all Spain's American possessions, producing about half of all colonial revenues for the crown. Here Humboldt devoted himself to something he had promised the king of Spain: evaluating colonial mining techniques. Humboldt's many-faceted expertise included formal training in mineralogy. Humboldt being who he was, he saw room for improvement in New Spain, but less in the mines than in the overdependence on mining itself. For centuries, the Spanish crown had privileged the great silver mines of Peru and New Spain, organizing its entire American empire to serve mining interests. Given the fabulous wealth of these mines at their height, one can see why. At the time of Humboldt's visit to Guanajuato, north of Mexico City, a single mine there, the Valenciana mine, was responsible for fully one-fifth of all world silver production. The 20 percent tax on minted silver had been the Spanish crown's chief economic interest in América for centuries.

But Humboldt thought that the fertile lands of New Spain could produce even more wealth than its mines and employ more people, too. Employing people seemed urgent, because economically marginalized indigenous farmers composed half the population of New Spain. From a different perspective, "marginalized" Indians were enjoying reliable subsistence agriculture. Many of them, in fact, saw it just that way. Overall, indigenous people, accustomed to providing for their own needs, showed little interest in trade or in wage labor. Humboldt argued, however, that if Spain did not want to lose its colony, "the copper-colored race" would have to be better integrated into it and share the prosperity. Otherwise, he explained, there could be more bloody indigenous uprisings such as Peru's Tupac Amaru rebellion of the

1780s. That rebellion was the largest ever to occur in colonial América. Tens of thousands died. Once they had repressed the savagery of the rebels, the Spanish applied their own, pulling Tupac Amaru apart, limb from limb, before a jeering crowd and distributing fragments of his corpse as gruesome warnings about the perils of rebellion.

Enter Father Hidalgo

In New Spain Humboldt found people who shared his critique of Spanish imperialism, though he did not meet a dissident priest named Miguel Hidalgo. Hidalgo shared many interests with Humboldt and would have delighted in hosting our travelers. Besides, Hidalgo lived not far from the silver mines of Guanajuato, the greatest ones in New Spain, which Humboldt intended to visit.

Father Hidalgo agreed with Humboldt that diversification was essential to the economy of New Spain and that "the copper-colored race" needed opportunities to prosper. And like Humboldt, he pondered many sorts of practical innovations, things that could provide gainful employment for the Indians and mestizos. He proposed to plant some olive trees and also some vineyards. Why import olive oil and wine from Spain if New Spain could produce them? The practical answer was that Spain's monopoly trading system prohibited the colonies from competing, but Hidalgo had no patience for that. He proposed to plant mulberry trees, because he wanted to cultivate silkworms, which feed on those leaves. Breaking the profitable Chinese monopoly on silk manufacture was then being attempted in various places. Why not New Spain? Local clay would produce good pottery, and Hidalgo had specific ideas about what kinds of pots to make and sell. The rich mining city of Guanajuato would provide a nearby market, an important consideration because pots are heavy to transport. A tannery made good sense, too. After all, domestic animals were slaughtered every day for food; why not tan the hides for use as leather? In addition, one could always consider textile manufacture—on a small scale, of course, and utilizing wool; who could afford cotton? Hidalgo envisioned these as enterprises that would be owned and worked in common by the people of the village. They would produce for the market, but the organization of production would be communal rather than capitalist.

Hidalgo's friend Manuel Abad y Queipo, recently selected as bishop of Michoacán, did get the opportunity to meet Humboldt as well. Abad y Queipo had gained some notoriety in 1799 by writing a letter of protest to the Spanish crown. Abad y Queipo explained that nine-tenths of the people of New Spain, by his estimate, were Indians and poor mestizos and pardos whose destitution gave them no investment in the colonial order. They resented the whites who had everything while they had nothing. The Indians protested at the special tribute they had to pay, while mestizos and pardos chafed at the caste system that limited their social mobility. Among the bishop's recommendations were elimination of the tribute and caste distinctions and free distribution of all the vacant lands in New Spain. The bishop's main recommendation, though, was more royal support for the church, most especially for the parish clergy. Only the parish clergy, according to Abad y Queipo, could exert the moral suasion needed to maintain Spanish rule in the villages of New Spain. Abad y Queipo and Hidalgo sometimes discussed such topics, as well as French books and "utilitarian arts and sciences" such as silk production, in which both had a special interest. The two were old friends.

Lately, though, the bishop had been concerned to hear that Hidalgo was under investigation by the Holy Inquisition. The investigation stemmed from indiscreet remarks made at a gathering in 1800. Hidalgo had supposedly declared disbelief in Christ's virgin birth. Hidalgo's educational views, too, were branded unorthodox—influenced by the French thinker Jean-Jacques Rousseau. Hidalgo had supposedly declared himself in favor of "French liberty." In fact, his house in the parish of San Felipe had acquired the nickname "Little France" because, according to witnesses, Hidalgo gathered all sorts of people there in a spirit of equality, without due attention to caste distinctions or social hierarchies. Hidalgo's legendary parties at Little France included dancing, theatricals, and card playing, as well as serious discussion. Hidalgo made fun of church rituals and incense, discovered the inquisitors. His assistant, another French-reading radical priest who often substituted for Hidalgo at mass, had to be alert for his superior's practical jokes. On more than one occasion, when the faithful were already kneeling, the assistant found that Hidalgo had hidden the communion wafers. In addition, Hidalgo declared fornication to be not so bad, and he put that conviction into practice. Over the years, he lived with several women who bore him children. Josefa Quintanilla, one of these women, commonly appeared with leading roles in the theatricals that Hidalgo liked to stage at his house from time to time.

Abad y Queipo did not approve of all this, obviously. He had watched Hidalgo's behavior destroy a promising academic career. A boy from a middling family of españoles americanos, the son of the administrator of a rural estate, Hidalgo had gone away to school at the age of twelve. He excelled, and for the next twelve years immersed himself in Latin literature, rhetoric, logic, ethics, theology, Italian, and French, as well as two indigenous languages, Nahuatl and Otomí. Despite certain escapades and a nickname (*el zorro*, "the fox") that gave a hint of his future trespasses, the well-liked Hidalgo gradually rose to become the rector of his school, one of New Spain's best, San Nicolás College in the provincial city of Valladolid.

Hidalgo immediately tried to modernize the curriculum and texts of San Nicolás College, moving away from a medieval-style focus on rhetoric, logic, and theory toward a focus on applied, practical knowledge. Given the large personal investment of the college faculty in the old subject matter, reform was an uphill battle. Still, to that point, Hidalgo's academic career had been a smashing triumph, one that brought sufficient financial reward to enable the purchase of considerable property. But then Hidalgo's fast living caught up with him. He mismanaged college funds and developed a large personal debt, probably betting on cards, one of the most popular pastimes in colonial New Spain. His enemies at the college demanded his ouster, and given the untidy details of Hidalgo's personal life (which included a son and a daughter), they succeeded in forcing his resignation in 1792. Since that time, Hidalgo had spent a decade as parish priest in the town of San Felipe.

As Humboldt and Bonpland made their way from Acapulco to Mexico City, Hidalgo was preparing to leave San Felipe and move to the nearby village of Dolores, a smaller, poorer, more Indian parish. In Dolores, he would have a chance to try all his projects—the silkworms and vineyards and olive orchards, the looms and pottery and tannery. Miguel Hidalgo was then fifty years old, already completing an average life span for his day, and he looked older still. He was a bit weary of all the partying and wanted somehow to make a difference in the world. He must have believed, as he moved his household (including his companion Josefa Quintana and their two children) in creaking carts to Dolores in August 1803, that he was opening his life's final chapter. But the book had an ending he couldn't foresee.

Considering Liberty and Tyranny

In August 1803, Humboldt and Bonpland were no more than a day's travel away from Hidalgo, visiting Guanajuato and its mines. Humboldt had spent 1803 busily visiting mines and collecting economic and demographic data in New Spain. New Spain was another great heartland of indigenous América rather than a frontier to be explored—except, that is, for the extensive and sparsely populated provinces of the distant north, including Texas and California. Humboldt spent his time in New Spain's offices and libraries rather than tromping through the wilderness. Mexico City, the third viceregal capital on his tour of América, was by far the most impressive. Large, prosperous, bustling, spaciously planned, with imposing public buildings, Mexico City was in fact one of the most impressive capital cities anywhere, which it had been since Aztec times.

But Humboldt and Bonpland were now eager to return to Paris. First Humboldt wanted to visit the United States, however. He hoped, above all, to meet the U.S. president, Thomas Jefferson, whom he fervently admired, and so he wrote to Jefferson (in French) immediately upon landing in Philadelphia. The travelers did not have to wait long for Jefferson's enthusiastic response. Jefferson had a special interest in the geographical data Humboldt had gathered in New Spain. As president, Jefferson's grand gamble was the Louisiana Purchase—a huge tract of the North American continent that doubled the territorial claims of the young United States overnight. Jefferson had bought the territory from Napoleon, who needed money and had his hands full in Europe and in Haiti, where rebellious former slaves led by Toussaint Loverture and his successors had decimated several large French armies. The Louisiana Purchase bordered Texas, a northern province of New Spain, but the border was entirely theoretical and still largely uncharted and unmarked in 1804, when Jefferson received Humboldt's visit. The Lewis and Clark expedition had embarked to explore the Louisiana Purchase a few weeks earlier. They would not return for years. Hence an invitation to Jefferson's county estate at Monticello.

Humboldt traveled through a still half-built Washington, D.C., to the ridges of western Virginia, where he and Jefferson talked animatedly about the emerging map of the United States. They doubtless spoke as well of their shared conviction that the New World constituted a space where liberty would create a better society. In 1804, *liberty* was a very important word, one that no longer has the same ring it once did. As a big idea, liberty implied the freedom to exercise rational self-interest, free from arbitrary governmental interference or tyranny. Humboldt believed that the United States understood liberty—with the glaring exception of slavery in the southern United States, of course. The first American republic had made a portentous entrance onto the world stage. It had enjoyed favorable European trade and weathered a series of political crises, the election of "French-loving" Jefferson being the greatest of these. Humboldt took note, and back in América, so did people such as Hidalgo. But the U.S. example did not appeal to many of Hidalgo's countrymen. After all, English-speaking Protestants had been enemies of Spanish-speaking Catholics for centuries. América's freethinkers admired England and the United States, but they tended to feel more passionate about the French Revolution.

By August 1804, Humboldt and Bonpland were in Paris, where they (or rather Humboldt, always alone in the spotlight) met wonderful acclaim. At that moment, only Napoleon was more famous in Europe than Alexander von Humboldt. Napoleon seemed not to relish the competition. After Napoleon crowned himself in Notre Dame Cathedral, Humboldt attended the coronation gala and congratulated the new emperor, only to be snubbed by him: "I understand you collect plants, monsieur. So does my wife."[9] The idealistic early phase of the French Revolution was now over.

Simón Bolívar, too, was in Paris during Napoleon's autocoronation, distracting himself from the grief of María Teresa's death, often in the company of her wealthy kinsman Fernando Toro. In the heady atmosphere of the French capital, the young Venezuelan was undergoing a political metamorphosis, becoming an exponent of liberty. At stylish gatherings, he spoke in impassioned tones about Spanish tyranny and about creating new republics in América. When Humboldt and Bolívar were introduced in a Parisian salon, where elegant ladies and gentlemen gathered to socialize, Humboldt was not very impressed, but Bonpland liked Bolívar and encouraged him to keep thinking. Bolívar was raw at being a revolutionary, but it had given his energies a new focus.

A critical element of Bolívar's metamorphosis was the presence at his side of his former schoolmaster from Caracas, Simón Rodríguez, an in-your-face nonconformist, scornful of all social conventions. Rodríguez had fled Venezuela following the 1797 "French" conspiracy there, in which he was implicated. The freethinking schoolmaster escaped under an assumed name, Samuel Robinson, which he took from the book *Robinson Crusoe* to signal his self-reinvention as a political castaway. Rodríguez went first to Jamaica, where he improved his conversational English, then to the United States, and then, of course, to France, the original homeland of liberty, where he lived as "Samuel Robinson of Philadelphia" and shared a house, for a while, with Servando Teresa de Mier, a radical priest who had fled New Spain for political reasons. Rodríguez eventually traveled throughout Europe, learning more languages and trying his hand at a variety of trades. Rodríguez was a passionate exponent of Rousseau's educational theories, which emphasized practical experience and discovery over simple memorization of prepared lessons.

Shortly after meeting Humboldt in Paris, young Bolívar left with Rodríguez, now acting as his tutor and legal guardian, for an educational walking tour from France to Italy, a sort of crash summer-abroad course in the philosophy of liberty. While in northern Italy, tutor and student saw Napoleon in person, a defining moment in the life of Bolívar, who afterward was often compared to Napoleon. Perhaps he had Napoleon in mind when, weeks later, the young Venezuelan vowed amid the inspiring ruins of ancient Rome that he would free América from the yoke of tyranny. Also in Rome, Bolívar crossed paths again with Humboldt. Humboldt did not record his impressions of Rodríguez/Robinson, which is a shame. Instead, Humboldt hurried off to climb another volcano, Vesuvius, where he hoped he might be present at an eruption.

José Bonifácio Yearns for Brazil

In March 1805, an old acquaintance of Humboldt's, a Brazilian named José Bonifácio de Andrada e Silva, felt like erupting in a different way. José Bonifácio, whom we will call by his given name as Brazilians do, had come from his native Brazil to pursue a university education in Portugal. For postgraduate study, the Portuguese government had sent the bright young colonial to acquire a technical specialization in mineralogy at the Freiberg mining school in Germany, where he met Humboldt. After many years of postgraduate training in northern Europe, José Bonifácio had returned to Portugal, where the government quickly put him to work creating a mineralogy program for the national university, Coimbra. In addition, to take advantage of his expensive training and multifaceted talents, the Portuguese government assigned José Bonifácio a truly amazing number of additional projects. When would he ever go home to Brazil? He had not seen his mother in twenty years.

In the meantime, he was comforted in Portugal by the company of his younger brothers Antônio Carlos and Martim Francisco, who had confirmed the Andrada family's academic inclinations by making the transatlantic journey to get Coimbra degrees as well. Both had stayed in Portugal afterward, seeking their fortunes. The Voltaire-reading, love-sonnet-writing José Bonifácio obviously adored Europe and its intellectual opportunities, not to mention the women he met there as a graduate student. Ultimately, he had settled down with an Irish girl (who, his mother could console herself, was at least Catholic). Like Humboldt, José Bonifácio had experienced the excitement of Paris in the summer of 1790. Being older and more conservative, however, he soon soured on the revolutionary vision. By 1805, José Bonifácio could nod in agreement when his government patron, former foreign minister Rodrigo de Souza Coutinho, railed against "abominable French principles." He agreed with Coutinho, too, about the promise of Portugal's enormous claims in América. As Napoleon careened around Europe, Coutinho went so far as to propose that the Portuguese monarchy relocate its royal court to Rio de Janeiro. That would be an extraordinary measure indeed—the first time a European monarch had erected a throne outside Europe.

Living next door to the French Revolution had not been easy for Spain and Portugal. Since 1793, Spain had generally succumbed to French pressure and accepted a French alliance, at the cost of almost constant British hostility. The powerful British navy made British hostility disruptive indeed to Spain's communication with its American colonies, as we have seen. Portugal had made the opposite choice, defying France and opting instead for England, its age-old ally. But Napoleon became ever more menacing. He reiterated demands that Portugal close its ports to British ships, arrest British subjects, and confiscate their goods.

Extraordinary times called for extraordinary leadership. On that point José Bonifácio, although a loyal Portuguese americano, had to throw up his hands. The Portuguese royal family was not strong on leadership. The queen, Maria I, was incurably insane. For the last fourteen years, her son João had governed in her name as prince regent. João was a kind soul but no leader. In the geopolitical free-for-all of Napoleonic Europe, João was a cringing spectator. In late 1805, he began to sink into a depression and despondency that his wife, Carlota Joaquina, vociferously compared to the onset of his mother's madness. Carlota Joaquina's intervention was actively hostile to João, though one can forgive her: Carlota Joaquina's parents, the king and queen of Spain, had married her to João at the age of ten, and a royal marriage being, after all, a matter of state rather than sentiment, neither her preference nor his was consulted in the least. Now an active and strong woman who had given birth to seven princes and princesses for the

Portuguese royal house of Braganza—another matter of state—Carlota Joaquina cordially despised her husband and wanted to undermine his regency. Next in line for the throne after João was her son Prince Pedro, only seven years old and not, at this point, the object of high hopes, at least on the part of José Bonifácio. What, indeed, could one expect of a child reared amid such bitter discord in a gloomy palace presided over by a mad grandmother?

José Bonifácio wrote to his patron Coutinho saying that he was sick and tired and would soon be ready to plead, "facedown at the king's feet," for permission to leave royal service and return to Brazil.[10] Now in his forties, he yearned to become a gentleman farmer, applying his scientific training to improving agricultural techniques, selective breeding, and plant propagation, just as Humboldt's friend Thomas Jefferson liked to do in the backcountry of Virginia. Indeed, José Bonifácio was already raising grain, vegetables, and flowers on a piece of land he rented near Coimbra, a fact that he cited to Coutinho as evidence of his serious desire to farm in Brazil.

Despite his long absence in Europe, José Bonifácio knew Brazil well. If he were to describe it for our benefit, he would probably start by pointing out that Brazil contained many separate, hardly connected settlement areas, called captaincies. Brazilian plantations, worked by African slaves, had pioneered large-scale export sugar production in América. Three major port cities framed the sugar-growing main area of Portuguese colonization: Recife, Salvador, and Rio de Janeiro. Each of these Atlantic ports stood where a large bay (or, the case of Recife, a series of reefs) and navigable rivers facilitated water transportation of the exported crates of sugar. In José Bonifácio's day, Brazil's sugar trade had declined somewhat from its glory days in the 1600s, but more than half of Brazil's entire population of two million lived in these three major coastal settlement areas. Many others lived in a string of secondary ports that stretched from the mouth of the Amazon almost to the Río de la Plata.

By José Bonifácio's day, Portuguese claims (not settler population, which remained mostly coastal) had expanded inland to cover about half the South American continent, mostly because that continent is so much easier to penetrate from the Atlantic side. José Bonifácio would not be shy about describing Portugal's westward-advancing claims, because they were especially the work of people from his own captaincy, São Paulo. Today, São Paulo is the most dynamic of South America's megacities, and to fly over the thirty-mile climb from the Atlantic shore to the original Jesuit mission settlement area of São

Paulo is to see one continuous urban sprawl up the hilly slope. In José Bonifácio's day, the same short climb from the coast put the small town of São Paulo in a world apart. São Paulo marked the coastal terminus of several well-established Indian transportation routes that followed rivers into the heart of the continent. During the 1600s, men of São Paulo trekked into the interior along these routes to explore, to capture Indian slaves, and to claim new territories for the Portuguese crown.

Along the way, the trekkers of São Paulo found gold and diamonds. As a mineralogist, José Bonifácio took a great interest in the potential of Brazilian mines. Even though the Brazilian gold rush of the 1700s was over, it had transformed Brazil by drawing more settlers inland. In José Bonifácio's day, the primary mining captaincy, Minas Gerais, remained the only well-settled district of the Brazilian interior. Mining had created only a few islands of dense population in what remained a very sparsely populated Brazilian frontier, a vast open range where bands of indigenous people and widely separated cattle ranches coexisted uneasily.

José Bonifácio had reason for his booster-style optimism about Brazil. Overall, Portuguese America had fared better economically than had Spanish America of late. The 1791 Haitian Revolution, ending sugar production in what had been the Caribbean's greatest (or most gruesome) plantation colony, had created a large opening for the Brazilian product on the international market. Slaves on Brazilian sugar plantations felt the lash as their owners ramped up production. Meanwhile, some former sugar planters found an even better market for cotton, responding to the demand created by the textile factories of England's Industrial Revolution. By 1800, cotton was the second most important product of Brazilian plantations. Portuguese trade had become dependent on Brazilian agricultural products, which it reexported to the rest of Europe, supplying Brazil with English manufactures on the return voyage. Despite its relative prosperity, Brazil, like Spanish America, was limited by a monopoly trading system designed to benefit the mother country. Consequently, British smuggling was on the increase in Brazil, too.

José Bonifácio's description of Brazil in 1805 probably would not have included the various conspiracies that French liberty had inspired there. He was not a proponent of revolution. Moreover, the various conspiracies that occurred in late colonial Brazil were small, isolated, and quickly repressed. We note them only because they indicate the presence, and also the limits, of ideological ferment. The first conspiracy occurred in Minas Gerais in 1789. In addition to a pile of confiscated French books, the evidence against the conspirators included portions of the U.S. Constitution. The man most interested in that document was a pardo military officer who pulled teeth to supplement his income. Tiradentes, "Tooth-puller," as he was known, became the scapegoat, the only conspirator executed, because the others, who were white, used their wealth and influence to escape that fate. Tiradentes's consolation prize has been to become posthumously a Brazilian national hero. Each of Brazil's chief port cities—Rio, Salvador, and Recife— then discovered a "French" conspiracy of its own. Pardo artisans, exactly the sort who were harkening to revolutionary ideas in Venezuela during these years, figured prominently in both Rio and Salvador. A pardo tailor in Salvador was spreading the word that "all should become French and live in equality."[11] Portuguese authorities in Recife detected a group of plantation owners who they thought were meeting to discuss founding a republic under the protection of Napoleon Bonaparte.

Finally, if asked to describe Brazil in 1805, José Bonifácio no doubt would have taken the opportunity to denounce slavery and the slave trade, institutions that truly pervaded the Portuguese captaincies in América, from Pará and Maranhão in the Amazon basin to Rio Grande do Sul in the far south. José Bonifácio might not have believed in democracy, but he did know that slavery was bad, and he did not hesitate to say so at a time when few dared to, especially in Brazil.

Humboldt's Famous Travelogue Appears

In September 1805, Humboldt finally returned home to Berlin. The Berlin Academy of Science made him a member, and the king of Prussia provided him a pension. In Paris, the French edition of his gargantuan travelogue began to appear: *Voyage aux régions équinoxiales du Nouveau Continent, fait en 1799, 1800, 1801, 1802, 1803, et 1804, par Alexandre de Humboldt et Aimé Bonpland*. Humboldt had collected enough data for a lifetime of publishing projects. He had a lot to say, and the reading public was eager for it. Beginning with the first landing in Cumaná in 1799, Humboldt gradually filled volume after volume, thirty-five in all, with details of his adventurous exploits and scientific observations.

In addition to his multivolume travel account, Humboldt also wrote systematic statistical studies of the Mexican and Cuban economies. He concluded the first of these, translated into English as *Political Essay on the Kingdom of New Spain*, just as the Spanish monarchy was about to enter the shattering crisis that would send everything spinning out of control and precipitate movements for independence in América. Humboldt dedicated the volume to Carlos IV, who had given him permission to explore Spain's American dominions. Humboldt had not found Carlos IV's American colonies seething with rebellion, but, characteristically, he did have a number of recommendations for reforms that, his *Essay* hinted, might help the king retain and improve his colonies. "How can we displease a good king when we speak to him of the national interest?" he concluded hopefully, and signed it, "Your Catholic Majesty's Very Humble and Very Obedient Servant, the Baron von Humboldt."[12]

Before Carlos IV ever saw the book, his kingdom had begun to crumble. But the blow that knocked it apart did not originate anywhere in América. Instead, it came from neighboring France, which had been giving Spain and the rest of Europe cause for alarm for more than a decade.

Two

PILLARS OF THE CROWN

1806–1810

Napoleon's invasion of Spain and Portugal, chronicled in this chapter, provoked rage and rejection in América. Crucially, but very confusingly, América's struggles for independence began with a virtually unanimous outpouring of loyalty toward the hereditary monarchies of both Spain and Portugal. This fervent loyalty appeared with crystal clarity when two expeditions of English-speaking adventurers tried to pry pieces of América away from Spain in 1806.

Miranda Invades América

The English language echoed eerily through the deserted streets of the small Venezuelan city of Coro in August 1806 as a few hundred armed men, most of them from the United States, marched into it. Almost all had come strictly for the pay, but it seems a bit unfair to call them mercenaries, because they had been recruited under false pretexts, supposedly to guard a mail shipment. Their leader—definitely *not* there for the pay—was a revolutionary americano named Francisco Miranda, who had lived most of his life in Europe and was returning to Venezuela after a thirty-year absence. Unfortunately for Miranda, the people of Coro heard he was coming and evacuated the city before his men entered it. The only shooting occurred when, at one point, groups of jittery invaders mistakenly fired on each other. Then, at a signal,

Miranda's men brandished linen handkerchiefs as a sort of invasion souvenir and promotional item. The handkerchiefs featured several inspirational portraits, including one of Miranda himself, as well as images of George Washington and two British officers, Admiral Home Popham and General William Beresford. As if this were not inspiration enough, the handkerchiefs offered optimistic slogans, such as "Let Arts, Industry, and Commerce Flourish."[1]

Miranda had also made other preparations to attract the multitudes to his cause. His expedition had sailed with a printing press on deck, turning out proclamations and tracts on French subjects such as liberty and the Declaration of the Rights of Man, sheet by sheet, two thousand copies each. Miranda's whole life of fifty-six years could be construed as grooming for the role he was playing at Coro: his military training, his reading of French political philosophy, and above all, his many years as a self-styled revolutionary. Miranda had toured the American Revolution of George Washington (whom he met) and Tom Paine (who became his friend and advocate). From there, he traveled to Europe and toured England, Holland, Germany, Austria, Italy, Greece, Russia, Scandinavia, Switzerland, and France. Everywhere in his four-year European odyssey, Miranda talked about his revolutionary project.

Miranda culminated his international journey in Paris in May 1789, on the eve of the French Revolution, which he joined, becoming a general and eventually getting his name inscribed on the Arc de Triomphe. Despite his name being on that grand revolutionary monument, however, Miranda was not a very triumphant general, and his military failures brought him down. In 1797, he abandoned France and the French Revolution to promote his project in London. Before leaving France, he had gathered with a few other expatriate americanos to start a movement. As a result, Miranda arrived in London sporting pseudo-diplomatic credentials as the principal agent of the Spanish American colonies. He was soon busy lobbying and publishing for his cause. Among other projects, he translated and disseminated Juan Pablo Viscardo's *Open Letter to the American Spaniards*, an argument for the independence of América. Miranda even sketched a vague plan for an entity to be called Colombia (in honor of Columbus) but to include rulers called "Incas" and a federal capital to be located on the isthmus of Panama (in honor of the meeting place of ancient Greek city-states on the isthmus of Corinth).

In the meantime, Miranda settled into London life, bought a three-story town house near the British Museum, married a young woman from Yorkshire, and socialized with leading intellectuals such as the antislavery crusader William Wilberforce, the utilitarian ("greatest good for the greatest number") philosopher Jeremy Bentham, and the pioneer educator ("each one teach one") Joseph Lancaster. Miranda had always identified more with the English than with the French. Now he made his London house the center of an international conspiracy to promote the independence of América. A vital element in that conspiracy was his Society of Rational Gentlemen, a Masonic lodge he founded in London for americanos only. Masonic-style lodges were spreading throughout the Atlantic world in the early 1800s, becoming a key mode of elite political organization.

A fellow Mason, Admiral Popham, whose approximate likeness graced Miranda's invasion souvenir handkerchiefs in Venezuela, was Miranda's most enthusiastic British supporter and collaborator. Popham viewed Spanish America as a field for the expansion of liberty (and British commerce). Spain was benighted and backward, in his view—a common one at the time in Britain and the United States. Without Spanish rule, alleged Popham, América would be better off, free to trade, develop, and enjoy the benefits of (British) civilization. In practical terms, the immediate result would be opening América to (British) trade and closing it to Napoleon, whose shadow was gradually extending over Spain. The Foreign Office promised aid, but Popham and Miranda waited in vain for it.

In late 1805, Miranda traveled to seek support in the United States. Unlike Britain, the United States was not at war with Spain, and President Thomas Jefferson committed no resources to Miranda's project. But he did not stop it, either. Fortunately for Miranda, British aid finally materialized. With that aid, and also by hocking his valuable library, Miranda managed to equip a small ship in New York and attract U.S. volunteers for his mysterious but well-paid expedition. One of them was the grandson of former U.S. president John Adams. The expeditionaries spent a month preparing in revolutionary Haiti. There the improvised invaders of this so-called Army of Colombia underwent some rudimentary military training and swore an oath "to be true and faithful to the free people of South America, independent of Spain."[2] Miranda hoisted the new flag that he had designed for the expedition: the yellow, blue, and red tricolor that still forms the basis of the Colombian, Venezuelan, and Ecuadorian national flags. Miranda had also written and printed two thousand copies of an elegantly worded "Proclamation to the Inhabitants of South America." It included provisions for military conscription for all adult males into the hypothetical Army of Colombia and provisions stipulating that Viscardo's *Open Letter to American Spaniards* should be read aloud daily in public buildings.

But Miranda's careful plans to drum up a mass following for his invasion of Venezuela elicited little or no response among Venezuelans in August 1806. Despite Miranda's confident predictions, the loyal Spanish subjects of Venezuela clearly had no intention of being liberated in the manner he proposed. Instead, as days passed in the occupied ghost town of Coro, Miranda became aware that local militias were massing to crush his small force, some (though Miranda did not know this) led by the uncle of Simón Bolívar, who was soon to return from Paris. On 13 August 1806, just eleven days after landing at Coro, Miranda's force withdrew. Then, quickly, it dispersed.

The outcome of Miranda's 1806 expedition shows that "French ideas" alone could not create movements for independence in América. The people of Coro looked on Miranda as a foreign invader, with some reason. In the United States, an angry public controversy followed the failure of Miranda's project because it had violated U.S. neutrality and because the capture of his auxiliary vessels had left fifty-seven U.S. adventurers prisoner. But a strong current of anti-Spanish feeling led to the acquittal of all those charged. Meanwhile, a British warship took Miranda home to England, where church bells greeted him as a hero. Along with his English wife, Sarah, and their two children, several friends were waiting to greet Miranda when he arrived at his London townhouse. One was his friend Admiral Popham, who had quite a story of his own to tell.

British Invasions in the Río de la Plata Also Fail

On 12 August 1806, the day before Miranda's invasion of Coro ended with a whimper, far away another invasion ended with a bang. Clouds of smoke spouted from muskets amid explosions and the confusion of house-to-house fighting in the streets of Buenos Aires. British soldiers had occupied Buenos Aires for three weeks in Admiral Popham's own renegade military operation. Popham had taken his fleet to Buenos Aires without orders to do so, after leading a successful British takeover of Cape Town, South Africa (which he *had* been ordered to do). As long as his force was in the South Atlantic, the admiral reasoned, it would be a shame not to "liberate" Spain's trade-hungry Viceroyalty of the Río de la Plata.

The Spanish viceroy, Sobremonte, fled ignominiously at the first sign of Popham's ships, allowing a startled Buenos Aires to fall virtually without resistance. The general commanding the invasion force was Beresford, the second face on Miranda's invasion souvenir handkerchiefs. To understand what Popham and Beresford were doing, one must consider that British commerce was driving the early 1800s version of economic globalization. Although the word did not exist, proponents of globalization, then as now, rationalized their own gain as a universal good. In fact, large-scale smuggling of British goods in América did reveal high demand for those goods, and British commercial interests urgently desired to break into the Spanish system of colonial trade. Therefore, General Beresford announced liberation from the Spanish trade monopoly immediately after occupying Buenos Aires. Inhabitants of the city could now enjoy the benefits of liberty and civilization, he explained, as well as international products at moderate prices. A number of Buenos Aires slaves misinterpreted his explanation of liberty, escaped their masters, and had to be returned by Beresford, who did not intend to create economic disruptions. Spanish monopoly merchants shut their doors in protest, but Beresford ordered them open for business. A few inhabitants of Buenos Aires, however, were actually eager for this sort of liberation.

Mariquita Sánchez, a young woman of the city, longed for the fresh breeze of the quickening Atlantic world. Mariquita was nineteen, newly wed in an era when marriage defined a woman's life, and her marriage had been a dramatic affair. Mariquita's father was a merchant and therefore, unsurprisingly, a europeo whose success within the Spanish monopoly system depended on his transatlantic connections in Spain. Ideally, business connections were family connections, and that is what Mariquita's father had in mind when, around the time Mariquita turned fourteen, he chose his preferred future son-in-law, a merchant and a europeo like himself. Mariquita refused to marry the man, and she did, after all, have to say "I do," even in an arranged marriage. So her father deposited her in a convent for safekeeping while his friends deployed her beau, a vibrant young americano naval captain of English descent, to Spain. The lovers kept passionately faithful and legally defended their right to marry for love, eventually triumphing in a case personally decided by the viceroy. At the time, marrying for love rather than family interest constituted a sort of radical individualism, part of the raft of new ideas floating out of Europe, most especially France. At least one of these ideas, though—free trade—found its supreme exponents in Britain. Therefore, Beresford's "liberation" of Buenos Aires seemed pregnant with enticing possibilities to certain dissident free-thinkers such as Mariquita and her husband, who invited Beresford to gatherings at their house.

Freethinkers were few in 1806 Buenos Aires, though, and resistance to Beresford's invasion came quickly. In three weeks, Buenos Aires forces regrouped in Montevideo, and, with help from that city, the other Spanish stronghold in the Río de la Plata, recaptured Buenos Aires from the invaders. José Artigas was present at the final battle, sent by the governor of Montevideo to bring word of the outcome. As militias of Buenos Aires and Montevideo converged on the main square of Buenos Aires, Beresford quickly surrendered and withdrew to Popham's warships offshore. The heroes of the recapture of Buenos Aires were the local americano militias, led by Santiago Liniers, a French officer in the service of the Spanish crown.

Artigas rushed home to Montevideo, where joy greeted the news that the "heretics"—that is, Protestants—had been defeated, having found only a few more supporters than had Miranda in Coro. The Spanish imperial government granted Montevideo a new honorific title, "Most Loyal and Reconquering," for its role in the recapture of Buenos Aires. Montevideo was in fact a more important naval and military base than Buenos Aires itself, and better fortified, with a fine harbor that Buenos Aires emphatically lacked. Popham's reconnaissance vessels had given forewarning of his invasion in late 1805 by showing themselves on the coast of the Río de la Plata, and Montevideo had actively prepared to face the threat. A Montevideo-based beef jerker—which is to say a leading industrialist or the closest thing to it in the Río de la Plata—had offered to fund a force of 280 volunteers, recruited from the countryside, against the British threat.

The officer charged with sifting through the gaucho riffraff to create such a force was the former contraband trail boss José Artigas. Artigas had recently married and received permission to leave the mounted police force that he had captained, by now, for about ten years. His bride was not Isabel Velásquez, who apparently had died a few years before, but rather his first cousin Rafaela, a woman eleven years younger than he. If Artigas had been looking forward to settling down, however, he forgot about that as he rode around the frontier in search of roving gauchos who habitually lived off the land for months and required little or no training to become light cavalry. Artigas was empowered to offer various contrabandists, renegades, and bandits among his acquaintances the kind of amnesty he had received himself a decade earlier. He also visited Montevideo's prison and recruited several dozen likely candidates there. The recorded testimony of Venancio Benavides, "When I need a shirt, I stop and work, and when I get the shirt, I ride," can function as a concise rendering of the care-free gaucho lifestyle.[3] His file showed that the police had captured Benavides only by shooting his horse, and then, when he was already a prisoner with hands tied, Benavides had suddenly leaped onto a guard's horse and thrown the guard off it, whereupon the police had to shoot that horse, too. Here, obviously, was the sort of recruit that Artigas sought.

Larger assets than this would be required, however, to resist what came next. General Beresford's withdrawal from Buenos Aires proved merely tactical. In October he and Popham were back, strongly reinforced, and this time they planned to take Montevideo first. They landed at the nearby town of Maldonado, sacked it, and waited. The proven vulnerability of Buenos Aires had awakened official British support for Popham's rogue expedition, and in mid-January 1807 scores of British vessels, an entire fleet, began disembarking along the beach outside Montevideo. Fortunately for the British, Viceroy Sobremonte had taken personal command of Spanish troops in Montevideo and, as usual, he did everything wrong. Ill-led, overmatched, and outnumbered, the defenders surrendered the city to the British two weeks later, leaving four hundred dead. Sobremonte himself had withdrawn discreetly before the British closed the siege.

The British occupiers announced a new dawn, including free trade, of course, as well as Montevideo's first newspaper, *Southern Star*, to be published in English and Spanish. Mostly, though, they prepared their assault on Buenos Aires, where Liniers was organizing local militias for the defense. London sent a new general, John Whitelocke, to command the operation, but the British attack on Buenos Aires ended in a defeat so convincing that the terms of Whitelocke's 6 July 1807 surrender included total British withdrawal from the Río de la Plata. Deserted by their incompetent Spanish viceroy, americano militiamen had trounced a well-armed force of professional European soldiers. A new spirit of self-sufficiency infused the defenders. Riding a wave of popular support for Liniers and scorn for Sobremonte, and clearly exceeding their authority, the Buenos Aires militias and city council declared Liniers viceroy. The confidence gained by the militias of Buenos Aires would have a clear impact during the looming crisis of the Spanish monarchy.

The most important lesson of both Popham's and Miranda's plans for the liberation of América is how little popular support they received.

The new political philosophy of the Enlightenment might be, or rather was, tremendously influential for a few French- and English-reading intellectuals in the Spanish colonies. Overall, however, the language of liberty rang false for most inhabitants of América in 1806–7. Nor were British offers of economic benefits enough to make people betray king and country and embrace invading "heretics." But a pivotal moment in world history was about to begin: Spain's hereditary British enemies would soon become allies.

Prince Regent João Sails for Brazil

Napoleon's 8 September 1807 letter to Prince Regent João of Portugal, interrupting the seclusion of João's life at the royal residence and monastery called Mafra, was a stark ultimatum: pick a side, England or France, and pick *now*. Faced with an urgent decision, João did what he habitually did. He stalled, closing Portuguese ports to British ships but *not* arresting British subjects or confiscating their goods as Napoleon demanded. The crafty, procrastinating prince also offered his firstborn son, Pedro, now nine years old, as a husband for Napoleon's niece. João reasoned that the upstart emperor would be eager to see his family marry traditional royalty. Furthermore, Napoleon's niece was the daughter of the French general Murat, who was now poised to lead the French invasion of Portugal. So it would have been a brilliant stroke of diplomacy indeed had Murat and João become in-laws just at that moment.

But Napoleon was not inclined to marry his relations into the Portuguese royal family. Instead, he made plans to invade and partition Portugal. To secure Spanish cooperation, he offered southern Portugal as a prize to be ruled by the infamous Godoy, lover of the Spanish queen. Murat's troops began marching through Spain on their way to Portugal, while Spain's own army prepared to collaborate with the French invasion.

Reluctantly, João began to ready the Portuguese fleet. The old idea of moving his royal court to Brazil had gained new appeal. Still, he wavered. Perhaps it was shameful not to stay and fight. As a sort of dynastic insurance policy, a few princes or princesses could be sent to Brazil, out of French reach. On 11 November 1807, news reached Lisbon that French soldiers had entered Portugal and were marching toward the capital. That same day, the British fleet arrived at Lisbon with instructions to evacuate the Portuguese royal family. "We all go or none of us goes," said João's mother, the mad Maria I, who supposedly settled the matter.[4] The whole Portuguese royal court, including thousands of courtiers and servants, would move to Brazil. Tentative preparations for the voyage had been secret until then for fear of alarming the populace. As the preparations became frantically public, the people of Lisbon expressed dismay at seeing their royal family abandon them in the face of an invading army. The Lisbon waterfront was a swirling mass of wagons and carts, a jumble of chests and wardrobes and boxes containing everything from china to silver services to linens to family portraits in heavy carved frames. Crowds of commoners shouted and sobbed as they watched.

Murat's soldiers were marching into the outskirts of Lisbon when João and Carlota Joaquina arrived at the waterfront in separate coaches and embarked on the separate ships that would carry them to Brazil. Young Prince Pedro arrived with his mad grandmother, who shouted at the coachman not to drive like a fleeing bandit. João issued a final proclamation explaining that his departure from Portugal would prevent the country from suffering for his sake. Seeking conciliation to the last, he gave instructions for Murat's troops to be well fed and well housed. France and Portugal were destined to be friends, João declared. The entire Portuguese royal family then sailed away with every vessel in the Lisbon harbor fit to put to sea and a British naval escort hovering around.

José Bonifácio de Andrada was not among the thousands of Portuguese evacuated to Brazil with the royal court. He clearly could have accompanied his patron, Rodrigo de Souza Coutinho, who did make the voyage. José Bonifácio's brothers Antônio Carlos and Martim Francisco had already returned to Brazil and now occupied prestigious positions in the Andrada family's home province of São Paulo. José Bonifácio was no longer a young man, and he dearly wished to see Brazil again. But when the last sails of the departing fleet disappeared over the Atlantic horizon, José Bonifácio turned his attention to organizing a corps of academic volunteers at Coimbra University to fight the French invaders.

Meanwhile, in the middle of the Atlantic, the Portuguese royal family and courtiers began to endure the inevitable result of hurried and incomplete preparations. Potable water, passable food, and space itself were at a premium aboard ship. Landlubber courtiers in luxurious garments turned green and vomited copiously all over themselves. Meanwhile, Prince Pedro's new tutor kept him busy with his Latin lessons, reading Virgil, or at least trying to. Prince Pedro was far from studious, but the plot of Virgil's *Aeneid*, in which an exiled king crosses the sea with his ailing mother and young son to found a new kingdom, understandably caught the nine-year-old's attention.

Finally, in late January 1808, João's fleet and its British escort sailed into the beautiful Bay of All Saints, site of Brazil's first capital: Salvador, Bahia. The people of Salvador erupted with jubilation, and the city fathers tried mightily to convince their sovereign to make his new capital right there. João had his heart set on Rio de Janeiro, however, and tactfully declined the Bahians' fervent plea. Before continuing to Rio, he declared Brazilian ports open to trading ships from all nations, most especially from Britain. On one hand, ending the Portuguese trade monopoly was mere necessity. Portugal, previously the destination of all Brazilian trade, lay under enemy control. On the other hand, free commercial access to Brazil constituted an urgent goal of João's new British allies. Not by accident did João begin a century of British commercial domination in Brazil within days after setting foot on Brazilian soil. That was, in effect, a condition of his being there.

On 8 March 1808, João and company finally disembarked in Rio de Janeiro as fireworks exploded overhead, church bells pealed throughout the city, and warships fired salvos in spectacularly beautiful Guanabara Bay. The city fathers and excited populace crowded the waterfront to greet the royal family, and João went straight to hear mass in a solemn procession, a silk awning held over his head, the streets packed with onlookers. The prince regent loved Rio immediately, and Rio loved him. Most Portuguese courtiers liked Rio considerably less than did the prince regent, however. Carlota Joaquina liked it least of all.

Napoleon Invades Spain, Too

Meanwhile, in spite of growing resistance from people such as José Bonifácio, combined French-Spanish forces still occupied Portugal in March 1808. Among the soldiers in the occupying army was a thirty-year-old Spanish officer named José de San Martín. San Martín was a seasoned veteran from a military family. He was an americano, born at a remote outpost called Yapeyú during his father's tour of duty on the Plata frontier, but his childhood residence in América lasted only a few years. By the time he reached school age, San Martín's family had returned to Spain. When he was eleven years old, San Martín and his two brothers followed their father into the Spanish army, becoming career officers and witnessing the tumultuous European events of 1791–1808 from the vantage point of men who wore a Spanish uniform. In March 1808, San Martín was on the staff of the general commanding Spanish troops in Portugal when news began to arrive of breathtaking events in Spain.

Northern Spain was filling up with a hundred thousand French troops, far more than required to support operations in Portugal. Consequently, Spanish queen María Luisa's lover, Godoy, who had instigated the French incursion for his personal benefit, had risen to new heights of unpopularity, and María Luisa along with him. The Spanish people blamed Carlos IV for not controlling his wife. The disgraced royal family and royal favorite stayed away from Madrid, residing in outlying palaces, in order to avoid the hostility of urban crowds. The crowds, in turn, began to view Carlos IV's son and heir, Prince Fernando, as the kingdom's only hope. Unfortunately for the kingdom, Fernando's popularity had little basis in the prince's true qualities. Instead, Fernando's popularity expanded, as a sort of equal and opposite reaction, in direct proportion to the growing hatred of Godoy. It was no longer necessary even to say the prince's name. Instead, he became simply *el deseado*, the Desired One.

Gradually, as Napoleon's troops occupied much of northern Spain, the French emperor's aggressive purpose became unmistakable. Upon receiving a Napoleonic ultimatum to surrender their kingdom, the Spanish royal family, then lodged at their palace at Aranjuez, near Madrid, prepared to retreat south. Rumors flew through Aranjuez and beyond saying that the royal family intended to flee across the Atlantic to New Spain. No such plans existed, but the idea was plausible enough in light of João's departure from Lisbon. The Spanish people thought that an idea so awful could have come only from Godoy, and first hundreds and then thousands of rioters streamed into Aranjuez looking for him. Godoy had to hide in an attic for more than a day to escape their wrath, his days of political influence ended forever. The Spanish military detachments around the palace at Aranjuez shared the sentiments of their rioting countrymen and eventually joined them. On 19 March 1808, the Aranjuez riot came to a head when the crowd forced Carlos IV to abdicate his throne in favor of Prince Fernando, who was acclaimed as king that same night. Fernando's entry into Madrid days later was celebrated by delirious multitudes that lined sidewalks and filled balconies.

The Desired One began to disappoint his yearning subjects immediately. Under the protection of French troops, his father, Carlos, asked for the Spanish throne back, pointing out that he had not abdicated of his free will. With disastrously poor judgment, father and son accepted an invitation from Napoleon to settle the matter at a friendly meeting in southern France, at Bayonne. Once in Bayonne, however, both Fernando and Carlos became, in effect, Napoleon's prisoners, and the foxy emperor forced both to renounce their claims to the Spanish throne in favor of a new dynasty, the Bonapartes. The first Bonaparte king of Spain would be Napoleon's brother Joseph. Carlos and María Luisa went into Italian exile. The Spanish people did not want them back. But Spain *did* want Fernando, who would remain in French custody for the next six years, giving his loyal subjects further opportunity to yearn for him as a symbol, the Desired One, without really knowing him.

News of Napoleon's treachery spread through Spain and also to Spanish forces in Portugal. On 2 May 1808, a famous day on the Spanish patriotic calendar, the people of Madrid rose against the occupying French army, which quelled the uprising with mass executions. Throughout the remaining Spanish provinces not yet under French occupation, provincial leaders formed committees of resistance called *juntas*, refusing to recognize the legitimacy of a new Bonaparte dynasty and declaring that in the king's absence, sovereignty reverted to the provincial level. Among the first initiatives of the provincial juntas was an appeal for help to Napoleon's archenemy, Britain. As this earthquake rocked the political landscape, San Martín's unit separated from its erstwhile French allies, withdrew from Portugal, and returned to Spain.

In Spain's principal southern port, Cádiz, San Martín, a member of the commanding Spanish general's inner circle, learned as much as anyone could about these confusing events. General Solano, his commander, was his friend and confidant, no doubt in part because Solano, too, was an americano. The two socialized together despite the difference in rank. They even resembled each other, which was too bad for San Martín on a day in late May 1808 that marked him for life. General Solano had just announced his decision *not* to lead his troops into revolt against the French occupation. The weakened Spanish army was in no shape to fight their powerful former allies, he reasoned. British helpfulness remained to be tested, and Solano had little faith in the success of the popular uprising against the French. Unfortunately for him, the popular uprising had an equally skeptical view of General Solano, whose reputation in the Spanish army rested on his advocacy of French-style organization and tactics. Accusing

Solano of treacherous pro-French sympathies, a patriotic crowd seized San Martín's friend, patron, and mentor and tore him to bits. San Martín himself was mistaken for Solano at one point and barely escaped with his life. Ever after, San Martín carried a medal with Solano's image in his pocket, and from then on he equated democracy with mob rule.

Meanwhile, Spain's mobilization of national resistance against French occupation was becoming a reality. Among all the provincial juntas, Seville's grandly titled Supreme Junta of Spain and the Indies was the strongest, and for logical reasons, such as the city's size, wealth, and overseas connections, not to mention its location as far from France as possible. In combination with the nearby port of Cádiz, Seville had dominated trade with América for centuries and served as well as the primary administrative center for Spain's overseas colonies. Seville's Supreme Junta got a major boost also when its armed forces scored two victories against the French. The first of these, which occurred in late June 1808, was an extremely minor skirmish. Still, it was the first Spanish victory of the war, and so the patriots celebrated. For our purposes, its only significance is the name of the junior officer commanding Spanish forces that day: José de San Martín. San Martín also distinguished himself the next month at the larger battle of Bailén, which caused Joseph Bonaparte to flee temporarily from Madrid, at great cost to his dignity, only ten days after arriving there to claim his throne.

For seven years, Spain and Portugal (together, the Iberian Peninsula) became the battleground of what the English call the Peninsular War and remember as the campaign in which the Duke of Wellington emerged as Napoleon's battlefield nemesis. For Spain and Portugal, the Peninsular War was a national uprising against armies of occupation, a patriotic war of national independence. Civilian volunteers such as José Bonifácio composed the chief Portuguese and Spanish forces, the regular troops being mostly English or French. The British counterinvasion began around Lisbon, where General Beresford was on hand to organize the Portuguese volunteers.

Napoleon's 1807–8 invasion of the Iberian Peninsula triggered sweeping but gradual changes in América. It provoked the Portuguese monarchy to do what no other European monarchy ever had—leave Europe, making Brazil, for the time being, the seat of the Portuguese monarchy. And it provoked in the Spanish colonies a slow-motion crisis of political legitimacy. Who should rule in the absence of the king?

News of the European crisis arrived in New Spain with a delay of about six weeks. Sporadic, contradictory reports of the most dramatic possible character—concerning the French invasion of Spain, the uprising at Aranjuez, the fall of Godoy, the forced abdication of Carlos IV, the fleeting reign of the Desired One, the 2 May massacres in Madrid, and the formation of Spanish regional juntas—surged through the country, week after shocking week, during the months of June and July 1808. The spontaneous public reaction in New Spain included righteous satisfaction at the eclipse of Godoy, angry condemnation of France, and tender concern for Prince Fernando, whom the people of New Spain immediately accepted as king, swearing obedience to him in solemn public ceremonies as Fernando VII. Overall, americanos seemed just as loyal as europeos to the Desired One, but americano attitudes toward the Spanish juntas were much brisker. Did the juntas speak for the king? No. And unless they spoke for the king, who were the juntas, after all, but simply bossy gachupines giving orders?

In August 1808, when emissaries sent by Seville's Supreme Junta of Spain and the Indies appeared in Mexico City, New Spain's small, but rich and powerful, community of europeos wanted the government of New Spain to recognize the Seville junta's paramount authority. Given the Seville junta's strong links to commercial interests, this europeo pressure was predictable. Europeo merchants were the chief beneficiaries of the monopoly mercantile system. Overall, europeos controlled the ruling institutions of New Spain, but americanos did predominate on the Mexico City council, where the representatives of Seville's self-styled Supreme Junta presented themselves in August 1808, calling for aid and obedience.

What happened next was an event that requires special terminology. The emissaries of Seville were invited to an open meeting of the city council, called a *cabildo abierto*. Cabildos abiertos constituted the grassroots of traditional Spanish self-governance. A cabildo abierto included anyone believed deserving to be heard, which meant, basically, a wealthy few. Those in attendance would include an honor roll of civil, military, and church officials, including (in a major capital such as Mexico City) justices of the high court, called the *audiencia*, and members of the official monopoly merchant's guild, called the *consulado*. In Mexico City, as throughout América, these dignitaries were predominantly europeos. But the members of the normal city council also attended the cabildo abierto, obviously, and they were predominantly americanos.

At the 1808 cabildo abierto in Mexico City, various americanos—most notably a city councilman, José Primo Verdad, and a friar, Melchor de Talamantes—declared that during the captivity of the king the sovereignty of New Spain reverted, by rights, to the people of New Spain. Many suspected that the main interest of the europeos, even during this crisis, was preserving their special economic advantages, a sore point. As with the systematic preferment of europeos for office holding, Spain's trade monopoly showed that New Spain was treated as a colony. But the americanos of New Spain preferred to think of themselves as the descendants of valiant conquerors who had defeated the Aztecs and carved out a new kingdom in América. In an argument later heard across the hemisphere, the bold americanos of Mexico City's 1808 cabildo abierto cited political traditions with an impeccable Spanish pedigree to deny that the king's American kingdoms were, by rights, colonies of Spain at all. Spain and New Spain, they insisted, were separate kingdoms ruled by the same monarch. Americanos owed no obedience to europeos, only to Fernando. According to a metaphor often heard in these months, Spain and América were separate and equal pillars of Fernando's crown. Spanish juntas spoke only for Spain, and New Spain should speak for itself.

This argument was all the more persuasive because of the confusion that reigned among the Spanish juntas themselves. Although Seville's junta had styled itself the Supreme Junta of Spain and the Indies, it was just a regional junta with outsized ambitions. The other Spanish juntas did not accept the authority of Seville. In fact, during the meetings of Mexico City's 1808 cabildo abierto someone read a letter from a different Spanish junta, warning against Seville's false claims to supremacy. Briefly, the city council began to consider the idea of forming their own junta in support of Fernando VII.

Meanwhile, Iturrigaray, the viceroy of New Spain, had suffered the climate of uncertainty more than most, being a political appointee who owed his job to the despised Godoy. Iturrigaray had so many enemies among the europeos of Mexico City that only support from the americanos could save his political skin. But Iturrigaray's pro-americano sympathies smacked of danger to powerful europeos in the royal administration, church hierarchy, merchant community, and mining aristocracy. To guarantee the security of Spain's most profitable colony, the europeo faction organized a preemptive coup and, in mid-September, arrested Iturrigaray to replace him with someone they could control. Less than two years after the disgrace of Sobre-monte, a second Spanish viceroy had toppled. A major shake-up was beginning in América.

For the present, that shake-up was most meaningful to the wealthy. Take Leona Vicario, a recently orphaned young woman of nineteen who lived in Mexico City. Leona's father was a rich europeo merchant who had married a poor but respectable and attractive americana, a common pattern. Leona's family fortune allowed her guardian uncle to make her the mistress of a big house all her own, with many ser-vants. Young, smart, and talented in addition to wealthy and orphaned, Leona was extremely marriageable. During the exciting political events of 1808, her engagement to a young man equally opulent and attractive dominated her attention. Indeed, Leona's fiancé belonged to a branch of the family that owned Guanajuato's fabled Valenciana silver mine. And Leona's future father-in-law was close to Viceroy Iturrigaray, so close, in fact, that the overthrow of Iturrigaray dragged him down, too. Leona's fiancé had to leave her and flee New Spain for fear of europeo reprisals. The widening divide between europeos and americanos defined Leona Vicario's political orientation in the years to come.

Meet Manuela

Something similar happened in the life of Manuela Sáenz, a twelve-year-old girl living in the distant and far smaller city of Quito. Manuela was not rich. Her father, like Leona Vicario's, was a europeo merchant, quite prosperous but not married to her mother, an americana who had borne Manuela out of wedlock. One early afternoon in late March 1809, Manuela and her mother went running to the open window, called by the sound of many horses' hooves echoing on the cobblestone streets of Quito. Flanked by guards, Juan Pío Montúfar, the Marqués de Selva Alegre, head of one of Quito's leading americano families (who had hosted Humboldt's stay in the city and whose son Carlos climbed Chimborazo with Humboldt), entered the city under guard as a prisoner, arrested for plotting against the Spanish government.

In Quito, as throughout América in early 1809, people were strug-gling to gather, interpret, and assimilate news of European events. Hardly had they heard that Fernando had mounted the throne when they learned that Joseph Bonaparte had pushed him off it. No sooner had they heard of Seville's Supreme Junta of Spain and the Indies than they learned that a new Central Junta claimed supremacy over *it*. Who now represented legitimate royal authority? Throughout América, the argument made in New Spain sounded again and again: no Spanish junta spoke for the king; americanos owed no obedience to Spain per se. In the absence of the legitimate king, Fernando, went the argument, his subjects should do exactly the same in América as in Spain, that is, form caretaker juntas to rule in his name until he returned. The March 1809 conspiracy in Quito had exactly that very popular aim. Bowing to public pressure, the Spanish president of the city's *audiencia* (high court) eventually released Montúfar and the others, to the glee of Quito's defiant americanos.

These political events concerned Manuela's family directly. Her europeo father was prominent in Quito and a sworn enemy of the Montúfar clan. Manuela's mother's family, on the other hand, being americanos, likely harbored contrasting sentiments and regarded Montúfar not as a criminal conspirator but as a hero. Manuela's adolescent sympathies soured toward europeos partly for personal reasons, but similar changes of heart were then occurring throughout the Andes, most notably in the cities of Chuquisaca and La Paz, in Upper Peru.

Chuquisaca, like Quito the location of an audiencia, overthrew the Spanish president of that body. The Chuquisaca rebels included everyone from audiencia judges and americano lawyers to angry crowds of mestizo townspeople motivated by the rumor that the audiencia president had been accepting diplomatic overtures from Carlota Joaquina, the Portuguese prince regent's wife and chief detractor, now residing in Rio de Janeiro. Carlota Joaquina was a Spanish princess, after all. In fact, she was Fernando's sister, the only member of her family not under Napoleon's thumb in 1809.

The fracas in Chuquisaca encouraged the city council of nearby La Paz to depose its own royal administrator, amid loud declarations of loyalty to Fernando VII, in July 1809. The La Paz uprising went further than Chuquisaca's, founding a junta and reaching out for support to the Quechua- and Aymara-speaking Indians of Upper Peru. The leader of the movement, Pedro Domingo Murillo, was a mestizo, although an exceedingly rich one. The declarations of the La Paz junta were the boldest claims of americano independence so far— independence from Spain, but not from the Desired One, of course. Less than a month after the creation of the La Paz junta, americano conspirators in Manuela's Quito were at it again. Fifty or so delegates met on an August 1809 evening (at the house of a freethinking patriotic lady) and moved to depose the audiencia president and form a junta of their own in the name of Fernando VII but under the leadership of the Marqués of Selva Alegre. The people of Quito lit their windows with candles for three nights in celebration. The junta quickly imprisoned hostile europeos such as Manuela's father.

Unfortunately for the juntas of La Paz and Quito, the Spanish viceroy in nearby Lima was among the most able colonial administrators ever sent to América. And by 1809 Viceroy Abascal was a seasoned ruler with wide experience, having served in the Caribbean, New Spain, and the Río de la Plata, including seven years as audiencia president in Guadalajara, before becoming viceroy of Peru. At the helm of Spain's chief South American viceroyalty, Abascal had been notably effective, building fortifications, introducing steam power in Peru's deep-shaft silver mines, founding a botanical garden and a medical school, and more recently raising unimaginable sums of money for patriotic Spanish resistance against Napoleon. Under Abascal's stern influence, the americanos of Lima swore an oath of allegiance to the new Central Junta without a peep about Peru not being a colony of Spain.

When word reached Lima of juntas in Quito and La Paz, Abascal responded with quick and deadly force. By November 1809, the viceroy's soldiers had erased all trace of upstart juntas in the Andean highlands. In La Paz, they executed Pedro Domingo Murillo and eight other rebels. Abascal's forces put down the Quito junta as well. None of Quito's more aristocratic rebels got a death sentence, but sixty were imprisoned indefinitely. Among those leveling accusations at the americano rebels of Quito was Manuela's father, newly released from prison.

Despite the drama of these events, however, other things filled Manuela's adolescent days. Her slave Jonatás, for example, a girl only two or three years older than Manuela, was an ever-present and truly important companion, and would be that throughout her life. When Manuela's half sister by her father's wife married a Spaniard twice her age and left for Spain, Manuela shared the family's flurry of excitement. Her relationship with her father, however, remained troubled. And that was not her only trouble. Manuela's indocile temperament created constant friction in socially conservative Quito, where women and children were to be seen and not heard. Soon her family would intern her in a convent school, not at all the place for a free spirit such as Manuela. For the next ten years, her rebelliousness would have a personal rather than political focus.

Manuela Sáenz, Leona Vicario, and Mariquita Sánchez—destined to become the most famous americana patriots—had in common an unusual degree of independence from their fathers. Manuela was estranged from hers, Leona's had died, and Mariquita faced hers down in a court battle. In a society ruled by patriarchy, these young women had lost, escaped, or resisted patriarchal authority. No wonder that eventually they would not hesitate to defy the rule of the "father king," as he was frequently called.

Resistance to Napoleon Collapses in Spain

Back in Spain, José de San Martín was working to help organize the resistance against French occupation in the province of Catalonia during November 1809. Spanish patriot volunteers did not compose regular uniformed army units, but rather, as in the case of the Portuguese patriots fighting with Wellington, were members of irregular forces who seldom confronted the French army directly in the fixed battle formations of the day, drums beating and flags waving. Instead, Spanish patriot volunteers fought the "little war" (*guerrilla*, in Spanish) of secrecy, surprise, and hit-and-run tactics against superior arms. They did not invent these tactics, of course, but they gave them the name we still use today. San Martín's part in this war was training, organization, and liaison and did not involve combat because he fell gravely ill. Apparently this was the first major onset of the lung disease, tuberculosis, against which he struggled for decades.

Convalescing in Seville during the eventful early months of 1809, San Martín witnessed firsthand the evolution of Spanish attempts to form a unified government of resistance. During most of that year, Seville hosted the Central Junta, an umbrella organization consisting of two delegates from each of Spain's regional juntas. Seville's so-called Supreme Junta resisted the authority of the Central Junta at first. Eventually, however, the Central Junta did gain recognition throughout unoccupied Spain.

But the Central Junta could not hold back the French invasion gradually pouring south across the Spanish countryside. A crushingly superior French army of more than two hundred thousand led by Napoleon himself had restored *frère* Joseph Bonaparte to the Spanish throne in Madrid by the end of 1809, when Spanish patriot resistance collapsed altogether and the Central Junta had to flee from Seville to the nearby port of Cádiz. Eventually, Spain's government of national resistance had lost control of all Spanish territory outside Cádiz, a near-island, where it could be defended by the guns of British warships and maintain communications with América. No sooner had the Central Junta arrived in Cádiz, than it dissolved, transferring its sagging authority to a newly formed Council of Regents that claimed, unconvincingly, to speak directly for Fernando. The existing regional juntas, including the one in Cádiz itself, were slow to accept the authority of the regency. The Cádiz junta was so concerned about the demoralizing effect that all this bad news might have in América that it prohibited the departure of ships. But bad news does not sail, it flies.

Americanos Organize at Querétaro

The apparent collapse of Spanish resistance to Napoleon emboldened americano militia officers to make a new try at a junta for New Spain. Americano sympathies for the now deposed, pro-americano Viceroy Iturrigaray had first arisen during militia exercises that Iturrigaray ordered in 1807. New Spain's twenty battalions of infantry militia and twenty-four of cavalry militia had converged on a high plain near the city of Jalapa, a strategic strong point for the defense of New Spain against invasion by sea, and engaged in several months of training and male bonding. Recent invasion attempts at Coro, Montevideo, and Buenos Aires gave them much to talk about. When Iturrigaray went to direct their maneuvers personally, each unit vied to surpass the next in skill and enthusiasm. Whatever his failings, Iturrigaray possessed a winning manner in the rough male society of a military camp, and a number of americano officers became personally devoted to him during the weeks of maneuvers.

The most important of these officers, for our story, was Ignacio Allende, a forty-year-old americano of considerable wealth from the town of San Miguel, not far from Hidalgo's village of Dolores. When Mexico City europeos overthrew Viceroy Iturrigaray in 1808, Allende was spurred to action against the europeos and joined a major plot, the so-called Valladolid Conspiracy, to create a junta in New Spain. Unfortunately for Allende, word of the plotting reached the ears of the Spanish government. The government responded with leniency, its customary attitude toward disgruntled americanos, in contrast to the harsh treatment of mestizos such as Pedro Domingo Murillo and others executed in La Paz. As soon as he was released, though, Allende went back to organizing.

In March 1810, Allende and other militia officers began to visit Miguel Hidalgo at his house in the village of Dolores. Supposedly the military men were showing an interest in the worldly priest's famous parties, but really they had come to invite Hidalgo into the conspiracy. Hidalgo was now fifty-seven years old and enjoying the fruits of his diverse agricultural and other projects. He was comfortable and respected, and he had a scandalously gratifying personal life. But Hidalgo was also an idealist and a dreamer, and he had always been reckless. Furthermore, he had believed for years in the same liberty that inspired Humboldt, Jefferson, and so many others. Hidalgo remained interested in French ideas even after Napoleon invaded Iberia. He traveled frequently to Guanajuato and to Allende's hometown, nearby San Miguel. Such cities buzzed with apprehensive conversations in 1810. The catastrophic collapse of Spanish resistance to Napoleon had left only the symbolic, almost literally offshore, Cádiz government intact. Even that might soon vanish. Would Napoleon and the puppet Spanish king Joseph I then try to assert control over New Spain? The case for a junta in New Spain seemed stronger than ever. It did not take many visits from Allende before Hidalgo agreed to join what became known as the Querétaro Conspiracy.

The city of Querétaro stands on the north side of the Lerma River valley, whose middle stretch constituted one of New Spain's richest regions, the Bajío. The Bajío was simultaneously a great breadbasket and the location of the mother lode of silver, more or less directly underneath the city of Guanajuato, where Humboldt had lingered and marveled during his visit to New Spain. The Querétaro Conspiracy brought together militia officers such as Ignacio Allende and educated urban people including apothecaries, judges, and clergymen. Even Querétaro's chief royal official participated. The conspirators of Querétaro planned to announce the formation of an americano junta to defend the rights of Fernando VII on an occasion propitious for a popular uprising—the teeming country fair at San Juan de los Lagos, where tens of thousands of people, especially Indians and people of mixed descent, formed a two-week encampment every December to trade horses, mules, and burros and carouse in honor of the Virgin of Candelaria.

Hidalgo agreed to play a crucial role in the Querétaro Conspiracy. Well known and well liked by the indigenous peasantry, Hidalgo could be very influential in rallying them to the cause of revolt. And the conspirators deemed an uprising of the peasantry to be crucial. The Bajío contained untold numbers of rural people who no longer lived in traditional Indian communities and served instead as agricultural wage laborers, a much more precarious life. Here, famine was a familiar companion of the poor. Throngs of Bajío peasants had joined large anti-gachupín protests in 1766. The Querétaro conspirators wanted Father Hidalgo to help them rouse a similar anti-europeo sentiment now. Hidalgo possessed prestige among the Indian peasants because he respected them, organized among them, and was clergy.

But any talk of French liberty would sour things totally with the pious folk who gathered at the San Juan de los Lagos country fair. Allende felt he had to stress the point to Hidalgo, who was already manufacturing slings, pikes, machetes, and other crude weapons to be distributed on the day of the uprising. Always avid for a practical challenge, Hidalgo had even tried to cast a few cannons. Allende did not want things to get out of control. The common people of New Spain might join a revolt against europeos as colonial rulers, particularly if the latter were tarred as sellouts to Napoleon, he told Hidalgo, but they would never rise against the Desired One, nor had they the slightest interest in republics. The planned rallying cries of the uprising at San Juan de los Lagos would have to be "Death to the gachupines! Long live Fernando VII!"[5]

Wearing the Mask of Fernando

In 1810, twenty-seven-year-old Simón Bolívar was back in Venezuela. Although he had theoretically embraced liberty and endorsed the superiority of republican over monarchical government, Bolívar continued to behave in his daily dealings like a great landowner from one of Venezuela's overweening mantuano families. Imagine him arriving with a party of armed slaves to plant a crop of indigo on land disputed by another landowner. The other landowner and *his* slaves, also armed, take up the challenge. The two plantation owners end up tussling in front of their slaves, who separate them. Bolívar regrets that he must inform the authorities about his neighbor's "strange conduct" and has him arrested. A bit later, when those same authorities ask the young mantuano plantation owner to take a turn serving as a local official in the vicinity of his plantation, Bolívar can't find the time and delivers a supercilious rebuff. Who do these insignificant local authorities think he is?

Meanwhile, the legitimacy crisis of the Spanish monarchy was growing in Caracas. News of Napoleon's usurpation of the Spanish throne arrived in July 1808, and the immediate, spontaneous, and overwhelming reaction of all Caracas was fervent loyalty to the good king Fernando. For once, though, people's fears of French influence among their colonial rulers were well founded. In April 1810, the captain general of Venezuela was Vicente Emparán, the same Spanish official who had welcomed Humboldt to Cumaná in 1799 and encouraged his work. Emparán (like Hidalgo or San Martín's unfortunate superior, General Solano) was the sort of person called, at the time, an *afrancesado*—which meant he had been "Frenchified" by excessive admiration of French scientific, literary, and political culture. Only Emparán's many years of excellent governance in Venezuela compensated for his unattractive Frenchness. Emparán's friends and associates tended to be "Frenchified" as well—among them Simón Bolívar and Bolívar's in-law and fun-loving companion from Paris, Fernando Toro. At one gathering Bolívar went so far as to toast the end of Spanish tyranny in the captain general's presence—plainly an odd situation.

On 19 April 1810, only four days after a ship docked at La Guaira with news of the apparent collapse of Spanish resistance to Napoleon, a cabildo abierto met in Caracas to form a junta, with crowds outside shouting, "Death to the French! Long live Fernando VII!" Emparán surrendered his staff of office to the head of the city council. Humboldt had regarded the elite of Caracas as among the most outward-looking (and therefore progressive) in América, and his attitude was confirmed by the junta's abolition of trade restrictions, export tariffs, Indian tribute, and the slave trade. In addition, now that Britain supported the cause of Fernando VII against Napoleon, the Supreme Junta of Caracas planned to send a diplomatic mission to London.

Simón Bolívar offered himself as envoy, but the junta hesitated. Was the scrappy and undisciplined young militia officer the right man for this delicate mission? Bolívar terminated the discussion by offering to pay for the whole mission out of his own deep pockets. However, as a precautionary measure, the Caracas junta sent several older-and-wiser types to London with Bolívar. One was Andrés Bello, who had once tutored Bolívar and who spoke English. (Fortunately for Bolívar, Andrés Bello and Simón Rodríguez turned out, in vastly different ways, to be the greatest educators of their generation in all of América.) The junta supplied Bolívar with diplomatic credentials from "Don Fernando VII, King of Spain and the Indies, and in his Royal Name, the Supreme Junta for his Rights in Venezuela."[6] Knowing Bolívar, they added strict instructions against spendthrift behavior that would create the wrong impression in London. Finally, the junta admonished Bolívar that

Francisco de Miranda was *not* a loyal subject of Fernando VII. Although it might be necessary to approach him in London, Bolívar should keep Miranda at arm's length and definitely not encourage his return to Venezuela. Bolivar agreed to their terms, but, like Allende and Hidalgo in New Spain, he concealed his true intentions behind "the mask of Fernando," as insincere use of the king's name by republican revolutionaries would later be termed.

The envoys of the Caracas junta embarked on a British warship in early June 1810 and enjoyed a quick passage, landing in England just one month later. Bolívar went straight to see Miranda, who used his Foreign Office connections to arrange an informal and totally fruitless interview between the envoys and a British diplomat. Miranda also introduced his visitors to other dissident americanos, with whom Bolívar and Bello spent some time exploring pubs in London. Bello, in Europe for the first time, liked the expatriate life so much that he never returned to Venezuela. It was a good time to arrive in London with a Spanish accent and representing a junta. Like the Spanish words *liberal* and *guerrilla*, the word *junta* was entering the English language at this time with a stylish and friendly ring. Directly disobeying his orders, Bolívar persuaded Miranda to return to Venezuela, betting that the aging revolutionary's savvy, prestige, and connections would help win whatever battle had to be fought against Spain and against Fernando VII. Miranda, ever the dreamer, decided on one more try and bid farewell—forever, as it turned out—to his English family.

Meanwhile, like the Supreme Junta of Seville, the Supreme Junta of Caracas was having trouble getting recognition among its neighbors. Venezuela lacked strong centralist traditions, and Caracas had become the capital rather recently. Before then, Cumaná and Coro had been the capital cities, respectively, of eastern and western Venezuela. Cumaná, which had formed its own junta, decided conditionally to recognize the leadership of Caracas, but Coro refused. Smaller cities followed one lead or the other, raising the specter of civil war within Venezuela. This specter soon haunted many parts of América.

Buenos Aires Has a Revolution

Mariano Moreno, a young americano revolutionary of Buenos Aires, also wore the mask of Fernando in 1810, becoming known (especially to his enemies) for his revolutionary zeal. Moreno's was a shooting star. He helped launch the most durable of all the americano revolutions of 1810, but Moreno's own participation lasted only a few months.

In May 1810, Moreno possessed an excellent job on the staff of the audiencia of Buenos Aires, a job that, given his family's modest means, he could count as a significant personal achievement. Only because his brilliance as a student had attracted a generous patron, an admiring bishop, was Moreno able to attend the chief university of the Viceroyalty of the Río de la Plata, far away at Chuquisaca. Moreno's early life was sheltered, almost cloistered. He spent a lot of time in the home of his ecclesiastical patron. Moreno earned a degree in theology and another in law, then disappointed his family (who had hoped he would enter the priesthood) by getting married. Moreno also visited nearby Potosí—the "mountain of silver," the main reason for Chuquisaca's existence—and came away horrified by the mistreatment of the indigenous miners who still groaned under the infamous colonial labor draft called the *mita*. After briefly practicing law in Chuquisaca, Moreno decided to return to Buenos Aires—just in time, as it turned out, for the British invasions. Even before Popham's rogue expedition appeared, the smart and ambitious Moreno had become a secretary of the high court.

During the 1806 British occupation of Buenos Aires, when British trading vessels rapidly clustered offshore offering attractive goods, Moreno became convinced of the necessity and virtues of free trade, although not under British rule, of course. After the British had been ejected, Moreno argued publicly for an end to the official trade monopoly. That argument brought him powerful enemies, but friends as well. The circle of quiet dissidents who often met socially at the house of Mariquita Sánchez de Thompson (her married name) agreed with Moreno. In addition, the landowners of Buenos Aires, as a group, urgently desired free trade. Even the longtime secretary of the city's merchant guild, Manuel Belgrano, argued that direct trade with Britain had become an economic necessity. Belgrano was a trade analyst of considerable sophistication, but his argument was simple. As Spain fell gradually under French occupation, Spanish ports became enemy ports. In the meantime, Britain and Spain were now allies. So why not trade with Britain? Whether legal or contraband, trade with Britain seemed destined to happen. Indeed, aside from a few monopoly merchants, there were not many inhabitants of Buenos Aires who did not favor free trade. Viceroy Liniers himself tolerated it until replaced by a new man sent from Spain.

Mariquita Sánchez and her husband, Martín Thompson, had been thoroughly swept up in the political ferment of 1808–10. Mariquita presided over evening gatherings modeled on French salons, where guests enjoyed music and dancing as well as discussion of literature and current events, even the occasional scientific demonstration. But the young mother already had two babies and another on the way. While her children were keeping Mariquita busy, several of her habitual salon guests, Belgrano among them, became chief players in the upcoming revolution. Buenos Aires had become rather assertive since trouncing two British invasions with its own militia forces. So when news arrived in May that the French had swept Spanish resistance practically off the map, the americanos of Buenos Aires reacted quickly.

Belgrano and Juan José Castelli (Belgrano's cousin, longtime co-conspirator, and another friend of Mariquita's) demanded a cabildo abierto, and to back up their demand, they called on Cornelio Saave-dra, the popularly elected commander of the Buenos Aires militia. A crowd of supporters filled the main plaza in front of the cabildo hall as inside Castelli delivered his version of the argument being heard that year all over América: that in the absence of Fernando, his American subjects should constitute their own juntas. A preponderance of amer-icano votes inside the hall and a preponderance of americano forces outside it together guaranteed victory. On 25 May 1810, the cabildo named Saavedra president of the new junta, which also included Bel-grano, Castelli, and, in the post of secretary, Mariano Moreno.

Although only secretary, Moreno became the driving force of the Buenos Aires junta, its minister of war, the interior, and foreign rela-tions. He approached the task with ruthless single-mindedness. Moreno devoted himself to consolidating the May 1810 revolution, as it was called, building the junta's armed forces and promoting its ideology in a newspaper that began to circulate in June. The junta had been con-stituted in the name of Fernando VII, of course, and its president, Saavedra, was a conservative monarchist. Therefore, Moreno, Bel-grano, and Castelli all kept the mask of Fernando securely in place. But Moreno's true intentions included the formation of a South American confederation, for which he translated the U.S. Constitution as a model. Moreno earned his reputation as a ruthless revolutionary by persecuting resident europeos, and when he learned that the deposed viceroy Liniers was plotting against the junta, Moreno had him uncer-emoniously executed. Meanwhile, Castelli and Belgrano set out to assert the Buenos Aires junta's authority militarily in Upper Peru and Paraguay, respectively.

After only a few months of Moreno's activities, the conservatives forced the young radical off the Buenos Aires junta and sent him to London on a diplomatic mission, where he would be safely out of the way. The man whom some had called the Robespierre of the Buenos Aires junta died during the voyage to London. Some said that he was poisoned.

New Granada Gets Juntas Galore

Americano juntas in Caracas and Buenos Aires were joined by many others as word spread of military and institutional collapse in Spain. One of those spreading word was Carlos Montúfar, Humboldt's young traveling companion from Quito, who had accompanied Humboldt and Bonpland back to Europe and returned to América in 1810 as an exponent of liberty. Montúfar was supposedly a representative of the Cádiz Council of Regents, but he encouraged the creation of juntas in América. In May 1810, Montúfar arrived in Cartagena, Spain's great fortified naval base on the Caribbean shore of New Granada. Cartagena's powerful merchant community already demanded the right to trade with British vessels as an absolute commercial necessity, in defiance of the wishes of Cádiz. Montúfar's bad news from Spain galvanized the Cartagena city council. In June a ten-hour cabildo abierto ousted the royal governor of Cartagena and established a local junta in the name of Fernando VII.

One can imagine the excitement of Antonio Nariño, an emaciated prisoner whom new americano authorities released from Cartagena's fetid dungeons. A native of Bogotá, Nariño, who was now in his late forties, had spent much of the last fifteen years in prison for his republican ideas. Nariño was a Moreno born twenty years before his time or, perhaps, a Miranda who stayed home. In 1781, after witnessing the grisly executions of several rebels who protested new taxes, Nariño had renounced his militia officer's commission and turned dissident. Like Moreno, Nariño was a studious reader who fell under the spell of French books and a successful bureaucrat in the royal government, in his case as treasurer; he was also administrator of the royal quinine monopoly and, most significantly, operator of the official press. When the French Revolution began in the 1790s, Nariño hosted evening salon gatherings to discuss French political philosophers and news from Europe, just as Miguel Hidalgo was doing. Nariño acquired a collection of banned books presided over, in his private library, by a bust of Benjamin Franklin, whom Nariño particularly admired. Like Miranda—and partly, as we will see, because of him—Antonio Nariño became an outright revolutionary at an unusually early date.

In 1794, Nariño read a history of the French revolutionary constitutional assembly that contained the full text of the Declaration of the Rights of Man. He translated the document into Spanish and, having access to a press, printed a hundred copies. Nariño paid dearly for that mistake, because it was soon discovered by the royal authorities, who located and confiscated Nariño's banned books. Banned books were the purview of the Inquisition, which publicly burned Nariño's translation, then tried the flaming revolutionary himself and sentenced him to ten years of hard labor in one of Spain's North African penal institutions.

Nariño somehow escaped during his ship's stop in Cádiz, however, and made a beeline for revolutionary Paris. In Paris, the persistent americano dissident met with Francisco Miranda, who had not yet transferred his activities to London. In April 1797, within a year of his departure from New Granada, Nariño returned there, disguised as a priest, attempting to enact the vision that he and Miranda shared with an infinitely tiny number of other Frenchified americano intellectuals. Traveling around the New Granada countryside, Nariño found few, if any, subscribers to his republican vision, and by July he was again a prisoner. A prisoner he would remain until his health deteriorated so severely that he received a humanitarian parole in 1803.

Nariño was still convalescing in 1809 when news of Juan Pío Montúfar's Quito junta inspired patriot stirrings in Bogotá. A Bogotá cabildo official named Camilo Torres submitted to the viceroy a petition denouncing royal misgovernment and demanding that americanos have the right to form their own juntas. The disgruntled viceroy cracked down on americano agitation, and among those netted for conspiring to displace royal authorities was—again, unfortunately—Antonio Nariño. Nariño was sent to the impenetrable dungeons of Cartagena. Escaping en route, he was recaptured and subjected to such brutal conditions of imprisonment that he was almost dead when the formation of the Cartagena junta rescued him in June 1810.

But the coming weeks presented the gaunt revolutionary with the scenario of his dreams. The secondary cities of New Granada were following the lead of Cartagena and forming juntas for home rule. Cabildos abiertos established juntas in Cali, Pamplona, and Socorro. On 20 July 1810, americano patriots in Bogotá intentionally provoked an incident with a europeo merchant on the main plaza of the city, triggering a riot. The americano militias whose job it was to quell riots declined to interfere in this one, and the city council convinced the viceroy that only the formation of a local junta in the name of Fernando VII would satisfy the crowd. Although the viceroy was to preside over the new junta himself, the rebellious mood in the plaza led in a different direction—toward the arrest of unpopular europeos, including the viceroy, who was so roughly treated by the excited crowd that friends had to spirit him out of harm's way and, eventually, out of Bogotá. The chain reaction continued, and secondary cities throughout New Granada formed juntas.

As Antonio Nariño made his way up the Magadalena River from Cartagena to Bogotá, New Granada, always the most decentralized Spanish viceroyalty, was generating more cabildos abiertos and competing juntas than any other region of América. It would be Nariño's self-appointed task to bring order out of this chaos—if his health lasted and he could stay out of prison for a while.

Chile Gets a Junta, Too

Chile was the part of América most remote from Spain. In 1810, few ships made the difficult passage around Cape Horn, at the southern tip of the continent. Normal communications between Chile and Spain came down the Pacific coast, necessitating transshipment in Panama and Lima. So news of the Central Junta's retreat to Cádiz and its subsequent dissolution arrived in Chile after everyone else in América had already heard it. The Chilean capital, Santiago, called a cabildo abierto and formed a junta in the name of Fernando VII on 18 September 1810. The Carrera family, among Santiago's most influential, led in organizing the festivities, which of course included a glittering celebratory ball. In charge of preparations was the elegant Francisca Javiera Eudoxia Rudecinda Carmen de los Dolores de la Carrera y Verdugo—Javiera Carrera for short—an aristocratic young woman who, like Mariquita Sánchez, hosted an evening salon that functioned more or less as a revolutionary cell, bringing together the brightest stars of Santiago's intellectual firmament. Several men who attended Javiera Carrera's gatherings (including three of her own brothers) were to assume leading roles in Chile's new government.

The dominant member of the Santiago junta, however, was Juan Martínez de Rozas, who had merited membership partly because of his renowned learning and partly because of his sway in Concepción,

Chile's second city. Martínez de Rozas hosted gatherings in Concepción where guests discussed more or less the same things as at Javiera Carrera's house, though in less sumptuous surroundings. Sometimes in attendance was a young man for whom Martínez de Rozas had a special affection, the illegitimate son of a former governor of Chile, a governor who eventually received a title of nobility and become the viceroy of Peru. The viceroy's surname, O'Higgins, requires some explanation.

Viceroy Ambrosio O'Higgins had left Ireland as a boy to visit relations in Spain and never came back. He worked with Irish merchants in Cádiz, shipped out to Buenos Aires, found himself constructing fortifications in Chile, entered Spanish royal service, and did very well in it. During his period as royal administrator of Concepción, he met and seduced Isabel Riquelme, a young americana, whom he declined to wed when she became pregnant. Ambrosio's and Isabel's son, Bernardo, was born in 1778 and lived his first twelve years on Spain's most remote American frontier, the region of the Bío Bío River, beyond which dwelled the warlike Araucano people, never conquered by Spanish arms.

Bernardo's absent father sent him to school, first in Lima (the viceregal capital of Peru, where Ambrosio was currently viceroy), then in Cádiz. Young Bernardo Riquelme (as he was then called) left Cádiz for a five-year stay in London, where he mastered his father's native English, read too many French books, and acquired republican convictions. Naturally, he became a protégé of Francisco Miranda. Bernardo's father, understandably, was less than thrilled by his son's ideological evolution and eventually cut off the boy's money altogether. Bernardo could not even afford passage home to Chile until his father died in 1801, leaving him a bequest.

Bernardo's inheritance made him a frontier landowner with three thousand cattle and a seat on the local cabildo. His mother and half sister went to live with him on his estate. Despite his illegitimate birth, Bernardo's European education made him welcome at salon gatherings such as those hosted in nearby Concepción by Martínez de Rozas. In a bid for higher social status, Bernardo petitioned the royal government for permission to use his father's prestigious surname, O'Higgins. Because the boy's father had never legally recognized his paternity, however, the courts asked for sworn testimony from men of sterling reputation, and Martínez de Rozas provided it. The royal government never granted permission, but amid the excitement of the founding of Santiago's junta, that no longer mattered. In the end, Bernardo

Riquelme adopted the name O'Higgins on his own, a step in his metamorphosis from viceroy's bastard son into americano militia officer wearing the mask of Fernando.

In 1810, in response to the apparent collapse of Spanish resistance to Napoleon, americano rebels reacted with impressive unanimity, forming caretaker juntas that asserted the right to home rule in the absence of clear royal authority. The crown of Fernando VII, they explained, rested on two pillars, Spain and América. One pillar had been shattered, but the second stood strong. Thus the huge majority of people in América, americanos españoles, Indians, mestizos, and pardos, swore their oaths of loyalty to Fernando with utter sincerity even while raging against the europeos in their midst. Without using the term, they were claiming popular sovereignty, América for americanos. Directing the new juntas, in many cases, were radicals who actually wanted to create republics similar to the United States. For the time being, the republicans had to wear the so-called mask of Fernando, disguising their true intentions for lack of majority support. Their numbers were few, but their influence would be great.

The situation in Brazil, meanwhile, was infinitely less complicated. Royal authority there had actually been strengthened, with João VI comfortably ensconced in Rio de Janeiro and no crisis on the horizon. The contrast was stark, and it was about to get starker, as the Spanish-speaking lands of América descended into not-so-civil wars.

Three

NOT-SO-CIVIL WARS

1810–1812

B Y SEPTEMBER 1810, Portuguese patriots and their British allies had retaken Lisbon, and, in Spain, Cádiz still defied Napoleon. Overall, however, French armies dominated the Iberian peninsula. Meanwhile, in América, juntas multiplied. All of them proclaimed loyalty to Fernando VII while denying their subservience to Spain and asserting their status as separate and equal kingdoms. If made effective, these claims themselves would end Spain's colonial system, so the Spanish resistance government at Cádiz could never accept them. For the moment, though, the Cádiz government was tiny, fragile, isolated, and fighting for its own survival. Americano juntas in Caracas, Buenos Aires, Bogotá, and Santiago had little need to fear retaliation from Spain. Their problem for the time being lay in their own backyard, as various sorts of fighting began to tear América apart. Events in New Spain were the most dramatic.

A Multitude Rampages Through New Spain

Before dawn on 16 September 1810, Hidalgo and Allende learned that the Querétaro Conspiracy had been outed. What had happened is what so often happens: someone got cold feet and ratted to the authorities. But Querétaro's royal administrator was one of the conspirators, and he stalled while his wife warned Allende and Hidalgo, who were at

Hidalgo's house in the village of Dolores. Today Mexican schoolchildren learn to recite the woman's famous message to Hidalgo: "On the heels of these words come the threat of prison and death. Tomorrow you will be a hero or you will be a prisoner."[1] In other words, the only alternative to flight or surrender was to raise the cry of rebellion immediately. Hidalgo did not waver at all. He calmly invited Allende to breakfast before assembling the nucleus of their insurgent army, comprising the thirty-man militia of Dolores and a dozen or so workers from Hidalgo's ceramic factory. Their first act was to imprison the local europeos.

It was Sunday, market day in Dolores, and early-rising Indian peasants had already begun arriving to trade their wares. This was not the great San Juan de los Lagos fair that the conspirators had originally targeted, but still, a gathering of hundreds of country people. Hidalgo was a figure of respect to these humble people, mostly of indigenous descent, and he addressed them that day wearing the mask of Fernando and playing on their strong piety. Various versions exist of this often reenacted speech, but the gist is always the same: *The kingdom of New Spain must be preserved for Fernando VII against the godless French. The perfidious españoles europeos cannot be trusted. Many serve Napoleon. We must arrest all gachupines and confiscate their wealth to defend Fernando!* Hidalgo loathed wearing the mask of Fernando, but he saw it work that day, because spontaneous volunteers offered themselves by the hundred.

The rather surprising basic themes of the uprising had been clearly announced. Scapegoating europeos was obviously one. The handwritten flyers made during the uprising's early weeks blasted europeos insistently. Hidalgo began his march by mounting the europeos of Dolores on donkeys and forcing them to ride near the head of his column as objects of derision. Affirmations of popular sovereignty constituted a more subtle complementary theme. At a village called Atotonilco, Hidalgo entered the church and brought out an image of the Virgin of Guadalupe. This painting of Guadalupe, surrounded by flames, became the official standard of the rebellion, carried at the head of the army, and Guadalupe's name became the revolutionary password. Hidalgo's choice was far from accidental. A legend described Guadalupe's miraculous appearance to an Indian boy outside of Mexico City, and over several centuries she had become a focus of americano pride in New Spain. Her appearance, according to this idea, showed God's blessing of América. And she was often painted with a dark face, endearing her to the Indian peasantry, who sometimes called her by a name in Nahuatl, the Aztec language. When Hidalgo raised Guadalupe's image before his followers in 1810, she represented religious fidelity, of course, but also the collective identity of New Spain—including americanos, the indigenous majority, blacks, and mixed-race people in between. Hidalgo had three *vivas* inscribed on the bottom of the painting: one for Guadalupe, one for Fernando, and one for América.

Country people flocked to the banner of Guadalupe, and Hidalgo's army met little resistance as it moved toward Allende's nearby hometown of San Miguel. The army was growing huge, and Allende feared looting. Looting would alienate property-owning americanos, the people whose support he most wanted. Besides, these were Allende's own neighbors. But he got little help from Hidalgo, who had begun to imagine for New Spain something like the French Revolution—a total social, economic, and ideological transformation whereby españoles of both the europeo and americano varieties would lose their privileged status—something that would necessarily involve considerable violence. To achieve such a revolution, moreover, Hidalgo was ready to unleash the whirlwind, the accumulated resentment of the oppressed against their oppressors. Allende, and most americanos, trembled at the thought.

Volunteers swelled the ranks of Hidalgo's army to many thousands in the next few days but, just as Allende predicted, few americanos joined. Approaching the larger city of Celaya, a major center of New Spain's breadbasket Bajío region, the multitude had swelled to around twenty-five thousand, a truly staggering size in this era of small populations. To call this an army may be misleading, though, if by an army one means a group of soldiers. Allende had brought about one hundred militiamen with training, weapons, and uniforms. The other 24,900 "combatants" constituting Hidalgo's force were poor rural people, including many women and children, armed mostly with farm implements and soon encumbered with a variety of modest loot, such as chairs, goats, and chickens. Celaya offered no resistance, and the city's americanos even proposed the creation of a local junta. Hidalgo's triumphant multitude acclaimed him captain general and Allende lieutenant general. Hidalgo composed an ultimatum to the Spanish governor of Guanajuato, announcing his march in the direction of that city and advising capitulation, or else.

Guanajuato, with its fabulous Valenciana silver mine, was an important city (by Humboldt's calculations, América's third most populous, after Mexico City and Havana) with many rich europeos. Because

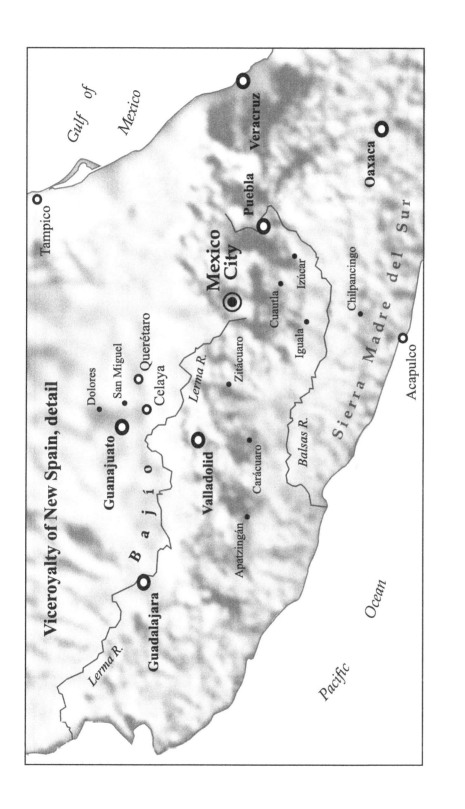

Viceroyalty of New Spain, detail

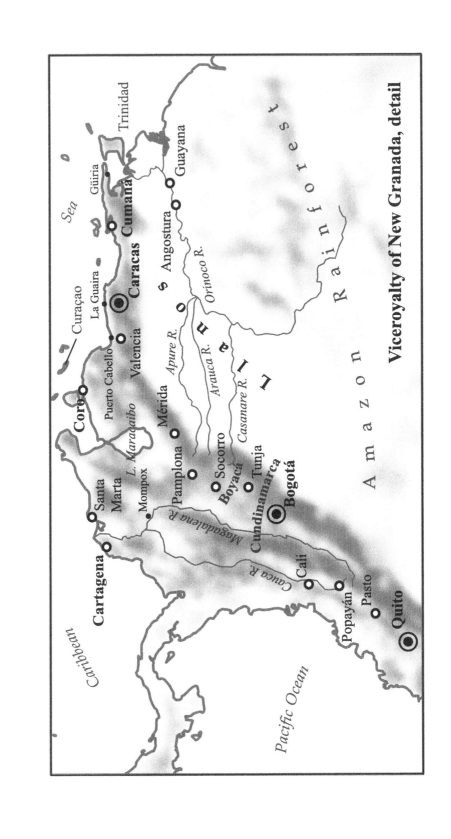

Viceroyalty of New Granada, detail

Guanajuato lay at the bottom of a steep canyon, the city was extremely hard to defend. In fact, the Spanish governor chose not to defend Guanajuato at all. At Celaya, Hidalgo had threatened to execute his seventy-eight europeo prisoners if the city resisted, and Hidalgo's menacing ultimatum to Guanajuato made clear that europeos would be targeted there as well. So the royal administrator of Guanajuato gathered local europeos inside the thick, high stone walls of the city granary, leaving the rest of the population to fend for itself. With a well-armed garrison to defend the walls, abundant grain, their own well, and twenty-five women to cook tortillas, the defenders of the granary were prepared for a lengthy siege.

They lasted only five hours. Hidalgo's multitude arrived at Guanajuato, and, finding its terrified inhabitants barricaded in their houses, descended directly on the city granary, shouting "Death to the gachupines!" Shooting down from the towering walls, the defenders killed hundreds of attackers in the first minutes, but on came hundreds more, determined. The hero of the day was a young miner who managed to set fire to the granary's heavy doors, allowing the attackers to pour inside and finish the job. Many of the three hundred people who died in the granary, largely europeos, were noncombatants. Their deaths—along with the several days of looting that followed, including the destruction of mining equipment and the emptying out of every europeo-owned store in town—became key points of anti-Hidalgo propaganda. Shocked at what had happened, Guanajuato's remaining officials refused to follow the example of Celaya and formed no junta when the smoke cleared.

Hidalgo's multitude continued to grow, but its next destination, the quiet provincial city of Valladolid, was a personal rather than military or political target. Valladolid was the scene of Hidalgo's earlier life as student, professor, and rector—the scene, too, of his eclipse and disgrace. Hidalgo's former friend Abad y Queipo, now bishop of Valladolid, had lost no time in excommunicating him when the rebellion began. The bishop's edicts were nailed to the city's church doors, and Hidalgo, at the head of his multitude, marched to Valladolid to tear them down.

The Cortes of Cádiz Offers a Deal

Four days before Hidalgo's attack on Guanajuato, an assembly of Spanish patriots met in a Cádiz church claiming to embody the sovereignty of the whole Spanish nation. Taking the traditional name for such assemblies in Spain, they called themselves the *cortes*. But this was unlike any previous cortes in Spanish history, not least because it included delegates representing América.

Before dissolving earlier that year, the doomed Central Junta had called elections for this cortes. Because regular elections were impossible under French occupation, however, the group of men who assembled in 1810 represented little more than the patriot resistance based in Cádiz. Its members were mostly quite young, and despite their devotion to the great symbol of resistance, Fernando VII, they tended to believe in radical new ideas such as elected, constitutional government. In a word, they were exponents of liberty (which they carefully did not call *French* liberty, in the current situation). Instead, they called themselves liberals, a new moniker just coming into existence. Among these original liberals was José Mejía Lequerica of Quito, leading the thirty or so delegates who, because they happened to reside in Cádiz, were "representing" América.

Delegates representing América were unprecedented in a Spanish cortes. Inspired by the crisis of French occupation (and following the lead of the defunct Central Junta), the Cortes of Cádiz had expanded the definition of the Spanish nation to include América, which therefore merited representation in the national assembly. The problem, according to the americano delegates organized by Mejía, was inequity. By any estimate, América's population was much larger than Spain's, but Spain got three times more representatives in the cortes. On the second day of the assembly, Mejía petitioned for equal representation according to population, which, if it were to be implemented, would have put the cortes under americano control.

The Spanish delegates summarily rejected the suggestion. They would never voluntarily accept equality with América, which they regarded as a colony. That, however, was something that they could not admit on the floor of the cortes. The whole point of including americano delegates was to maintain their loyalty in this moment of desperate peril for Spain. Therefore, the Spanish delegates offered racial explanations for their desire to maintain Spain's numerical predominance. Indians and people of African descent, because of their racial inferiority, could never count as españoles or be represented in a Spanish cortes, they insisted. And if only americanos were counted for representation, Spain's delegates would outnumber América's at least five to one.

The americano representatives were just that, americanos, so they were not personally implicated in this racial innuendo, but it still disempowered them. So, playing the other side of the race issue, Mejía, a man renowned for his learning and by all accounts one of the most eloquent orators in the cortes, decried the injustice of excluding from political representation the king's loyal subjects of Indian and African descent. But the Spanish delegates would not budge. So, on 1 October 1810, Mejía was ready with another proposal. What if only people of African descent were disqualified from political representation? That way, Indians, the original and still most numerous inhabitants of América, would be enfranchised, along with americanos and mestizos. Mejía and the other americano representatives could live with that, and, it was concluded, so could Spain.

The delegate from Puerto Rico offered the perfect language for the compromise. To satisfy the europeos, he specified "the indisputable concept that the Spanish dominions of both hemispheres form a single monarchy, a single nation, a single family." But the new wording also specified, as the americano delegates insisted, that "natives derived from said European and overseas dominions are equal in rights."[2] The word *native* was construed to mean americanos, Indians, and mestizos—but *not* free pardos, by the logic that their African ancestors came neither from Spain nor from America. Pardos, being part white, had Spanish ancestors as well, but the cortes conveniently ignored that complication and promulgated the decree on 15 October 1810.

The formula "one transatlantic monarchy" was the cortes's answer to American juntas' formula "a crown with two pillars." To sweeten the deal, the cortes decreed an amnesty for rebels in América. The rebels it had in mind were those of the recently formed American juntas. News of Guanajuato had not yet arrived.

Hidalgo's Multitude Is Defeated

The city of Valladolid surrendered to Hidalgo without resistance on 17 October 1810, two days after the Cortes of Cádiz adopted a compromise decree excluding people of African descent from citizenship. So Hidalgo's gigantic, ragtag rebel army made a triumphal entrance into this small, provincial city that he had left under a cloud years before. To savor his personal comeback in Valladolid, Hidalgo donned a resplendent military uniform, a gold image of the Virgin of Guadalupe hanging at his throat. Let the bishop's henchmen try to arrest him now.

Bishop Abad y Queipo had fled the city already. His repeated published denunciations of Hidalgo stemmed from a sense of personal betrayal, surely, but also from the threat of guilt by association. Abad y Queipo, like Hidalgo, had experimented with silk production, and he too had recently come under suspicion by the Inquisition. Another who fled Valladolid at Hidalgo's approach was a dashing young americano officer named Agustín de Iturbide, who one day would become emperor of Mexico, albeit fleetingly. For now, though, and for many years to come, Iturbide remained staunchly loyal to colonial rule. Meanwhile, a village padre named José María Morelos, a former student of the College of San Nicolás, where Hidalgo had been rector, put himself at Hidalgo's orders. Another radical priest in an army that already had several in leadership positions, Morelos would eventually become Hidalgo's successor.

In Valladolid, Hidalgo went beyond his earlier affirmations of religious fidelity and crossed-finger endorsements of Fernando VII to decree revolutionary changes in the social order. His first major one was the total, unconditional abolition of slavery. The impatient approach was pure Hidalgo. Slave owners, be they europeos or americanos, were to free all their slaves immediately or face execution. No exceptions for slave owners who joined the revolutionary cause, no provisions for monetary compensation for their expensive human property. Furthermore, Hidalgo decreed that freed slaves, be they Africans or native to América, became immediately equal to whites. In practical terms, these things happened only in Hidalgo's dreams. His army controlled only a minuscule portion of New Spain. Still, Hidalgo's pronouncements concerning people of African descent contrasted notably with those of the Cortes of Cádiz, which never considered abolishing slavery. Nor did Hidalgo declare the abolition of slavery just to gain recruits for his army, which was already too large an army. He did so because he knew it was right, and he pronounced freed slaves equal to whites for the same reason. This philandering priest and inept general, this occasionally reckless and consistently vain man, was boldly embracing principles of justice that the respectable moralists of his day denied totally.

After a few days in Valladolid, Hidalgo's enormous multitude, numbering now something like eighty thousand souls, lumbered toward Mexico City. To get there, it would have to transit a narrow pass at Monte de las Cruces, a bottleneck guarded by a small but disciplined and well-armed force of twenty-five hundred troops loyal to the viceroy. Unfortunately for Hidalgo and his cause, an unarmed multitude without military experience was worth little in that situation. At the battle of Monte de las Cruces, 30 October 1810, Hidalgo's followers were unable to force their way through the pass during a day's bloody fighting. Two thousand of them died, and many more thousands were wounded. Deserters flooded to the rear in panic. So when the viceroy's forces retreated the next day, leaving the pass open, it seemed a pale victory for the rebels. Still, the way forward lay clear, and the wounded throng shuffled through the pass toward Mexico City, the ancient viceregal capital of New Spain, now almost within view. Sobered by the outcome at Monte de las Cruces, however, Hidalgo expressed second thoughts. His followers had expended their scarce ammunition, and another army of troops loyal to the viceroy was approaching from behind. This second force was led by Félix María Calleja, Allende's own former superior. Allende urged an assault on the capital before Calleja had time to reinforce its defenses. But when Hidalgo insisted on retreating toward Valladolid, Allende could only assent. The americano militias he had hoped to recruit for the rebellion—who would have followed him rather than Hidalgo— had shunned his call after the pillage of Guanajuato. In any dispute, the multitude would obey the charismatic padre rather than Allende.

Calleja's fast-moving force of seven thousand militiamen, brightly uniformed and lavishly equipped by recent contributions to the viceroy's cause, caught up with the rebel army on 7 November 1810 at a place called Aculco. The battle of Aculco again displayed the weakness of Hidalgo's inexperienced fighters when a horseman, decapitated by a cannonball but with his foot still caught in the stirrup, was dragged through the ranks by his galloping horse, provoking horror and confusion. To escape Calleja, Hidalgo and Allende divided their remaining followers, Hidalgo heading for Valladolid and Allende for Guanajuato, to regroup.

Hidalgo had been brilliantly successful in attracting the largest mass of followers ever seen in América. There was no doubt about the appeal of his message, but his message could not reach very far. He did not yet have a printing press, for example, to disseminate his proclamations. Outside the Lerma River valley, most of New Spain had remained steadfastly loyal to the viceroy. Gone now were rebel hopes of quickly toppling the viceroy and forming a junta of americanos for New Spain. The fearful people of Mexico City had collaborated wholeheartedly with the viceroy's preparations to defend the capital. Now they celebrated their deliverance, giving special thanks to the Virgin of los

Remedios, whose image had been brought into the city to save it from Hidalgo's multitude. The Virgin of los Remedios would compete symbolically against the insurgent Virgin of Guadalupe for the rest of the war.

Back in Valladolid by mid-November, Hidalgo forged ahead with the popular rebellion. His scapegoating of gachupines reached a new level when he authorized the mass execution of more than sixty prisoners in Valladolid. Obliged by Calleja's forces to abandon Guanajuato, Allende also permitted executions. He did not specifically order the deaths of more than a hundred europeos confined in the city granary, now a makeshift prison, but furious locals predictably did the job for him after Allende left. When Calleja entered Guanajuato, he initiated a bloody tit for tat, selecting scores of ordinary residents at random and having them shot against the gore-spattered walls of the former granary. Both halves of the insurgent army now retreated west along the Lerma River valley toward the city of Guadalajara, where the executions would continue. Although there were some exceptions, the general principle was firm: Hidalgo executed europeos; Calleja, people born in América.

On 26 November 1810, Hidalgo's much-reduced force entered Guadalajara amid music and cheering spectators. Hidalgo rode in a closed coach, apparently accompanied by a woman referred to as *la capitana* because she wore a military uniform—a bit of gossip picked up from the wagging tongues of Hidalgo's detractors. It would be odd, however, if it weren't true, given what we know of the man and his times. The slightly unhinged leader began to let the mask of Fernando slip as he formed the nucleus of an insurgent government. "The rights of Fernando VII in América" became an obligatory, formulaic reference remote from everything that Hidalgo was really doing. Hidalgo had portraits of the Desired One removed from official settings and dropped the term *royal* from the titles of government offices. He called for elections for a national congress and designated an ambassador to the United States, from which he evidently expected support. At last Hidalgo's message began to appear in print as well. He published his decree abolishing slavery and another ending the yearly tribute that Indians had to pay merely for being Indians. He decreed the return of lost Indian lands to Indian communities. Also in print appeared the official newspaper of the new government, *El Despertador Americano*, loosely *Wake Up, Americans!* After the first issue, it omitted all mention of Fernando VII and invoked the idea of a new nation comprising everyone born in América.

Hidalgo's magic worked again in attracting new volunteers around Guadalajara. Five weeks after arriving there, his multitude was back up to about eighty thousand. Still, the new battalions of poorly armed volunteers proved no more effective on the battlefield than had their predecessors. As Calleja's army of seven thousand well-armed and well-disciplined troops approached Guadalajara, Hidalgo's army marched out to meet them in high spirits. But the battle of Calderón Bridge on 17 January 1811 was an unmitigated disaster. As at Aculco, the panic of inexperience defined the outcome instantly when an ammunition wagon exploded in the middle of the insurgent ranks. Calleja lost only fifty men at Calderón Bridge, while over a thousand of Hidalgo's men died, and the other seventy-nine thousand insurgents scattered in all directions.

Two days later, Allende and the remaining officers of the rebel army stripped Hidalgo of military command, retaining him only as a figure-head leader. Then the dwindling insurgents fled north into the sparsely populated frontier provinces of northernmost New Spain, where their uprising had found a faint echo, as local americano leaders declared their defiance of Mexico City. In February 1811, when Hidalgo and Allende finally received the offer of amnesty made months earlier by the Cortes of Cádiz to all insurgents, they proudly refused it. Perhaps there was still hope.

But in March 1811, the entire leadership of the revolt rode into a trap and was captured without a fight.

Paraguay Resists the Buenos Aires Junta

Civil war spread quickly in América during the year 1811. More common than Hidalgo-style uprisings from below, however, were battles between entire provinces. In the former viceroyalty of the Río de la Plata, for example, Asunción, the provincial capital of Paraguay, held a cabildo abierto that refused to recognize the Buenos Aires junta. When Buenos Aires sent Manuel Belgrano to bring the Paraguayans into line, he failed totally.

Admittedly, Belgrano was a bookish sort ill suited to war, but probably no one could have subdued the Paraguayans with the few hundred soldiers Belgrano commanded. Paraguay, a tough, isolated frontier province deep in the interior of the continent, was the seedbed from which much of the Plata frontier had been populated, a settlement older than Buenos Aires. Paraguay's frontier location endowed it with military capacity because so many Paraguayan men were in the militia. Fighting on their own ground, Paraguayan militias defeated Belgrano's forces of Buenos Aires decisively at the battle of Tacuarí on 9 March 1811.

At the time of the battle of Tacuarí, Paraguay still had a europeo administrator, but he was soon replaced by an americano junta. The architect of that junta, José Gaspar Rodríguez de Francia, placed an indelible stamp on Paraguayan history. Francia had a doctorate, one of the few in Asunción, and he espoused certain ideas of the French revolution. He gained control of the Asunción junta as a populist who channeled the resentments of upwardly mobile mestizos against their supposed "betters." His biggest popular issue, the one that he rode until it delivered him total control of Paraguay, was provincial autonomy. Doctor Francia, as he is generally known, vowed above all that Paraguay would never again be ruled by Buenos Aires, an attitude enthusiastically endorsed by Paraguayans as a whole. From this time on, Francia's Paraguay would be effectively independent, not only from Spain but from Buenos Aires as well.

Paraguay was not the only case of civil war in the former Río de la Plata viceroyalty. In a military expedition parallel to Belgrano's, another original member of the Buenos Aires junta, Belgrano's cousin Juan José Castelli, had been sent to subdue a second disobedient province, Upper Peru, with its mountain of silver at Potosí and chief administrative center at Chuquisaca.

The Battle for Upper Peru Begins

Castelli's mission fared no better than Belgrano's, collapsing, after some initial successes, on an Andean mountainside called Huaqui on 20 June 1811. Castelli had traveled from Buenos Aires up the road that led northwest through Córdoba, Tucumán, and Salta to Chuquisaca and the silver mines of Potosí. Since 1776, Upper Peru had formed part of the Río de la Plata viceroyalty, and this north-south axis was its main road. Many young men of Buenos Aires studied in Chuquisaca, a graceful university town of whitewashed buildings, and the arduous trip from Buenos Aires was their famous initiation to student life. Mariano Moreno, the ex-secretary of the Buenos Aires junta, had been one of these, Castelli another. Castelli's reading in Chuquisaca—and then his participation in Mariquita Sánchez's salon conversations—had infected him with "French ideas," making him, like Moreno, one of the junta's more radical members.

Castelli traveled to Upper Peru not as a general per se but rather as the junta's political representative. He devoted all his efforts to spreading the revolutionary ideas that lurked beneath the Buenos Aires junta's formulaic loyalty to Fernando VII. Like Hidalgo, Castelli devoted special attention to the plight of the Indians, abolishing their ancient tribute and labor obligations with a stroke of his pen. When village leaders bowed down to him, as they had done for centuries to royal officials sent from distant capital cities, Castelli raised them to their feet. Those days were over, he told them. Now americanos, all those born on American soil, were equal to europeos. The Indians scratched their heads; since when had they been americanos? The meaning of the word *americano* was blurring in the bloodshed of civil war. Castelli chose to celebrate 25 May 1811, the first anniversary of the formation of the Buenos Aires junta, in the ruins of Tihuanaco to tie his patriotic message to imagery of Incan glories. Castelli, like Hidalgo, envisioned a new nation that included everyone born in América, who would all be called americanos.

But Castelli was overbearing and doctrinaire, and the native people of Upper Peru did not respond well to his revolutionary catechism. Where Hidalgo had used a saint's image as his banner, Castelli gained a reputation for blasphemy. The main problem was not Castelli himself but his associate Bernardo Monteagudo, another young Chuquisaca intellectual, author of a fanciful and influential 1809 political pamphlet in which the spirit of the last Inca, Atahualpa, endorses the cause of América. Imprisoned for his political activities, Monteagudo escaped to join Castelli. The dashing and iconoclastic Monteagudo delivered sacrilegious political sermons from the pulpit, believing that the church had contributed much to the colonial enslavement of the indigenous people and that its hold on people's minds had to be shattered in order for true liberation to occur. But a wide cultural breach separated Castelli from the people whom he hoped to inspire. The generally conservative people of Upper Peru, including the Indian majority, did not appreciate Monteagudo's style of psychological liberation and rather approved of the hellfire that, they were certain, awaited him and all the flatlanders in his company.

Fortunately for the rebels, scapegoating europeos was a winning strategy in Upper Peru, as everywhere else. Castelli found local city folk eager to free themselves from europeo merchants, mine owners, and crown officials. Castelli recruited americanos and mestizos in Chuquisaca, Potosí, La Paz, and Cochabamba. He also acquired several thousand Indian auxiliaries without firearms who mostly served as porters. Still, the armies of the junta of Buenos Aires were tiny miniatures by comparison with Hidalgo's multitude.

The worst problem was Castelli's Miranda-like inability to assess his real military prospects. Despite the precariousness of his patched-together army, he hatched the idea of marching on distant Lima, convinced that Spanish resistance would simply crumble away. Castelli's forces got only as far as the deep, sinuous gorge called the Desaguadero (literally "the drain"), through which the accumulated waters of Upper Peru's high plateau, after pooling in Lake Titicaca, spill toward the Pacific Ocean. All the roads from Upper Peru to Lima passed through the Desaguadero, and armies of the Peruvian viceroy Abascal controlled it tightly. Furthermore, to undercut Castelli's support, Abascal spread news of the concessions made to americanos by the Cortes of Cádiz and asked for a truce. Castelli accepted the truce, which Abascal then violated by ordering a surprise attack at Huaqui, scattering Castelli's inexperienced forces virtually without a fight. The defeat at Huaqui terminated Castelli's mission and permanently clouded his reputation. Ironically, the man known for his fiery oratory during the May Revolution of Buenos Aires soon lost his voice completely to a cancer growing on his tongue.

After the battle of Huaqui, Viceroy Abascal gradually reasserted Spanish control over Upper Peru. Indeed, the Andean highlands were to become the last great stronghold of Spanish colonial control in América. In the wake of Castelli's withdrawal, half a dozen rural guerrilla movements eventually formed enclaves to resist the reimposition of Abascal's authority in Upper Peru, however. *Republiquetas*, or "mini-republics," they were called later, because each (eventually six of them) held sway independently for a few years in a warren of mazelike canyons. One of these patriot mini-republics was led by a married couple from Chuquisaca, Manuel Ascencio Padilla and Juana Azurduy.

Padilla and Azurduy were natives of Chuquisaca's rural hinterland—not Indians themselves, but people who had grown up among indigenous people and spoke their languages. Juana was a mestiza who had learned Quechua from her mother and acquired a knowledge of Upper Peru's other main Indian language, Aymara, while helping administer her family's landholding. When her parents died, Juana clashed with her guardians and landed in a convent school where, her classmates later recalled, her main girlhood heroes were warrior saints. Juana's husband Manuel had begun his political career when events in Chuquisaca triggered resistance to Spanish authorities there and in La Paz. Then the town of Cochabamba announced its support for the

Buenos Aires junta in 1810, and Manuel went there to help recruit Indians. When Castelli's expedition arrived in Upper Peru, Manuel joined it. In the meantime, Juana stayed on the couple's land with their small children, supplying food and animals to the cause.

Spanish authorities confiscated her land and confined her and her children to a house outside Chuquisaca in hopes of luring her husband there to capture him. Somehow, though, Manuel Padilla managed to rescue Juana and the children and whisk them away to a mountain hideout, a veritable condor's nest hung between two peaks, where the local Indians promised that they would be safe. Ten days later, he departed again to organize patriot guerrillas. Juana awaited his return, took care of her children (one still a babe in arms), and began to practice using the firearms and swinging the sword Padilla had left her.

Venezuela Becomes a Republic

Castelli's downfall coincided with Francisco Miranda's hour of triumph. Convinced by Simón Bolívar to make a last hurrah in Venezuela, the aging revolutionary Miranda had met a much warmer reception than in 1806. Miranda was given a congressional seat, for example, without having to be elected—although he let it be known that Pao, the district he would represent, was too obscure and distant to suit him. Something in Caracas, perhaps . . .

Miranda remained a problematic figure from the perspective of most people in Venezuela. He arrived, for example, wearing the gold-trimmed uniform of a French revolutionary general, evidence of his past military experience, but something that Venezuelans failed to find reassuring. The common folk mistrusted Miranda's foreign airs, and the aristocracy regarded him as the troublemaking upstart son of a Caracas storekeeper. It took Bolívar a whole week to convince the Caracas junta to let Miranda into the country. The junta finally welcomed him, but somewhat to their chagrin, because Miranda soon behaved as if already in charge, responding to the most effusive toasts of greeting without raising his own glass.

On the other hand, Miranda was a committed abolitionist and effectively courted the political support of the city's large population of restless free pardos, people who had long strained against the limits of the colonial caste system. With the aid of Bolívar and other local revolutionaries, Miranda gave a populist tilt to the existing Patriotic Society of Caracas, inviting pardos to join and publishing a newspaper called the *Venezuelan Patriot*. Miranda's bid to raise revolutionary consciousness found a more receptive audience, it would appear, than did Castelli's simultaneous attempt in Upper Peru. The first anniversary of the formation of the Caracas junta was marked by a popular fiesta in which enthusiastic demonstrators torched Fernando VII's portraits, to the astonishment and horror of conservatives.

On 28 June 1811, just a week after Castelli's revolutionary dreams were shattered at Huaqui, Miranda took his place in Venezuela's first national congress, and he soon proposed a formal declaration of independence. Within a few days, one had been written. The congress formally declared Venezuelan independence on 5 July 1811, after commemorating the Philadelphia events of 1776 the previous evening. The new constitution, unveiled shortly afterward, also showed the strong influence of Philadelphia precedents, making Venezuela a republic, the first to emerge from the great crisis washing over América.

On the other hand, resistance to new claims of authority was rife in Venezuela. Three important cities—Coro, Maracaibo, and Guayana, each dominating an entire region of the country—had not joined the republic, and the city of Valencia, which did join, tried to back out almost immediately. At the same time, a protest demonstration by Caracas europeos shouting "Long live the king!" led to their arrest and the execution of a dozen of them. Such harsh treatment of europeos had become a universal attribute of americano movements.

Miranda led the republican army against rebellious Valencia with the help of his young friend Simón Bolívar, who received a special commendation for his actions. Miranda's victorious return to Caracas was his finest hour. Finally, he was publicly hailed as the Father of his Country. Virgins in white gowns scattered laurels in his path.

Portuguese Intervention Brings Further Complications

The crisis of legitimacy that wracked the Spanish-speaking world in 1811 sprouted a new international complication when Carlota Joaquina, sister of Spain's Fernando VII, asserted her authority over Spanish territory in her brother's name. Carlota Joaquina was still in Rio de Janeiro where she and her husband, João, prince regent of Portugal, had come to escape Napoleon. She had her eyes particularly on the Eastern Shore Province of the Río de la Plata, today called Uruguay, and dreamed of extending her control over the entire Viceroyalty of the Río de la Plata.

Montevideo, provincial capital of the Eastern Shore, was a royalist holdout against the Buenos Aires junta. Carlota Joaquina hoped to use Montevideo as her stepping-stone to a southern takeover, so she sold her personal jewelry to fund the city's defense and sent a printing press to turn out anti-revolutionary propaganda for distribution in the Río de la Plata.

The Portuguese throne in Brazil remained thoroughly insulated from events in the rebellious Spanish colonies. Domestic concerns rather than political ones dominated the life of a Portuguese royal family gradually becoming acclimated to its new home in the tropics. João and Carlota Joaquina liked each other no better in Rio than they had in Lisbon, though, and they occupied separate residences. Carlota Joaquina's favorite was the royal country house at Botafogo, where sheer green mountains rose spectacularly behind the beach. Now a graceful old neighborhood in the heart of the twenty-first-century metropolis of Rio, in 1811 Botafogo was a garden district outside of town. Courtiers who arrived in Rio with the royal family requisitioned many such houses from the native-born Brazilian elite who had lived in them previously. Such were the privileges of nobility. Prince Pedro, on the verge of adolescence, was extremely happy in Rio, where he and his brother, Miguel, spent their time much as they pleased. Both boys suffered from a mild form of epilepsy, including periodic seizures, but these seemed to trouble them less in their new home. Even João's demented mother, Queen Maria, seemed to gain a bit of clarity and tranquility in Rio.

Despite its natural attractions, Rio was not a very impressive city for a European royal court. Its principal modern improvements were a public park and a secure water supply provided by a Roman-style aqueduct. The streets were narrow and unlighted—unpaved, too, with sewage often running down the center of them. Heavy wooden grilles covered the windows, keeping the interiors cool but creating a forbidding appearance. Oranges, bananas, pineapples, and other tropical fruits abounded, but wheat bread was hard to find and worth its weight in gold. Fancy shops to cater to the refined tastes and deep pockets of the aristocracy did not yet exist. At the top of the city's social hierarchy, one encountered courtiers, bureaucrats, and merchants, as well as plantation owners who preferred to reside in town. Catholic clergy, lawyers, storekeepers, artisans, fishermen, soldiers, and tavern keepers made up the rest, not counting the slaves. About half the population of Rio was enslaved. While the male members of the royal family soon lost any desire to return to Lisbon, the same could not be said of their glittering entourage as a whole, nor of Carlota Joaquina, who was as restless as ever.

Claiming to act for her brother Fernando, Carlota Joaquina had contacted numerous parties in Buenos Aires, including the ex-viceroy Liniers and Manuel Belgrano, offering herself as princess regent of the Viceroyalty of the Río de la Plata. But she proposed to reign from Buenos Aires, and, although a princess, Carlota Joaquina had to ask her husband's permission to travel. João naturally refused to grant it. He wanted to limit her influence in the Río de la Plata in order to maximize his own. João was following the advice of Rodrigo de Souza Coutinho, José Bonifácio's former ministerial patron in Lisbon, a man who had for years envisioned the permanent transfer of the Portuguese crown to América. It was Coutinho and João who had commenced a troop buildup on Brazil's southern frontier, while the renegade princess continued to dicker separately through her own agents.

One success of Carlota Joaquina's agents, at least, was to establish friendly relations with the new viceroy sent out from Cádiz to try to recover control of the Río de la Plata—an experienced, hard-line Spanish colonialist named Francisco Javier de Elío. Montevideo became Elío's impromptu viceregal capital, Buenos Aires being unavailable. Montevideo's well-fortified location had allowed it to resist the Buenos Aires junta for over a year. But Elío's support did not extend far outside the port city. When Elío had declared outright war on Buenos Aires in the name of Fernando VII, an uprising in the countryside of the Eastern Shore had opposed him and recognized the Buenos Aires junta instead. The leader of those rural rebels was our old friend José Artigas. His tiny, ragtag army was joined a few weeks later by an expeditionary force from Buenos Aires, and together they laid siege to Montevideo. In July 1811, Elío decided to call his would-be Portuguese rescuers to break the siege.

Hidalgo and Allende Meet Their Maker

Meanwhile, Hidalgo, Allende, and many other rebel prisoners had been taken further north from their place of capture, like a dangerous virus that had to be isolated as far away as possible, to the frontier outpost of Chihuahua. There they had been interrogated and sentenced. The executions of lesser prisoners began in May, while Hidalgo's interrogation continued for months. He was the last to face a firing squad, or rather, the only one permitted to actually *face* one. Allende and all the others had been shot degradingly in the back, which was a standard procedure. On the day of his execution, 30 July 1811, Hidalgo thanked his jailors for their kindness to him and distributed sweets to the embarrassed firing squad.

Miguel Hidalgo died a broken man. Allende had fought his interrogators, at one point striking them with his chains, but Hidalgo appears sincerely to have repented. The record of the interrogation, at least, indicates that. And the Inquisition, always a stickler for true confessions, pronounced itself satisfied with the old man's repentance, affording some leniency, such as the privilege of facing the firing squad. Hidalgo died with no idea that 16 September, the date he began his uprising in the village of Dolores, would be celebrated in future years as Mexico's Independence Day—no idea, even, that seeds of his rebellion had already taken root in the south. Hidalgo's severed head, along with Allende's and those of several other high-ranking rebel officers, was transported back to Guanajuato; the grisly trophies were put on display in iron cages hung from the pockmarked walls of the city granary, where they rotted for ten years, reminding passersby of the fate that awaited traitors to the Spanish crown.

Nariño Becomes President of Cundinamarca

Imagine fireworks, a patriotic celebration, and an official reception on 29 August 1811 for the "incomparable, unconquerable, immortal hero" (and long-suffering political prisoner) Antonio Nariño.[3] Nariño was getting a lot of attention in Bogotá with his political periodical *La bagatela*—from now on *Wisecrack*, a nonliteral translation that captures the title's tongue-in-cheek spirit. *Wisecrack* commenced publication on Bastille Day amid the parades and fancy dress balls with which Bogotá that year celebrated the anniversary of the French Revolution.

Nariño's paper was part of an explosive proliferation of print media then occurring throughout América. Uncensored political publications had simply not existed in colonial days, and the crisis of legitimacy ripping spasmodically through the Spanish-speaking world since 1808 had provided both opportunity and subject matter for thousands of new publications. Admittedly, the scale of this print revolution remained relatively tiny. Most publications were small, four-page opinion sheets printed in runs of a few hundred by a lone editor such as Nariño. The population of América was largely illiterate, after all. However, literate people congregated in cities and were the principal power contenders, giving outsized importance to such small-scale publications, which, in addition, were frequently read aloud in taverns, workshops, and public places. Most people heard terms such as *constitution* and *Sovereign People* for the first time when read from one of these periodicals. The crusading journalist became a well-known figure. Nariño's *Wisecrack*, for example, was his catapult to the presidency, conferred on him by the Bogotá junta on 19 September 1811.

Bogotá was now capital of no more than the surrounding highland province called Cundinamarca, because the other provinces of New Granada had gone their own ways. Nariño aspired to reunite the fragmented former New Granada viceroyalty as a single republic, but there were large obstacles. Many provinces had formed juntas of their own. The fortress city of Cartagena, most notably, had its own junta and no patience for would-be republican overlords in Bogotá. Overall, there was a tendency for provinces with their own juntas to confederate more readily in opposition to Bogotá than in its support. To make matters worse, royalists still controlled some provinces, such as those of Santa Marta and Pasto. Simply put, civil war loomed in New Granada as elsewhere in América.

Ditto Chile

As Nariño rose to the presidency of Cundinamarca, young firebrand José Miguel Carrera (brother of Javiera Carrera) seized control of events in Santiago, Chile. José Miguel was an audacious character in his mid-twenties, a cross between Simón Bolívar, with his aristocratic family and habits, and José de San Martín, with his record of service as an officer of Spain's army of national resistance. The Carreras—Javiera, José Miguel, and other brothers, who were also army officers—espoused what insurgents were now calling "the cause of América," a rhetorical move beyond "the cause of Fernando VII." In September 1811, Carrera used his military clout and his political influence to engineer a takeover of the recently elected assembly, presenting a list of demands in the name of the people of Santiago.

Under Carrera's direction, the Santiago junta was several times reconfigured and eventually replaced by his personal dictatorship. Carrera oversaw some progressive legislation, such as laws forbidding the importation of slaves and a "free womb" law, later duplicated throughout the hemisphere, emancipating all the future children of enslaved women. But Carrera's rule also reflected his family's roots in the Santiago aristocracy. As always, the pretensions of the capital provoked a push-back from the provinces. At the south end of Chile's compact central valley, Santiago's old rival Concepción, home of Bernardo O'Higgins and his political patron, Juan Martínez de Rozas, wanted a junta of its own. Eventually, the provinces of Santiago and Concepción mobilized and deployed militias along the boundary between them.

Artigas Leads an Exodus

With João VI's Portuguese forces approaching to break the patriot siege of Montevideo, the Buenos Aires junta struck a deal with Viceroy Elío. Buenos Aires agreed to abandon the siege, and Elío agreed to curb the Portuguese invasion that was coming to his rescue. Consequently, on 14 October 1811, the junta's forces began to withdraw from the Eastern Shore and return to Buenos Aires. But local patriots under Colonel José Artigas had not been consulted in the agreement between Elío and the Buenos Aires junta. As the forces of Buenos Aires withdrew in the face of the advancing Portuguese, the remaining local patriots acclaimed Artigas general, in effect declaring autonomy from Buenos Aires.

A week later, the Army of the Eastern Shore, unable to maintain the siege, commenced its own withdrawal from Montevideo. It rode west through the rural neighborhood where it had originated, Soriano, where Artigas had once courted Isabel Velásquez. Along the way, ranchers and gauchos collected their families, each occupying a great two-wheeled cart pulled by several yokes of oxen. Hundreds and hundreds of such carts, full of women and children, flanked by riders, as well as people and livestock, moved slowly along in the dust, a line stretching many miles. Among those trudging along were many slaves owned by americanos. On horseback rode many more former slaves who had run away from europeo masters to join Artigas. Artigas's forces were a sampler of frontier social types, including auxiliaries from his old associates, the Charrúa Indians. The army and its accompanying families moved over a period of months up the Uruguay River, the old stomping ground where Artigas had roamed for decades on various sides of the law. Finally, they crossed over to the western shore and settled into a semipermanent camp at a place called Ayuí. There they huddled in the shelter of the low trees that line the prairie streambeds of the area to wait until the Portuguese left the Eastern Shore. Never again would they trust Buenos Aires. In future years, this "Exodus of the Easterners" would be remembered as the crystallization of a Uruguayan national consciousness.

Enter Morelos

Meanwhile, in New Spain, the new Viceroy Venegas had reason for alarm. Hidalgo's rebellious multitude had been dispersed and its top leadership executed in the distant north, but now events disturbingly close to home threatened a rekindling of the firestorm. This time the arsonist (in the viceroy's view) was Father José María Morelos, whom Hidalgo had sent to spread rebellion into "the hot lands" of New Spain's southern Pacific coast, around Acapulco. Morelos had done so successfully and then made a triumphal entry into the town of Izúcar, near Puebla, one of New Spain's principal cities. On 10 December 1811, Morelos won a big victory and took four hundred prisoners, including the europeo commander, who was executed. After being greeted in Izúcar with music, fireworks, and wooden triumphal arches erected over the streets, Morelos's army celebrated the Feast of the Virgin of Guadalupe. In addition, Mariano Matamoros, an obscure priest destined to become a famous patriot leader, joined Morelos at Izúcar.

The proliferation of priests in this story demands explanation. It may create the impression of a revolutionary impulse within the Catholic Church of América, whereas little such impulse existed. Clergy were among the most literate members of society and therefore had privileged access to banned texts about French liberty. Some, such as Hidalgo, clearly did extensive extracurricular readings of that kind, while most, like Morelos, stuck with their religious homework. The best explanation for the proliferation of priests in the independence movements is their general prominence in colonial society. The church had exercised tremendous authority in colonial América, as in Spain and Portugal, over many centuries. Churchmen were inevitably protagonists in any social event, so they naturally took prominent roles in these civil wars—on both sides of the conflict. Most priests, in fact, obeyed their bishops and remained loyal to Spain. Yet a significant minority of americano clergy converted to the gospel of independence. And, when churchmen enlisted in the patriot cause, they took leadership roles.

The paramount leadership of Hidalgo and Morelos, however, was unique to New Spain. Americano juntas elsewhere included lots of clergy, but the juntas' top leaders, following another centuries-old tradition, were usually men of the sword or the pen—that is, soldiers or lawyers, not churchmen. New Spain differed because, when nervous europeos made their preemptive strike against pro-americano viceroy Iturrigaray back in 1808, they scuttled the attempt to create a junta in Mexico City like those founded in Buenos Aires, Bogotá, and other capital cities. After Hidalgo unleashed the whirlwind, alienating New Spain's americano elite, Mexico City remained a bastion of Spanish colonial power. Because no high-level patriot figurehead emerged in the capital, national leadership was defined militarily in the provinces. A renegade junta eventually did emerge in the provincial town of Zitácuaro, near Valladolid, headed by a lawyer named Ignacio López Rayón, who had been Hidalgo's secretary. But the Zitácuaro junta had no army of its own. Father Morelos, on the other hand, did have an army. In late 1811, all New Spain began to see him as Hidalgo's successor.

José María Morelos came from a family of modest means in Valladolid. For years, he had to support his mother and sister after his father abandoned them. Morelos entered the priesthood after years of driving mule trains through the hot lands of the Balsas River valley, south of Valladolid. There he learned to tie a handkerchief around his head to soak up the sweat, as many muleteers did, and the garment became his trademark. At the College of San Nicolás, where he studied theology during Hidalgo's period as rector of that institution, Morelos was much older than his classmates and a mediocre student at best. His ambition was simply to make a respectable living as a village curate, as his mother had always wanted. After his ordination as a priest, Morelos was assigned to a series of parishes in the south, viewed by most people of highland Valladolid as unhealthy locations because of the torrid climate. Indeed, when Morelos invited his mother to come live with him there, she soon became ill and died. Morelos stayed on, however, for twelve long and not particularly happy years in the steamy villages of Carácuaro and Nocupétaro, periodically sending his sister money to have a house built back in Valladolid.

Learning of Hidalgo's revolt, Morelos did not hesitate to join it. Morelos had never been a reader of banned books and possessed only a sketchy idea of the French Revolution, but he revered Hidalgo and was ready for a change. Immediately, he threw himself into his new mission, to spread Hidalgo's revolution along the southern Pacific coast of New Spain, the "hot country" that Morelos knew only too well. He started in his own former parish of Carácuaro, where he tore down the edict excommunicating Hidalgo and drew on his local connections to recruit followers. Morelos did not accept all volunteers. As an ex-muleteer, Morelos had experience steering men and animals along the winding roads of the rugged south. He knew that he needed a force that was smaller, better-trained, and better-armed than Hidalgo's. Seasoned militiamen and a few powerful families joined him. The Galeana clan of Tecpán, on the Pacific Coast not far from Acapulco, constituted one example. They brought Morelos his first piece of artillery, a miniature cannon called El Niño that the Galeana family used to liven up fiestas on their estate. The Bravos, another family, assured Morelos of a warm welcome in what became the heartland of his movement, Chilpancingo in the Sierra Madre del Sur.

Chilpancingo lies just inland from Acapulco. To take Acapulco was Morelos's great objective, the mission he had received personally from Hidalgo before the battle of Monte de las Cruces. But the Spanish had heavily fortified Acapulco, and it easily repulsed Morelos. So, turning inland, Morelos had won a string of small victories, spent a few months training and provisioning his compact force of a thousand or so fighters, then appeared suddenly at Izúcar in December 1811, much too close to Mexico City, in the opinion of Viceroy Venegas.

On Christmas Eve, his forces were welcomed by the townspeople of Cuautla, even closer to Mexico City, and Viceroy Venegas appealed urgently to General Calleja, then busy attacking the junta of Zitácuaro, to stop Morelos. Calleja refused to be hurried, however. During the month of January 1812 he methodically captured or killed the remaining defenders of Zitácuaro and reduced the town to ashes, although the junta itself escaped. Not until mid-February 1812 did Calleja arrive with his battle-hardened and never-defeated force to besiege Cuautla, where Morelos awaited, thumbing his nose.

The Cortes of Cádiz Writes a Constitution

A month later, on 19 March 1812, in Cádiz, where Napoleonic troops still corralled Spain's isolated government of national resistance on a few sandy acres of Spanish soil, bells tolled as excited patriots swore allegiance to a new constitution. The Cádiz constitution, Spain's first, had been written by the cortes over the last year. It was a major innovation, and had it been fully implemented, it would have profoundly transformed the Spanish colonial system, limiting the power of the king and creating a permanent system of electoral representation that included América. The Cádiz constitution confirmed the compromise formula making americanos, Indians, and anyone descended from them—everyone without a trace of African descent—citizens of the Spanish nation, juridically equal to those born in Europe. Still, the americano delegates to the cortes could not rejoice wholeheartedly.

Exclusion of people of African descent meant that europeo delegates to the cortes would always outnumber americanos by a wide margin. In practice, this meant that americano demands could, and would, always be rejected. Europeo delegates were committed to maintaining the de facto colonial status of América. They consistently stonewalled americano requests for parity in government appointments or greater economic freedom, and they did so with racist slurs that rankled their americano colleagues deeply. Many americanos, while white by caste status in América, in fact had a trace of African or indigenous American descent that attracted ridicule in Spain. Racial innuendos added insult to injury when the cortes systematically rejected americano requests. Americanos who freely disparaged pardos, Africans, and Indians at home got a taste of their own racist medicine at Cádiz.

"Monstrous inequality," shouted Father Antonio de Larrazábal, unable to contain himself, on the floor of the cortes.[4] Normally this leader of the americano caucus, who often chaired sessions of the cortes, was more composed. Priests such as Larrazábal outnumbered delegates of any other profession in the Cortes of Cádiz, and most were hardly revolutionaries. Overall, demands advanced under Larrazábal's leadership basically constituted a project for home rule by América's dominant white minorities. The americanos at Cádiz accepted the Spanish monarchy but not the curtailment of their political representation in relation to Spain's.

In practice, the Cádiz constitution had little direct impact one way or the other. After all, the Cortes of Cádiz did not really rule Spain, which was still under French occupation in March 1812, and many parts of América totally refused to accept its authority. Even the viceroys of New Spain and Peru, while theoretically loyal to Cádiz, resisted implementing the more liberal aspects of the new constitution, such as freedom of the press. They did hold elections, albeit begrudgingly. Father Larrazábal's Kingdom of Guatemala, on the other hand, was a place where implementation of the Cádiz constitution went a bit further.

Until now we have had no reason to mention the Kingdom of Guatemala, which, despite its name, was simply a backwater Spanish colony, one that included all of Central America down to Panama, a territory one-third larger than Spain itself, but with only about one million inhabitants. Under the supervision of an effective Spanish administrator comparable, in some ways, to Abascal in Peru, the Kingdom of Guatemala, like Peru, had developed no independence movement and did not form a junta. The chief population centers of the Kingdom of Guatemala lay on the Pacific side, at the north end of the isthmus—isolated from the British-dominated Atlantic trade that so fascinated Caracas and Buenos Aires. The americanos of Guatemala ruled over large populations of subjugated Mayan Indians. Therefore, Guatemalan elites hesitated to make the populist appeals associated with americano juntas, dreading an outcome like Hidalgo's rebellion. Unlike New Spain, Peru, and Upper Peru, the Kingdom of Guatemala did not have rich silver mines, yet its tropical fruits and dyes could make modest fortunes for its leading families. Father Larrazábal proudly publicized a shipment of Guatemalan cacao and indigo that brought thirty thousand pesos to the Cádiz government. Various cities of the Kingdom of Guatemala—León, Granada, and San Salvador—had seen minor anti-europeo flare-ups in recent months, but nothing more.

Back in Cádiz, well before the completion of the 1812 constitution, some former americano supporters of the cortes had become frustrated by europeo obstructionism and deserted in protest. One of these was José de San Martín, who first joined a Cádiz branch of the Society of Rational Gentlemen, Miranda's secret organization for the independence-minded. San Martín got to know other Rational Gentlemen, americanos such as Father Servando Teresa de Mier, the dissident from New Spain, and Carlos Alvear, a young officer from a wealthy Buenos Aires family. The Cádiz branch soon had sixty-three members devoted to "the cause of América." As the Spanish delegates to the cortes systematically thwarted the initiatives of American delegates during the cortes debates, Mier, Alvear, and San Martín turned their backs on Cádiz and discreetly shipped out for London.

God Backs Fernando VII

On Holy Thursday, 26 March 1812, Caracas suffered an apparent act of God. Exactly on the second anniversary of the day when Venezuelans had formed a junta and unseated the Spanish administrator, a powerful earthquake shook Caracas apart. Thousands died, many in the great, crowded churches that collapsed on top of people hearing mass. In the context of the times, people might be excused for reading this as a divine referendum on independence. Clearly it seemed an unfavorable verdict. In the ruins of one church, the story circulated, a single pillar remained standing, the one emblazoned with the Spanish royal coat of arms. Simón Bolívar explored the corpse-strewn rubble of the cathedral that had stood on the main square of Caracas near his family's house, shouting in fury that Venezuelan patriots would, if need be, subdue Nature herself. But conservative clergy seem to have had more success than revolutionaries such as Bolívar in interpreting the meaning of the earthquake for the people of Caracas. The Holy Thursday earthquake of March 1812 signaled the beginning of the end for América's first republican experiment.

Indians, Mestizos, and Pardos Become Americanos

After more than seventy days under siege by the undefeated Spanish general Calleja, Morelos and the other defenders of Cuautla ran out of food and began to eat leather, iguanas, rats, and insects. They could stomach anything but surrender. "Intelligently fortified," in Calleja's assessment, Cuautla had decisively thrown back the initial assault of Calleja's five thousand veteran troops, including two battalions of europeos just off the boat from Spain.[5] Calleja consequently subjected the village to a steady artillery barrage and attempted to break the will of its defenders (half as numerous as their attackers) but to no avail. The people of the village, including women and children, collaborated enthusiastically in the defense. They amazed the besieging forces by defiantly dancing to celebrate their repeated survival of incoming mortar rounds and by singing at night around fires fed from the wreckage of Cuautla: "For a corporal, I'd give two pesos / For a captain, six or seven / But, oh, for General Morelos / I'd take a trip to heaven."[6]

The close alliance between Morelos's soldiers and the Cuautla villagers was notable because the villagers were strongly indigenous while many of the soldiers were pardos of the southern Pacific Coast. Among the defenders of Cuautla, people of diverse colonial castes came together as americanos. From now on, Morelos insisted, not just españoles americanos but everyone born in América was an americano—the old terminology of the caste system should be discarded. What mattered was the difference between americanos and europeos. From now on, Morelos announced, all public office would go to americanos, reversing the old preference for europeos. And debts owed by americanos to europeos were declared null and void. Morelos attracted followers by speaking to their interests but also by speaking their language. Compared with the Quixote-like figure of Miguel Hidalgo, Morelos was a bit of a Sancho Panza: stocky, folksy, and full of one-liners. Warned by the Zitácuaro junta of a plot in which a man described only as "pot-bellied" planned to assassinate Morelos, the intended victim almost died laughing: "The only pot-bellied guy around here is me!"[7] Morelos had guts, in more ways than one. On the day of Calleja's first attack on Cuautla, Morelos had personally led the counterattack. Separated from his men at one point, the reckless padre-turned-general fought off a circle of attackers at swordpoint for long minutes—a feat celebrated by his followers with tremendous gusto. Toward the end of April, more than two months into the siege, Calleja offered Morelos and his officers a pardon if they surrendered Cuautla immediately. In reply, Morelos, pinned down by a superior force, offered to pardon Calleja and his officers if they surrendered instead.

Then in the midnight darkness of 2 May 1812, the defenders of Cuautla, soldiers and townspeople, silently tiptoed through the besieging lines and escaped with almost total success. Calleja had planned to make the capture and destruction of Cuautla an object lesson to would-be insurgents, so instead of pursuing Morelos, he entered the village, executing the defenders who had been unable to evacuate and burning the remaining structures. Escaping from the clutches of Calleja was a feat worth celebrating. But Morelos's rebels would never again get so close to Mexico City.

By mid-1812, the impressive unanimity of América's initial reactions to the crisis in Spain had vanished. Loyalty to Fernando was not enough to maintain traditional lines of authority as americanos asserted home rule. The formation of americano juntas had disrupted old patterns of provincial subordination in Venezuela, New Granada, Chile, and the former Río de la Plata viceroyalty. New Spain had witnessed a vast and bloody uprising of downtrodden Indian peasants. These were civil wars. While important as leaders, españoles europeos constituted far less than 1 percent of the population. Therefore, the huge majority of people mobilizing on both sides of these not-so-civil wars were natives of América. Loyalty to Fernando VII remained strong. Yet, as the conflict radicalized, certain patriot leaders began to cast off the mask of Fernando. When they revealed their republican principles, however, their fortunes immediately took a turn for the worse.

Four

A LOST CAUSE?

1812–1815

NAPOLEON'S GRIP ON Spain finally did finally loosen. By the end of 1812, the Spanish nationalist resistance based in Cádiz had survived all French assaults, formed a government, and written Spain's first constitution. As Napoleon diverted troops from Spain to aid his disastrous Russian campaign, Spanish guerrillas continued to gnaw at the fabric of French control. Britain's Duke of Wellington (though he had not yet received that title) sallied on a rampage out of his base in Portugal and repeatedly trounced French armies. More Anglo-Spanish victories followed in 1813 and, toward the end of that year, Fernando VII finally emerged from his French captivity, vowing to recover control over Spain's colonies in América, as we will see. In the meantime, the cause of América was losing momentum.

The Venezuelan Republic Crumbles

The fortress at Puerto Cabello, where green mountains plunge steeply into the blue waters of the Caribbean shore, was the young Venezuelan republic's chief military installation—port, storehouse, stronghold, arsenal, and prison for dangerous royalist prisoners. Francisco Miranda had given command of Puerto Cabello to his protégé Simón Bolívar. But on 30 June 1812, royalist prisoners managed to spark a mutiny and take control of the fortress while Bolívar was outside its walls. Humiliatingly, Bolívar could only watch as his fortress artillery shelled the town it was supposed to protect. Four days later, his pride in tatters, Bolívar made an undignified exit from Puerto Cabello in a small boat with eight other officers—all that remained of the command entrusted to him by Miranda. The fiasco at Puerto Cabello constituted yet another in a string of catastrophes suffered by the Venezuelan republic during the past year. When the earthquake hit Caracas months earlier, a Spanish commander named Monteverde was already rallying royalist forces around Coro, and soon Monteverde marched on the devastated would-be capital, gathering support along the way. At that point, the patriots resorted to a Roman institution, the emergency rule of a "dictator" chosen to lead the republic through the crisis. Dictatorial powers were offered first to Bolívar's old ally, the Marqués of Toro, who prudently declined them, and then to Miranda, who accepted. As dictator, Miranda radicalized his populist appeals. "Liberty and equality" was the order of the day, and so was a hard line against europeos. More than a dozen Canary Islanders (equivalent to europeos in americano eyes) were executed after a not very menacing protest in which they paraded through Caracas wearing tin armor like Don Quixote and shouting "Long live the king!" Having abolished legal caste distinctions, the Venezuelan republic now courted further pardo support by opposing old racist customs, such as the special privileges reserved for white ladies in seating arrangements at mass. Miranda offered slaves eventual liberty in return for military service to the republic. But all in vain.

With Monteverde approaching Caracas from the west and a slave rebellion brewing in the east, Miranda's republic clearly lacked popular support in Venezuela as a whole. Next, news of the liberal Cádiz Constitution arrived—promising, in the name of Fernando VII, many of the same political freedoms that the republic offered. Then came the loss of the republic's key stronghold and arsenal at Puerto Cabello. Miranda believed that further resistance would be futile and result in needless loss of life. So he began secret negotiations with Monteverde. Secrecy would prevent panic and allow the negotiation of advantageous terms of surrender, Miranda alleged—but secrecy also permitted him to conveniently arrange his own evacuation on a British warship. The fleeing dictator neglected to inform his officers of these escape plans, however. Learning of them, Bolívar and several other furious officers declared Miranda a traitor to the cause of América and promptly turned him over to Monteverde. Still smarting from his disgrace at Puerto Cabello, Bolívar seems to have vented his frustration on his fallen idol. As a gesture of gratitude, Monteverde allowed Bolívar safe passage out of Venezuela and declined to expropriate Bolívar's property.

Miranda died in a Cádiz prison a few years later.

Rational Gentlemen Take Over in Buenos Aires

Carlos de Alvear cut a dashing figure in 1812. Imagine his impeccable blue uniform and aristocratic bearing, his strong chin and high forehead crowned by a curly plume of black hair, and his gallant reputation as a young veteran of the Spanish resistance against Napoleon. Alvear's rich and illustrious family in Buenos Aires, suitably proud of its twenty-three-year-old hero, politely welcomed the young man's older and also distinguished-looking companion, José de San Martín, whose military rank and experience far exceeded Alvear's, though he could not compete with the younger man in social prominence or social graces. San Martín had been born at the frontier outpost of Yapeyú, among soldiers, gauchos, and Indians, and had left for Spain as a small child, never to return to América until now. When this somewhat laconic career soldier opened his mouth in Buenos Aires, he sounded more *europeo* than *americano*.

Soon after arriving in Buenos Aires from London, San Martín and Alvear founded a new branch of the americanos-only Society of Rational Gentlemen that they had joined in Cádiz. The new lodge was to be the old one's most important offshoot, later famous as the Lautaro lodge. Masonic-style lodges were proliferating in these years as a vehicle for revolutionary organizing in América. They had written regulations and selective conditions for membership, clandestine meetings with candles and blindfolds, oaths of secrecy, pseudonyms, encoded symbols, and secret handshakes.

Martín Thompson, Mariquita's husband, also joined the Lautaro lodge, which Mariquita herself obviously could not do, because lodges were fraternal organizations for men only. But Alvear and San Martín became regular guests at Mariquita's famous salon gatherings, which had become a principal venue of patriotic social life in revolutionary Buenos Aires. A long room at Mariquita's house would accommodate a contredanse line of sixty couples, and there the patriot elite of Buenos Aires danced to celebrate the victories of their revolution. According to the story, the Argentine national anthem was first sung in chorus at one of Mariquita's gatherings, accompanied by her on the harp. Mariquita also offered her social support to another Rational Gentleman, Bernardo Monteagudo, the angry Chuquisaca radical who had accompanied Castelli in Upper Peru and whose poverty and dark mestizo coloring earned him a lot of dirty glances in Buenos Aires. In addition to being daring and eloquent, Monteagudo was devastatingly handsome, another quality that Mariquita appreciated.

More influential, however, were Alvear, San Martín, and other whiter—and notably less radical—Rational Gentlemen who gradually gained ascendancy within the Buenos Aires revolution. Their initial leverage came from a crack cavalry unit that San Martín recruited, outfitted, and trained in a few months after his arrival in Buenos Aires. Their political opponent was the junta secretary, Bernardino Rivadavia, who followed in the footsteps of the junta's first influential secretary, Mariano Moreno. Junta members were often figureheads, while their secretaries were full-time political operatives and more than one junta's driving ideological force. That was certainly the case with Rivadavia, as serious a revolutionary as Moreno or Monteagudo. Rivadavia regarded Alvear as a dilettante and an opportunist. As for San Martín, who was, after all, neither a democrat nor a republican, Rivadavia detested him. San Martín believed in the principle of popular sovereignty—América for americanos—but he did not think that the common people should rule, and he favored monarchical government. San Martín's expressions of monarchism made Bernardino Rivadavia throw objects across the room in fury.

Rivadavia's intemperate, heavy-handed style had offended a lot of people during his months as junta secretary, whereas the recently arrived Rational Gentlemen offered an appealingly fresh team. Carlos de Alvear, particularly, had many admirers. Steady, quiet San Martín, for his part, inspired confidence, and because of his efforts the Rational Gentlemen as a group possessed the persuasiveness of military force. By the end of October 1812, they had taken control of the Buenos Aires revolution.

Morelos Captures Oaxaca

While many village priests had joined the insurgency in New Spain, the church hierarchy remained staunchly loyal to its European leadership. This was especially true in Oaxaca, the chief city of southern New Spain. The bishop of Oaxaca hated Morelos, whom he preached against, excoriated, and described as having "horns and tail" like Satan himself.[1] Thanks to the bishop of Oaxaca's outspoken criticism of rebel priests, the Cádiz regency had promoted him to the diocese of Mexico City, but he had not yet traveled there to assume his lofty new position when Morelos and his small but seasoned army went to pay him a visit in Oaxaca.

In the six months since the siege of Cuautla, Morelos's forces had wound through the Sierra Madre del Sur, interrupting communications, capturing mule trains, occasionally occupying towns, and showing that the cause of América lived on. In Orizaba, on the road to Veracruz, Morelos's men seized and burned the warehouses of the lucrative royal tobacco monopoly, then doubled back south, toward Oaxaca. Oaxaca was effectively fortified and garrisoned, but Morelos's forces gained the benefit of surprise by appearing there suddenly after a two-week trek through the canyons and ridges of the Sierra Madre del Sur. The capture of Oaxaca took just two hours. The annals of Mexican patriotic history remember it for Morelos's pithy prediction to his troops, "Tonight we sleep in Oaxaca," and also for the dramatic gesture of a young man who had taken the nom de guerre Guadalupe Victoria.[2] One day he would be the first president of the Mexican Republic. On the day of the assault on Oaxaca, finding his path blocked by a water-filled moat, the young patriot officer inspired his soldiers by immediately throwing his sword across the water. It was too heavy to swim with, but to return from battle without his sword would mean dishonor. In the eyes of his men, Guadalupe Victoria had staked his life on victory, and when he dove in after his sword, they followed. Morelos's men did indeed sleep in Oaxaca that night, but not before they had thoroughly pillaged it and drunk a large quantity of high-quality mescal. The bishop had already fled, and the remaining Spanish commanders were summarily executed.

The 25 November 1812 capture of Oaxaca had considerable shock value. It constituted the military high point of the Morelos movement, bringing it new prestige and material resources. Oaxaca had, in fact, been a center of anti-insurgency efforts. Morelos freed hundreds of patriot prisoners from Oaxaca's royal dungeons, putting some of the most emaciated ones on horseback to publicize their ill-treatment. He also arranged two public ceremonies. The first was a mass of thanksgiving to the Virgin of Guadalupe, and the second a collective oath of allegiance to the National Junta founded at Zitácuaro by López Rayón. López Rayón's National Junta was mostly a fiction. After the destruction of Zitácuaro, it amounted to a few fugitive, frock-coated lawyers with letterhead stationery in their saddlebags. But at this point, the

National Junta and Morelos's army composed the entire americano cause in New Spain.

Bolívar Declares "War to the Death"

Bolívar arrived in Cartagena in late 1812, about half a year after leaving Caracas. He had spent most of that time with other political exiles on the island of Curaçao, off the coast of Venezuela, contemplating a discouraging panorama on the mainland. On the Caribbean coast, only Cartagena still defied Spain. Inland to the south, most of New Granada maintained the rebellion, but fragmented and torn by civil war. Antonio Nariño's government of Cundinamarca refused to accept the independence of other provinces, which he wished to reunite under the rule of Bogotá. The steeply Andean and strongly indigenous region of Pasto had become a royalist stronghold; Cartagena's old rival Santa Marta was likewise staunchly royalist. Amid these menacing surroundings, the republican government of Cartagena sorely needed experienced soldiers. Therefore, it gladly accepted the services offered by Bolívar and his fellow patriot refugees escaping from the fall of Miranda's republic.

On 15 December 1812, Bolívar published a manifesto, "To the Citizens of New Granada, from a Man of Caracas," explaining the collapse of the Venezuelan Republic and harping on the need to prevent Spain from using Venezuela as a platform for reconquering New Granada.[3] To explain the Venezuelan republic's untimely end, Bolívar primarily blamed Miranda's republican idealism and misguided coddling of europeos. The real problem, though, was that the early declaration of a republic had framed Venezuela's civil war as a conflict between republicans and monarchists. And republicans, with their newfangled French ideas, were likely to lose any popularity contest with monarchists in 1812 América. Bolívar had become convinced that to have a chance at victory, the struggle must be reframed as americanos versus europeos, pure and simple.

Cartagena assigned Bolívar a military command on the Magdalena River. At Mompox, where Humboldt had studied alligators during his ascent of the Magdalena a few years earlier, the headstrong aristocrat won a small military victory. Then, disregarding his instructions, Bolívar turned his gaze east toward Venezuela—the objective that really mattered to him, but not the mission given him in Cartagena. At the end of February 1813, Bolívar's men sacked the town of Cúcuta and began to advance toward Caracas. Although he occasionally sent reports to his supposed superiors in Cartagena, Bolívar continued to operate on his own initiative in the campaign he called "War to the Death."

Nativist venting was generally a crowd-pleaser, a tool too powerful for the patriots to ignore anywhere in América. To scapegoat europeos, with ubiquitous looting and lots of impromptu executions, had been common practice in all the rebellions since Hidalgo's. Bolívar's innovation was to make a merciless war of scorched earth into official policy and express it in a catchy slogan, which he did in June 1813. Threatening immediate execution of all europeos who bore arms in the service of Fernando VII, Bolívar's proclamation of War to the Death promised never to execute americanos, even if they fought against the republic. In effect, the new campaign redefined Venezuela's civil war between republicans and monarchists more advantageously as one between americanos and europeos.

Blood flowed, but War to the Death gave Bolívar's campaign new impetus. By early August 1813, Bolívar, who had just turned thirty years old, rode into Caracas at the head of his army of less than two thousand men. Many of the earthquake-shaken houses along his route remained roofless—walls surrounding piles of rubble—but they had been decorated for Bolívar's triumphal entry. Caracas seemed pleased to have its republic back and again produced virgins in white gowns to welcome a triumphant hero, proclaiming him "the Liberator." Twelve of the young women surrounded Bolívar's horse to crown him with laurels of victory, as in ancient Rome. The imagery was consistent with the stylistic imitations of Greece and Rome (considered models of non-monarchical government) practiced in other young republics of América. Consider, for example, the ubiquitous Greek temple motif in the city of Washington, D.C., under construction at this time.

But the second Venezuelan republic was far from consolidated— more precarious, even, than the first one. Bolívar's march had simply skirted the region of Coro, and Coro remained solidly royalist. Puerto Cabello along with Guayana and Angostura, two well-garrisoned cities on the great Orinoco River, highway into the interior, remained in royalist hands as well. Cumaná had become the center of an autonomous revolutionary movement to the east. In fact, Bolívar's republic really included only a small part of Venezuela around Caracas. From the outset, his government spent nearly all its energy prosecuting the war, which was Bolívar's forte anyway. The War to the Death was still on. Its deadly tit for tat continued as both sides accumulated prisoners and periodically executed some of them, ten americanos for ten europeos, then vice versa, and again and again. The republic could get no traction, it seemed. The populace of Caracas was tired of the fighting and each day less responsive to Bolívar's efforts to mobilize them militarily. Meanwhile, dark thunderheads towered over the Llanos, Venezuela's Orinoco River plains, where the most terrible reaction of all was brewing.

Vicario Goes on Trial

The rickety rise and rapid fall of Venezuela's second republic coincided, in Mexico City, with Leona Vicario's trial for treason. Imagine the shock, grief, and indignation of her guardian uncle, an outspoken royalist, who argued outright that disobedience to the "father king" was a sin against God. Yet Vicario's adherence to the patriot cause was undeniable. As Hidalgo's rebellion had burned out, then reignited under Morelos, Leona had been known to make highly impolitic public outbursts favoring the cause of América. Her participation went far beyond words, too. Vicario made her house in Mexico City into the unofficial communications nerve center of the patriot cause in New Spain. Indeed, Leona and a small network of secret patriot collaborators who called themselves the Guadalupes were the principal insurgent elements in the viceregal capital. Through a system of patriot couriers, Leona maintained correspondence with widely scattered rebel leaders, often in cipher, using code names that she assigned each of them. One of her more assiduous correspondents was Andrés Quintana Roo, a passionate patriot journalist from the far south of New Spain who worked with López Rayón's National Junta.

Vicario's treason was discovered when royal authorities arrested one of her couriers in early 1813. Fortunately for Leona, a patriot sympathizer warned her in time. It happened to be Carnival Sunday, creating confusion in the streets that facilitated her escape. In the company of several servants, she left Mexico City, supposedly to attend a party in an outlying town. Once outside Mexico City, however, she fell ill, and eventually surrendered to her royalist uncle. The discovery of Leona's "espionage" and, now, her detention were the talk of Mexico City. Leona faced down the judge who interrogated her, not revealing anything that might injure her cause. Her interrogation was not public, so her wit, resolve, and dignity under questioning were not generally known. People did hear, however, when she absconded from custody and disappeared into large, densely inhabited Mexico City, and many privately applauded the brave americana. Pioneer journalist and novelist Fernández de Lizardi, who was always in trouble with the censors, even hazarded an admiring comment in print. Subsequently, oral tradition memorialized the image of a mule train that left Mexico City weeks later, carrying loads of goods, attended by muleteers who rode alongside and by several women who rode atop the mules' burdens. All were pardos, as the muleteers of New Spain so often were—or pardas—including, on that day, Leona Vicario, who had darkened her skin and dressed as a parda to sneak out of the city, on her way to Oaxaca, where she hoped to find Andrés Quintana Roo.

Azurduy Creates a "Loyal Battalion"

Juana Azurduy had waited for Manuel Ascencio Padilla almost a year in her Andean condor's nest, caring for her brood of four and learning to swing a saber. The news that Manuel told when he returned, including his tale of patriot women's valiant fight in Cochabamba after the destruction of Castelli's expedition, only steeled Juana's resolve to become a patriot militant herself. When Buenos Aires sent a second expedition to secure Upper Peru for the cause of América, Juana and Manuel joined as a team, taking their children with them. This time the general coming from Buenos Aires was Castelli's cousin and cofounder of the original Buenos Aires junta, Manuel Belgrano. Belgrano was more affable and notably more sensitive than Castelli had been to the Catholic conservatism of the local people. Juana and Manuel Ascencio liked Belgrano, and he them. Even before arriving in Upper Peru, too, Belgrano had won a couple of welcome victories in Tucumán and Salta.

To win in Upper Peru, though, Belgrano needed the help of local people who could speak Quechua and Aymara, which, thanks to their rural upbringing, both Juana and Manuel Ascencio could do. Their assignment was to recruit Indians from the countryside. Juana did so on horseback, wearing a military uniform and carrying a saber. She made a strong impression on the Indians, to judge by the name that they began to call her—Pachamama, or Earth Mother—and by the fact that she brought ten thousand new fighters into Belgrano's forces. But Belgrano kept these large numbers of untrained and inexperienced volunteers (reminiscent of Hidalgo's followers) separate from his smaller, uniformed force. Juana's and Manuel Ascencio's volunteers, after all, were Indians, whereas Belgrano's flatlanders were whites and mestizos. The Indians fought with clubs and slings of the sort that David used against Goliath in the biblical story. Belgrano preferred to employ the Indians as auxiliaries, especially as porters to carry supplies and wrestle artillery and cannonballs though the mountains.

On 1 October 1813, Juana and Manuel Ascencio saw Belgrano's army defeated at a place called Vilcapugio while the thousands of Indians they had recruited were not allowed to fight. The story goes that after the battle Juana confronted Belgrano, who told her he feared her volunteers' lack of battlefield discipline. Knowledge of what had happened to Miguel Hidalgo's army at Calderón Bridge gave solid grounds for that fear. So Juana borrowed a training manual from Belgrano and went to work drilling a hand-picked Loyal Battalion, as she named it, to show what the Pachamama and her men could do. Only a few weeks later, Belgrano again confronted royalist forces, and he was again defeated, this time completely. But among the last to abandon the battlefield of Ayohuma, long after most of Belgrano's uniformed troops, were the Indians of the Loyal Battalion, whirling their slings defiantly amid the deadly rain of royalist bullets. After the battle, Belgrano gave his saber to Juana Azurduy in tribute to her battalion's bravery.

Manuel Belgrano is a sympathetic figure. He created the Argentine national flag, advocated for public education, and famously released prisoners awaiting execution. Unfortunately, he also tried to blow up the beautiful Potosí mint building as he retreated from Upper Peru after the defeat of Ayohuma. Granted, the mint was a symbol of Spanish power and a resource the enemy could use, but it was located in the center of town, and Belgrano's attempt to dynamite it endeared him to nobody in Potosí. In sum, the second Buenos Aires expedition to Upper Peru had reenacted the scenario established by the first. The flatlanders had arrived in a flurry of excitement, whipped everybody up, got beaten, and retreated—leaving the patriots of Upper Peru to suffer the persecution of the returning royalists.

Chilpancingo Gives Birth to a Nation

It called itself the Congress of Anáhuac, a small constituent assembly meeting under Morelos's wing in his southern base, Chilpancingo. Its aim was to found a nation. Only the nation hadn't found a name yet on 6 November 1813, when the Congress of Anáhuac declared independence. "Anáhuac," referring poetically to the ancient Aztecs, was more a literary motif than anything else. The name "New Spain" was a nonstarter. It would take a while for the name "Mexico" to be stretched from the ancient capital city around the whole country. So Mexicans prefer to remember this as the Congress of Chilpancingo, by the name of the dusty little town in the rugged Sierra Madre del Sur where the delegates met.

The main objective of the assembly was to write a constitution. Morelos told them briefly what he had in mind: no more kings. Enough kings. And no more castes. Enough castes. Slavery, too—enough of that. From now on, everybody would be just an americano, just as everybody should be Catholic. The two national holidays should be the day of the Virgin of Guadalupe and the anniversary of Hidalgo's 1810 uprising at Dolores village. After making these sentiments known, Morelos left the representatives to their work. He was a poor country priest, he explained, and the fancy literary stuff about Anáhuac was not for him. That was more for men of letters such as Andrés Quintana Roo, who, with Leona at his side in Chilpancingo, was vice president of the congress.

Meanwhile, Morelos had yet to lose a major battle. After taking Oaxaca the previous year, he had even captured Acapulco. But forcing the surrender of Acapulco in a protracted siege took the better part of 1813, with little immediate advantage. And, worse news, General Félix María Calleja had replaced Venegas as viceroy of New Spain by order of Cádiz. Calleja had sworn to get Morelos and was maybe the only person who could. Morelos does not seem to have felt intimidated, however. On the day after the Congress of Anáhuac declared independence, Morelos, who had decided that it needed a more appropriate venue for its further deliberations, launched his next military campaign. Why shouldn't the national congress legislate in cool and graceful Valladolid, Morelos's hometown, with access to the fertile Bajío and the silver mines of Guanajuato?

Fernando VII Turns Back the Clock

After six years of French captivity, the Desired One was back. The people of Madrid gave him a royal welcome on 13 May 1814, celebrating not only his adored self (at least, the self that they still imagined him to be) but also his recently unveiled rollback of everything the Cortes of Cádiz had done. Fernando turned back the clock of political change by restoring all Spanish public officials to the offices they had held when he became king in 1808. Fernando refused to be a constitutional monarch. He arrested liberal leaders, annulled the Cádiz constitution, and dissolved the cortes, saying he would call another one later. He never did.

Why Fernando wanted absolute power was less mysterious than why the Spanish people seemingly wanted him to have it. Perhaps they did not yet really know him. He had been their blue-eyed boy, snatched away too quickly into French captivity, desired since then, but always in his absence. As a whole, in May 1814 Spain seemed to accept that constitution-writing liberals were part of the whole French thing and best forgotten. And it was quite true, of course, that Spanish liberalism had many French inspirations—true, too, that the Cortes of Cádiz had been much more liberal than the country as a whole. Like the Congress of Anáhuac and other such wartime assemblies, it had symbolized the sovereign people without necessarily embodying their collective will in the absence of real elections. Therefore, the Spanish people might plausibly cheer as Fernando reassumed absolute power, restored the privileges of the feudal nobility, and even reestablished the Holy Inquisition, envisioning it all as a return to the good old days before the French Revolution.

Time to get the colonies back, too. The respectful petitions of the americano delegates to the cortes were off the table permanently. Fernando VII saw nothing to discuss with troublemakers such as Guatemala's Father Antonio de Larrazábal, who was one of the Cádiz liberals jailed at this time, much less with rebels who had infringed royal prerogatives. Fernando preferred a military solution to the problem of América. He ordered that a reconquest expedition, the largest military force Spain had ever sent to América, be prepared as quickly as possible. As for the equality of europeos and americanos proclaimed by the Cortes of Cádiz, perhaps it had never constituted more than lip service, but even that disappeared now, too.

Nariño Goes Back to Jail

The next day, in New Granada, the aging revolutionary Antonio Nariño was captured by Fernando VII's supporters while leading the Army of Cundinamarca against Pasto. This time Nariño almost didn't survive capture.

The Pastuzo people had proved to be among the toughest, most loyal, and most determined of Fernando's subjects in América. Pastuzo society was heavily indigenous, with a high-Andean flavor. Along with the local Pastuzo clergy and the city's elite of españoles americanos, the mestizo townspeople and Indian peasantry of Pasto were steadfastly royalist and had no wish to join a new republic that had renounced obedience to Fernando VII. Pastuzo loyalty responded to a native conservatism, no doubt, but also to the ancient rivalry between Pasto and Quito. Among the ideas that occurred to the first Quito junta had been to attack Pasto. The second Quito junta also failed to endear the Pastuzos to the cause of América when it captured and briefly occupied their city. In mid-1814, Pasto stood as the stubborn bastion of New Granada's royalist south—a royalist south into which Antonio Nariño vowed to introduce the benefits of liberty, whether the people there liked it or not.

Popayán, the chief city of southern New Granada, not far from Pasto, fell to Nariño's army by the first of the year. While his army rested in Popayán, Nariño wrote letters to the Pastuzos explaining that americanos shouldn't fight americanos, and that Bogotá had Pasto's best interests at heart. But the Indians collected round stones the size of grapefruit for their slings and placed boulders along cliff edges above the roads on which Nariño's armies would have to pass. The townspeople of Pasto likewise participated enthusiastically in the defense, which was fought in a string of holding actions as Nariño's force advanced toward the city. Finally, practically on Pasto's doorstep, the city's determined inhabitants scattered Nariño's forces and, on 14 May 1814, captured Nariño himself without knowing who he was. Nariño understood how the Pastuzos felt about him, so he dissimulated, claiming not to be Nariño but to know Nariño's whereabouts, which he promised to disclose if well treated. His captors marched him into the city to hear this information. Once safe in the custody of a Spanish general, the prisoner went out on a balcony and taunted the crowd with the information it sought: "Pastuzos! You're looking for General Nariño? Here he is!"[4]

In view of this revelation, the Pastuzos favored a summary execution, but the Spanish general protected his defiant captive, whom he thanked for preventing plunder in Popayán. Besides, Nariño was a valuable prisoner. Soon he was on his way to Lima, and then to Cádiz, in chains once more. He had been out of Spanish custody for not quite four years.

Meanwhile, Bolívar's fortunes, too, took a turn for the worse. A month after Nariño's capture, Bolívar lost the decisive battle of La Puerta, and the second Venezuelan republic quickly unraveled. Monteverde played no part in the luckless liberator's undoing. This time, Bolívar's nemesis was an entire region of the country called the Llanos.

The Llanos flank the Orinoco River on its course through the interior of Venezuela, which in 1814 was a sparsely populated cattle frontier inhabited by tough cowboys, *llaneros*, who now emerged as a potent military asset. The llaneros' advantage was old-fashioned. In global history the horse has been, above all else, a vehicle of warfare. In combination with the availability of mounts in the Llanos, the llaneros' skill as horsemen gave them tremendous military potency because it allowed them to use improvised lances. The iron bars of a single window grille of the sort common in colonial architecture, sharpened into lance heads, could turn a dozen bamboo poles into so many deadly weapons. Such improvised weapons were doubly valuable because firearms remained scarce. Frontier lancers, often pardos, figure importantly in the fighting of these years throughout América. They usually fought on the patriot side, but not always. African-descended horsemen from the Patía valley, near Pasto, were fearsomely effective allies of the royalist Pastuzos. Venezuela's llaneros were royalists, too, at least for now, under the leadership of a europeo "gone native" named Tomás Boves. Boves was a man of many talents, formerly a ship captain, who had stayed in Venezuela to live on the edge of the Llanos trading in horses, mules, and cowhides. His years in Venezuela had made Boves a horseman whose riding merited respect even among the discerning llaneros, but he became infamous for permitting, even encouraging, atrocities. If Bolívar wanted War to the Death, Boves gave him plenty of death.

On the patriot side, Bolívar had joined forces with another liberator, Santiago Mariño. Mariño led the republican movement of eastern Venezuela that had emerged around Cumaná, independently of Bolívar's Caracas-centered republic. On 15 June 1814, the liberators of east and west faced waves of charging llanero lancers at La Puerta and reeled away, shattered, in full flight toward Caracas. The population of Caracas evacuated the city, many thousands trekking east toward Cumaná to escape Boves. Their fear was not unreasonable. A single anecdote about Boves's macabre sense of humor will suffice for many. In the city of Valencia, which surrendered to Boves a few weeks after the battle of La Puerta, a smiling Boves invited the ladies of the city's upper crust to a dance in celebration of his triumph. They dared not refuse, but as they danced with Boves's men they heard what they later discovered to be the sounds of their husbands, sons, and brothers being slaughtered outside. The public plazas of Bolívar's republic, too, had echoed with the work of firing squads liquidating europeos without any sort of trial. Civil war had become bloodier in Venezuela than anywhere else in América.

In Cumaná, the fleeing Bolívar and Mariño once again clambered aboard small vessels and set sail for exile as Boves's lancers swept all opposition into the Caribbean Sea. Boves died mopping up the last republican forces left behind, but his llaneros had transformed the balance of military power in Venezuela. For the next two generations, whoever won the loyalty of the llaneros could rule, and whoever didn't, couldn't.

San Martín Hatches a Plan

José de San Martín's lung problems had started in Spain, but they became chronic, low-grade tuberculosis in América. On 7 September 1814, San Martín finished a long and, for him, physically torturous journey on horseback at the pleasant little city of Mendoza in the Andean foothills of far western Argentina. Perhaps, he hoped, the climate would improve his health. More important, however, it would allow him to advance his strategic plan (to be described shortly). San Martín's desire to do anything possible to further that plan was tested on the day of his arrival in Mendoza, when the cabildo proudly offered him a residence. San Martín's normal reaction to personal tributes was awkward refusal—and, true to form, he first spurned the cabildo's offer before finally accepting it to please the city fathers. He was going to need their help for his strategic plan.

San Martín had hatched his strategy during the past year, spent partly in Tucumán, where he replaced Manuel Belgrano, recently defeated in Upper Peru. Belgrano was San Martín's sort—consistent, reasonable, self-effacing. The two became friends in a series of letters exchanged before meeting. San Martín assumed command but kept Belgrano with him and defended the defeated general's reputation as he rebuilt his defeated army. The patient work of preparation, training, and supply, rather than battlefield heroics, had always been San Martín's specialty. In Tucumán he struggled to get uniforms for soldiers in rags and founded an academy to drill officers. San Martín made a good choice when he put Martín Güemes from the northern city of Salta in charge of training and deploying gaucho guerrillas there. Each time Buenos Aires forces had retreated from Upper Peru, royalist forces had advanced south in their wake. Güemes and his gauchos successfully snarled that advance, but their function was defensive.

Upper Peru loomed ahead, more impassable than ever for Buenos Aires forces. Talking with Belgrano and other veterans of the two failed expeditions to Upper Peru, San Martín decided that taking the highlands had become a fatal distraction from the ultimate strategic target: Lima, the chief command post of Spanish colonial power on the South American continent. Take Lima, decided San Martín, and the Andean highlands would necessarily follow in time. Meanwhile, Upper Peru—with its dizzying altitude, vast distances, and geographical bottleneck at the Desaguadero—posed insuperable logistic obstacles. San Martín's plan was to circumvent those obstacles, crossing the Andes at a narrow point much farther south, near Santiago, Chile. From there, a seaborne expedition could land troops practically on the viceroy's doorstep in Lima. San Martín's strategic plan called for the creation of a new Army of the Andes on the eastern slope of that range, at Mendoza, near the passes leading to Santiago. San Martín petitioned Buenos Aires for military command of the area.

Meanwhile, San Martín's former friend and associate Carlos de Alvear more or less held the reins of power in Buenos Aires. But San Martín expected no help from Alvear, whose priorities were entirely different. Alvear wanted above all to destroy the Eastern Shore forces led by Artigas, who still refused obedience to Buenos Aires. Alvear also wanted to send a third expedition to Upper Peru. And Alvear hoped to lead both expeditions, preferring to reserve as much glory as possible for himself. So he was happy to see San Martín posted to distant Mendoza, happy, too, to see Belgrano depart on a diplomatic mission to London.

So in September 1814, San Martín settled in for what appeared a long-term, long-shot project in Mendoza. His health did improve. Even better, his wife, Remedios, joined him there. The next two years would be their longest time together, probably the happiest in their marriage. Politically, though, the situation in Mendoza became more complicated when the fractious patriot government of Chile collapsed next door.

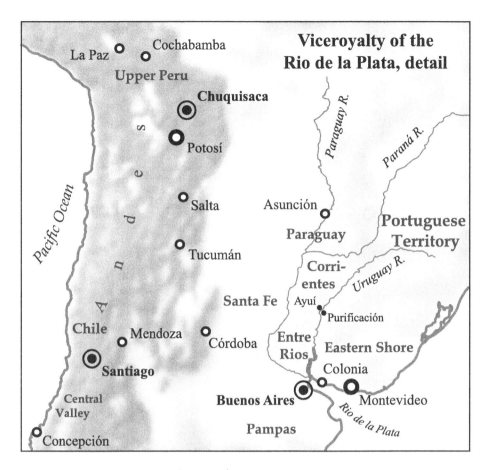

Remember Rancagua!

On 2 October 1814, Bernardo O'Higgins watched at dawn from atop a bell tower in the central Chilean town of Rancagua, searching for signs of a promised relief force. O'Higgins and his patriots had been corralled by royalist troops loyal to Peruvian viceroy Abascal and pushed into the town's central square, with barricades and cannon defending each of its four corners. O'Higgins's men were low on ammunition and water and could not resist much longer. Viceroy Abascal, victorious in Upper Peru and in Quito, was about to reconquer Chile for the recidivist absolute monarch Fernando VII.

As O'Higgins scanned the horizon for help, his stomach must have churned with the knowledge that help lay in the hands of his bitter rival José Miguel Carrera. O'Higgins and Carrera had started out the revolution as enemies, on opposite sides of Chile's regional divide between patriots of Santiago and those of Concepción. Those differences had been settled without bloodshed, but hard feelings lingered.

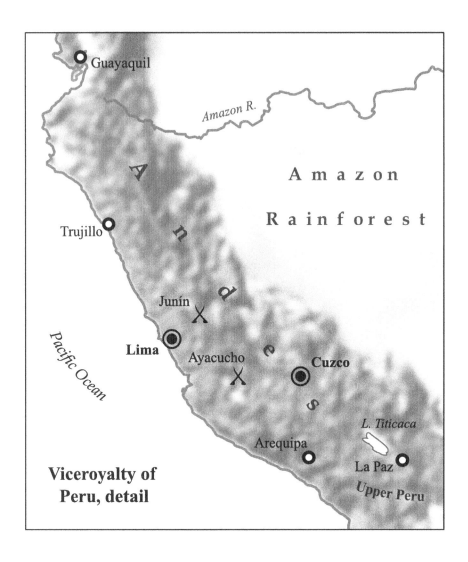

Viceroyalty of
Peru, detail

When Abascal's first expedition sent from Peru landed near Concepción, O'Higgins and Carrera tried to work together against the royalist invaders. Their mutual suspicions prevented effective collaboration, however, and a second Peruvian expedition soon reinforced the first one. O'Higgins's success in a few early skirmishes with the Peruvian force made him the patriots' military hero, but Carrera had stronger political connections. The arrogant Carrera regarded O'Higgins as a viceroy's bastard son, a social upstart of inferior breeding and intelligence. When Abascal's third expedition landed in the south and quickly advanced on Santiago, it found O'Higgins's soldiers maneuvering against Carrera's soldiers; taking all of them off guard, it easily trapped O'Higgins in Rancagua.

O'Higgins's lack of confidence in Carrera's promised relief force was prescient. Carrera said later that he turned back because he believed that Rancagua had already surrendered. Seeing him turn back, O'Higgins went down from the bell tower to face the final onslaught, which was not long in coming. As the ammunition dwindled to nothing, O'Higgins led all the remaining troops in a final attempt to break through the encircling force. Horsemen had the best chance of escaping, as O'Higgins himself managed to, along with a few hundred others. Of Rancagua's seventeen hundred defenders, though, about a thousand lay dead or wounded by the end of the day, and four hundred were captured. In the days after the defeat, civilian refugees streamed out of Santiago toward the Andes in a rout. Both O'Higgins and Carrera were part of that exodus, along with anyone who had participated in the various projects of home rule in Chile since 1810. From their initial base in Concepción, the Peruvian expeditions sent by Abascal gradually reestablished viceregal authority in Chile as a whole. Exiles such as O'Higgins and Carrera had to cross the Andes to Mendoza, providing San Martín with experienced recruits, but also problems, as the Chileans continued to feud with each other.

The battle of Rancagua, one could say, was the moment when Chile's first experiment with self-rule collapsed—*and* the moment when Chilean independence became inevitable in the long run. Somehow, the alchemy of hope turned this defeat into an inspiration. Like the patriots of Cuautla, the patriots of Rancagua had been bloodied but emerged proudly defiant. Chilean patriots would remember Rancagua the way that Sam Houston's Texans remembered the Alamo. The patriot cause gained new poignancy from its fallen heroes, new persuasiveness from the harsh royalist approach to reconquest. Such things were happening all over América in late 1814 as royalist forces reimposed royal control.

Abascal Snuffs Out Pumacahua's Rebellion

Early in 1815, at the Peruvian locality of Sicuani, sixty-seven-year-old Mateo Pumacahua found himself under the sort of summary interrogation that precedes summary executions. The Pumacahua Rebellion, about to end definitively that same day, was Peru's one large-scale local challenge to Spanish control. No doubt Pumacahua was regretting ever having joined the cause of América. For most of his long life,

Pumacahua had ranked among the most loyal and respected Indian defenders of Spanish rule in the southern Andes. All that had changed only a few months earlier, in Cuzco, the former Inca capital high in the Andes.

Spanish conquerors of the 1500s had created a new capital city on the coast to replace Cuzco. But the old Inca capital remained a rival center of power and authority in colonial Peru. Cuzco was the seat of an audiencia, for example, and Cuzco also boasted vestiges of an Inca nobility that retained prestige under Spanish rule. Pumacahua himself claimed descent from Inca royalty. Another who had claimed such descent was Tupac Amaru, who led a great uprising in the 1780s. The loyal Mateo Pumacahua, then in his prime, had fought against Tupac Amaru and even participated in the Spanish reprisals against the defeated rebels. Pumacahua's service to the Spanish crown had earned him social distinction and high rank in the militia. When the patriots of La Paz created their revolutionary junta in 1809, Pumacahua's men helped destroy it, and Cuzco was likewise the staging area for Abascal's successful counterstrikes against Castelli's and Belgrano's invasions of Upper Peru.

Cuzco's old rivalry with Lima found new expression when Viceroy Abascal reluctantly promulgated the Cádiz constitution in Peru. The americanos of Cuzco were eager to elect their own cabildo, which the constitution authorized, and they celebrated with fireworks and bull-fights. The indigenous people of the countryside had something to celebrate as well—the constitution's abolition of the annual tribute or head tax. Familiar patterns repeated themselves as Cuzco's europeo-dominated audiencia clashed with the americano-dominated cabildo, and urban crowds supported the cabildo. University graduates (especially an americano named José Angulo) and priests led Cuzco's patriot movement until Spanish authorities gravely insulted Pumacahua (by stripping him unceremoniously of his place on the audiencia, an insensitive blunder). The urban americano leadership then courted Pumacahua, blatantly using the mask of Fernando to hoodwink the old servant of the crown. They knew that the longtime militia commander, whose followers called him "Inca," could attract thousands of Indians to their cause.

And that is exactly what happened. At its high point, the brief Pumacahua rebellion captured both La Paz and Arequipa, two important Andean cities. But the Pumacahua rebellion suffered the same weakness exhibited by the Hidalgo rebellion in New Spain. In both cases, urban whites and mestizos had rallied Indian masses that they could neither arm nor discipline adequately. All but a fraction of Pumacahua's twelve thousand to fourteen thousand fighters carried slings and clubs rather than firearms. They responded to traditionalist imagery distant from the liberal agenda of the urban leadership. Pumacahua's men, like Hidalgo's, pillaged widely. Spanish property was their primary target, with the property of rich americanos a close second. Americano support for the rebellion waned rapidly as a result. It had almost disappeared by the time that Pumacahua's army was destroyed by a much smaller, better-armed, and more disciplined force analogous to the one that Calleja had used to rout Hidalgo's multitude at Calderón Bridge.

Soon after his army's defeat, Mateo Pumacahua had been captured, and on 17 March 1815 he responded with dignity to his browbeating interrogators, who repeatedly scorned the prisoner's answers to their questions. Pumacahua protested that he had agreed to raise Indian forces around Cuzco only because he was told by José Angulo that Fernando VII had died in French captivity and that the kingdom must be protected from usurpers. Asked why he signed documents organizing a new government, Pumacahua professed that those matters went beyond his understanding. He had merely endorsed what the rebellion's civilian leaders recommended. Asked why he had worn clothing that indicated his descent from the Inca emperor Huayna Capac, Pumacahua denied that he had ever worn anything except a military uniform. Asked if he knew the punishment suffered by traitors to the king, old Pumacahua said that he knew it was death. His testimony was then read back to him, and he signed it. He may have minimized his role in hopes of clemency. But as soon as he signed his testimony the old man was immediately hanged and his body decapitated, drawn, and quartered. Pumacahua's head was sent to Cuzco to be displayed on a pike in the main square of the city. One of his arms was sent to the city of Arequipa, scene of his greatest victory, to be displayed in a similar manner.

Peru, like Chile, was securely back under the control of the Spanish crown, where it would remain for years.

Enter Iturbide

By May 1815, royal control was being securely reestablished in New Spain as well. The Morelos movement had suffered a string of defeats since the Congress of Chilpancingo. Morelos's attempt to capture the city of Valladolid, where he had hoped to install the national congress, had failed abysmally. The rebel priest's long winning streak had come to a permanent end. Various small insurgent forces continued to exist in New Spain, but they became totally fragmented and, increasingly, fought among themselves. As Morelos's star declined, the star of another native son of Valladolid traced an ascendant path.

This star was Agustín de Iturbide, a rich young landowner and militia officer who had rejected Hidalgo's personal invitation to rebel and instead fought against Hidalgo at Monte de las Cruces. Iturbide had played a role in Morelos's humiliating defeat at Valladolid and personally led a brutal mop-up operation after the battle. The royalist officer had gained a reputation for ruthless treatment of patriot captives as Morelos's dwindling army and his portable national congress moved frequently, staying just one step ahead of their pursuers. One memorable stop was the remote mountain village of Apatzingán, where the tiny congress wrote a republican constitution that it would never be able to implement. Leona Vicario and Andrés Quintana Roo, now married, were an important part of this government on wheels, committed together to risk their lives for América. On 1 May 1815, Iturbide launched a new expedition in pursuit of Morelos and his congress, while Viceroy Calleja had the constitution of Apatzingán burned in the main square of Mexico City and ecclesiastical authorities declared that readers of the document would be excommunicated.

Artigas Builds a Federal League

The only place in América where royal Spanish authorities were not successfully reasserting their power was in the former Viceroyalty of the Río de la Plata. By mid-1815, in fact, Viceroy Elío had, at long last, surrendered Montevideo to the besieging Army of Buenos Aires and sailed back to Spain, leaving Carlos de Alvear to gloat in triumph. The people of Montevideo merely traded one occupier for another, however, because the Army of Buenos Aires dominated with an iron hand and took considerable spoils, including eight thousand urgently needed firearms, hundreds of cannon, and the printing press that Carlota Joaquina had sent to Viceroy Elío. But Alvear had spent all his political capital on the siege of Montevideo, and he had many enemies. In a surprising reversal of fortunes, Alvear's leadership abruptly imploded when his own troops mutinied against him. As a result, Buenos Aires withdrew its troops from Montevideo, leaving the rustic followers of José Artigas to enter the fortress capital of their own province for the first time in years.

Artigas had become the worst nightmare of the Lautaro Lodge, which was committed to establishing centralized control for Buenos Aires. A sworn enemy of Buenos Aires, Artigas had spent the last year assembling a Federal League, a loose confederation linking the Eastern Shore with four other autonomy-seeking provinces of the former Río de la Plata viceroyalty. The Federal League presented a serious economic as well as military challenge for Buenos Aires, thanks to its size, its well-watered pastures, and its location astride the Uruguay and Paraná rivers, which gave it independent access to Atlantic trade. Soon Federal League members began to export cattle hides and jerked beef from their own river ports, bypassing Buenos Aires. The Federal League had a military figurehead in Artigas, who assumed the title "Protector of Free Peoples." The closest thing to a federal capital was Artigas's encampment at Purificación.

Purificación—part frontier settlement, part military base—was a string of mud huts with thatched roofs on a plateau overlooking the Uruguay River. It also seemed part mission to visitors, surprised at the number of indigenous people in Purificación. Guaraní was no doubt heard there as often as Spanish. Purificación was also part prison camp. Artigas suggested that Spanish prisoners be sent there for a sort of rustic reeducation, learning republican values in contact with the American countryside. Artigas himself displayed the austere lifestyle that he advocated, living in rooms without furniture and often wearing ordinary country clothing instead of a uniform. He had always associated with the common folk of the plains frontier, with gauchos and Indians. He had adopted as a son a Guaraní youth, Andrés Artigas, to whom he wrote a letter at this time, explaining his plan to call a congress to create a defensive alliance with Buenos Aires against the coming "epidemic of Spaniards."[5] Artigas was referring to Fernando's great expedition being assembled in Cádiz to annihilate the remaining americano rebels. The expeditionaries, more than ten thousand of them on sixty ships, were seasoned veterans of Spain's war against Napoleon. The expedition's commander, Pablo Morillo, was a hero of that war. The Río de la Plata was his expected destination, and it promised to be easy prey if Buenos Aires and the Federal League could not present a united front.

On 29 June 1815 the tiny congress called by Artigas met at a place called Arroyo de la China, or "Squaw Creek," on the western shore of the Uruguay River, and agreed to send a delegation downriver to Buenos Aires to negotiate a defensive alliance. They found Buenos Aires in no mood to parley, however. According to news just arrived from Europe, the Morillo expedition had gone to Venezuela.

Bolívar Writes His Jamaica Letter

In Jamaican exile after his defeat by Boves (and after other adventures too involved to trace here), Simón Bolívar had plenty of time to brood about the discouraging turn of events in América. Since May, the once-opulent Bolívar had been penniless, living in rented rooms, sleeping in a hammock, dependent for food and spending money on the support of a British merchant friend. News of Napoleon's ultimate defeat by the Duke of Wellington at the battle of Waterloo had recently arrived in Jamaica as Bolívar sat down to write his famous "Jamaica Letter," dated in Kingston, 6 September 1815.

Bolívar's Jamaica Letter was partly a response to queries directed to him by a local British gentleman, but Bolívar wrote it for publication in the newspapers, hoping to reach a larger audience. It is essentially a plea for British aid. Like so many americano leaders, Bolívar was an Anglophile, and a bid for British aid seemed especially opportune at this moment. After a decade of war against Napoleon, the British army and navy would be much too large for peacetime; perhaps the expansive energies of the world's greatest power could be harnessed by americanos. If Britain wanted to assert itself in América, Bolívar wanted to guide it. In effect, he already saw Britain as what it would in fact become, the new hegemonic power in South America. But he did not expect the relationship to be conflictive. It was hard to tell who wanted British trade more, the British traders or the americanos. Bolívar's Jamaica Letter provides a rose-tinted survey of economic opportunities and of the bedraggled cause of América.

The Morillo expedition had occupied Venezuela, admittedly, but would fail to capture Cartagena, insisted Bolívar. He assured his readers, too, that Chile and Peru could revolt again at any time. He pronounced the situation in New Spain varied and confused, which was true. But only the Río de la Plata, which had indisputably managed to purge itself of Spanish control, really matched Bolívar's upbeat description—and even then not totally, because he forgot to mention the ongoing fratricidal confrontation between Buenos Aires and Artigas. Bolívar also announced that the "victorious armies" of Buenos Aires had reached as far as Upper Peru, without saying what happened to them there.

On the topic of América's economic potential, Bolívar threw up his hands in marvel. Untapped riches galore! Of course, much remained shrouded in mystery, protested Bolívar. Even Humboldt, with his encyclopedic knowledge, could not answer all questions about the region's future development. Bolívar also meditated on how an independent América should be governed, suggesting vaguely that new institutions would have to be adapted to the continent's particular social makeup. Then, without naming Britain directly, he repeatedly remarked on the need for some powerful, liberal nation to take América under its wing politically for guidance and protection. Where could such a nation be found? (Later Bolívar explained that Britain might, for example, take direct control of Panama and Nicaragua, create an interoceanic canal in one of those locations, and make the isthmus into the center of world trade.)

Bolívar decided to leave Jamaica and return to the fray when a request for his leadership came from besieged Cartagena. Cartagena's fortifications were almost impregnable, but its defenders had to eat. More or less when Bolívar was drafting his Jamaica Letter, Morillo intercepted a desperate plea for help from Cartagena, reporting that the city had only forty days' supply of food left, counting horses and dogs. Bolívar sailed to take command of the beleaguered city, but its defenders surrendered while he was still at sea. Bolívar learned of Cartagena's surrender from a passing ship and landed in Haiti instead.

João VI Creates a United Kingdom

British influence also interested the court of João VI in Rio de Janeiro, where by 1815 it was deemed too much of a good thing. João had opened Brazilian ports to international trade upon first arriving in América, and most of the ships that had arrived, by far, were British. Moreover, João gave other privileges specifically to Britain. British merchants were to enjoy a special legal status, and as a consequence, British traders often acted irritatingly above the law. British Protestants could practice their religion, a major concession for a Portuguese monarch to make. The British Foreign Office was not shy about exercising diplomatic pressure, either. Britain and Portugal had long enjoyed a close relationship, after all—most notably of late, when a

British fleet had escorted João across the Atlantic to escape the depredations of Napoleon.

But now British diplomats were pressuring João to make the return trip to Lisbon. Napoleon's defeat had inaugurated a new era in Europe. Napoleon's military adventures had disrupted old-regime monarchies and stimulated liberal revolutions throughout the continent. Even where republics did not succeed, constitutional monarchies had replaced the absolute kind. A reaction began immediately after Waterloo when Prince Metternich of Austria launched a campaign, based in Vienna, to restore the power and dignity of Europe's traditional monarchs, the ones who ruled supposedly by the grace of God and not because an assembly of elected representatives, exercising popular sovereignty, authorized them to do so. This was the so-called Holy Alliance. Spain's Fernando had opted for the absolutism of the Holy Alliance, but what of Portugal's João? Portugal had neither an elected national assembly nor a constitution. And it was undeniably odd to have a European ruler make his royal court in an American colony. Europeans, generally, including the British, thought it best that João return to his throne in Lisbon. The British even sent a naval squadron to escort him home.

João refused to go and resented the pressure. As soon as French troops had left Portugal, João's Portuguese subjects themselves called for his return. So, in a stunning gesture, João formally redefined Brazil as no longer a colony, issuing a royal charter on 12 December 1815 that raised Brazil to the status of kingdom, equal to Portugal. Furthermore, the charter joined Brazil and Portugal together in a single United Kingdom. With a few scratches of his royal quill, João thus granted Brazilians the legal equality that Spanish Americans had sought unsuccessfully for years, making Brazil and Portugal officially the two pillars of his crown. Moreover, the United Kingdom's royal court was to be not at Lisbon but at Rio de Janeiro. Brazilians rejoiced, while almost no one in Portugal was amused, save, perhaps, for José Bonifácio de Andrada and other Brazilians resident there. (José Bonifácio still had not received permission, as a servant of the crown, to return to his native Brazil. Now in his fifties, one might say that he was still paying off his student loans, tied to royal service because of his decade of scholarship support for his mineralogical studies in Germany.)

João also tried to counteract Britain's overwhelming influence by forming an alliance with Austria. In the monarchical way of doing things, the best sort of alliance is a princely marriage between allies. Therefore, João and Carlota Joaquina sent a secret mission to Vienna to arrange an alliance between their heir, Prince Pedro, and Princess Leopoldina of Austria. To appease Metternich, who was sure *not* to approve of João's throne moving permanently to América, João instructed his envoy to convey his royal eagerness to return to Lisbon, which he would surely do when Brazil was safe from infection by the revolutionary fever that still menaced Spain's colonies. Princess Leopoldina, for her part, was a smart and spirited young woman who brushed aside anxious whisperings about Brazil's deadly tropical climate and declared that she had always wanted to go to América. She also liked Pedro's portrait. By some miracle, Pedro was a fine specimen despite the notorious physical unattractiveness of both his parents.

As the curtain went down on the americano revolutions so optimistically surveyed by Simón Bolívar from Jamaican exile, old-style monarchy seemed stronger than ever in Brazil. The kindly but indolent João gave nightly audiences for petitioners, who knelt and kissed his hand before explaining their requests. Carlota Joaquina especially liked to see people on their knees; her guards habitually saber-whipped anyone who failed to kneel when her royal coach passed down the street. The presence of uppity foreigners caused some problems in this regard when, at one point, the diplomatic representative of the United States refused to kneel and even threatened to shoot Carlota Joaquina's guards if they attempted to administer the customary saber-whipping. Republicans, alleged the U.S. diplomat, did not kneel in the street. So João granted a special exemption to the whole diplomatic corps resident in Rio, much to his consort's displeasure.

Morelos Is Executed as a Traitor

Morelos, who refused to kneel before anyone but God, was executed as a traitor to his country and his king on 22 December 1815, while the people of Rio were still celebrating their new status as capital of João's United Kingdom. Morelos had appealed to Britain for support on various occasions, and more insistently to the United States, with no luck at all. Unfortunately, Morelos had his stronghold along the Pacific coast of southern New Spain, far from an Atlantic port that would have afforded him a direct sea route to either London or Washington. Therefore, he tried to gain U.S. support indirectly, working through various untrustworthy intermediaries who claimed connections in New Orleans and Philadelphia but who never put Morelos in contact with anyone worthwhile. Eventually, Morelos and his national congress decided to transfer their activities to the gulf coast of New Spain, precisely so as to achieve better communication with people in the United States—true republicans, it was hoped—who would aid republican brothers in need. It was while Morelos was escorting the portable congress east across the country that royalists finally captured him.

Viceroy Calleja had Morelos brought immediately to Mexico City for thorough interrogation by both royal and ecclesiastical officials. The radical priest's death sentence for treason was a foregone conclusion. Morelos seemed more disturbed at being convicted of heresy by the Inquisition. Fearing the damnation of his soul, he repented, for which good sense church authorities granted him the favor that his body not be dismembered for public display. In order that his execution not provoke a dangerous public reaction, Morelos was taken in a closed coach to the small village of Ecatépec, just north of Mexico City, where a firing squad shot him in the back and buried his body discreetly without identification.

During 1816, Morillo's expedition finished its reconquest of New Granada and reinstalled a viceroy in Bogotá. By that time, americano rebels retained control only in the former Río de la Plata viceroyalty, and even there, conflict between Artigas and Buenos Aires spelled patriot weakness. João's Portuguese forces would soon take advantage of that weakness. Elsewhere, Spanish arms had apparently crushed the insurgency. But appearances were deceiving. The brutal character of Spanish reconquest gave fresh appeal to the cause of América, even among people who opposed it. The period of not-so-civil wars was ending. As thousands of Spanish troops arrived to finish the reconquest of América, the conflict became more purely one of americanos versus europeos—a conflict that, in the long run, the cause of América couldn't lose. "It would be easier to have the two continents meet," wrote Bolívar in the Jamaica Letter, "than to reconcile the spirits of Spain and América."[6] He was right.

Five

INDEPENDENCE WON

1816–1824

O NLY THE SPARSELY populated provinces of the Río de la Plata remained in rebellion by 1816. To complete the reconquest of Spain's colonies in América, Fernando VII vowed to assemble a second expeditionary force at Cádiz, and this time the target would unquestionably be Buenos Aires. The situation in New Spain, Peru, and Upper Peru was by then so firmly in hand that the stalwart viceroys Calleja and Abascal could retire to enjoy their prestige as saviors of the Spanish empire. Portuguese king João VI (who had finally graduated from being prince regent because of the recent death of his mother, the mad queen Maria I) seemed totally secure on his Brazilian throne. Yet within a few years both Spanish and Portuguese control would dissolve with a minimum of resistance. What happened?

San Martín Begins to Turn the Tide

The americano resurgence started when San Martín's army executed the first step in the methodical general's master strategy, crossing the Andes to thrash a royalist army in February 1817. The ambitious trans-Andean assault was the culmination of two years of complex planning and dogged preparation on the part of San Martín. Essentially, he had built his Army of the Andes from scratch. Slaves expropriated from europeos and from church-run agricultural estates constituted the original nucleus of his force. San Martín worked hard to uniform and train them adequately. Chileans fleeing across the Andes after the battle of Rancagua provided veteran reinforcements. Bernardo O'Higgins became San Martín's close collaborator (making the Carreras, ipso facto, his enemies). San Martín's greatest collaborator, however, was the city of Mendoza itself.

Both the city council and the general populace cooperated with San Martín's project, a remarkable fact given that he had to levy taxes and exact loans to pay for munitions and provisions. San Martín intended to lead not a motley crew but a proper army, according to his concept as a career military officer, with regular discipline and equipment. The ladies of the city, proud americanas, famously offered their jewels for the patriotic cause and contributed their labor as seamstresses to produce hundreds of uniforms. Artisans manufactured gunpowder from naturally occurring nitrates and melted down church bells to make cannons.

This preparation happened in a climate of deepening uncertainty for the former viceroyalty of the Río de la Plata. The rising power of the Federal League provinces, led by Artigas, seriously challenged the control of Buenos Aires. When Buenos Aires organized a national congress to meet in the city of Tucumán, the Federal League provinces did not send delegates. Nor, of course, did Paraguay or Upper Peru send delegates. The resulting rump congress formally declared independence not only from Spain but also from Fernando VII on 9 July 1816. The new country's name was to be the United Provinces of the Río de la Plata.

San Martín's representatives at the congress of Tucumán supported independence, but what San Martín wanted was an americano monarchy, which he believed would provide more unity and stability than a republic—or, especially, a loose federation of republics—ever could. San Martín admired the British model of constitutional monarchy, a king subject to the laws made by parliament, rather like what the Cádiz constitution called for. That did not make San Martín pro-Spanish. He declared himself americano above all, and he believed in the principle of popular sovereignty. That is, he believed the right to rule flowed not *down* from God but rather *up* from the sovereign people, from a nation. Americanos had the right to choose their own form of government, including their own king.

The repressive Spanish reconquest of Chile made it ripe for a patriot uprising, in San Martín's estimation. He rushed ahead with preparations. Crossing the Andes from Mendoza to Chile could be done only in the Southern Hemisphere summer, when the high mountain passes would be free of snow and ice. So San Martín's Army of the Andes set out on its history-changing mission in the first week of January 1817. To show off his men's uniforms and discipline, and to motivate them for the grueling climb ahead, first he marched them from their camp into the main square of Mendoza, where the troops swore allegiance to their battle flag in a public ceremony, followed by three days of celebrations, including a high-spirited bullfight that featured officers of San Martín's army inside the ring. Then, at staggered intervals, detachments began to march up the eastern slope of the gigantic Andean range following various alternative routes designed to confuse the enemy. By this time, Chilean royalists knew to expect an assault, but San Martín was determined to retain elements of surprise by entering Chile simultaneously through multiple passes. To speed the army's progress, supplies had been cached at points along the climb, which would take several days. The army filed along narrow roads beside sheer drops into nothingness. San Martín dropped the reins of his sure-footed mule, letting it carry him without directions. After all, only one direction was possible at this point: ahead.

Descending the western slope of the Andes into Chile, the two main components of San Martín's army rendezvoused as planned and won a significant victory at Chacabuco on 15 February 1817, costing his enemies six hundred dead. The strategy had worked. The very next day, the vanguard of San Martín's invasion force entered the Chilean capital, Santiago. The partisans of Fernando VII remained strong in the south of Chile, especially in Bernardo O'Higgins's home region of Concepción—a situation that was logical enough, given the traditional presence of the royal army on the Spanish Empire's southern frontier. Nevertheless, the initial victory was cause for rejoicing, and the people of Santiago responded warmly to their liberators. Nothing had more clearly defined their will to be independent than subjugation by the army that Viceroy Abascal had sent from Peru to reconquer them in the name of Fernando VII. At a celebratory dance held in Santiago a few days after the battle of Chacabuco, the men attended wearing French-style "liberty caps" and offered toasts so portentous that each toaster shattered his wineglass after draining it, so that it might never be profaned thereafter. The giddy assembly sang the new national anthem of the United Provinces of the Río de la Plata all the way through, twice.

San Martín sang loudly that night, but overall his leadership faltered in the new setting. Absorbed in details and work, San Martín cared little for the adoration of crowds, and his public relations in Chile—a delicate and crucial matter for his strategic plan—were disastrous. In March, he refused a ten-thousand-peso donation by the city of Santiago to cover his personal expenses, donating the money to create a public library instead. He accepted the archbishop's palace as his residence but refused to use the luxurious silver service that went with it. He also refused a six-thousand-peso annual salary. One might think that these gestures of Spartan selflessness would be warmly received, but San Martín had a way of seeming ungrateful for gifts and unresponsive to his fervent well-wishers. Always a bit clumsy with personal relations, San Martín became reclusive as his tuberculosis troubled him more in Chile. Not only were people with tuberculosis commonly shunned for fear of contagion, but San Martín's preferred painkiller, opium, further addled his social graces.

San Martín's trans-Andean assault on Santiago was only the first stage in his grand strategy. The ultimate goal was Lima. Between Santiago and Lima lay a thousand miles, more or less, of the driest desert on earth. San Martín's plan was to cover the distance by sea and make an amphibious assault. But for that, he would need a navy, and creating one was a tall order indeed for a resource-strapped young republic without seafaring traditions.

Brazil Catches the Republican Contagion

Soon after San Martín's victory, the revolutionary contagion that worried João VI did erupt in Brazil. The contagion did not come from nearby, however. Brazilians caught it much as Chileans or Venezuelans had, from European sources. Recently created political lodges became the chief vector of infection. João's opening of Brazilian ports in 1808 had led to an influx of outside influences in port cities such as Recife, where the outbreak occurred. A recent cotton boom in the Pernambuco captaincy had attracted many European traders to Recife. One leader of Recife's March 1817 revolt was a local merchant who had lived in London and associated with Francisco de Miranda. At lodge meetings, local intellectuals (including clergy, along with military officers, merchants, and plantation owners) discussed the concept of popular sovereignty and other revolutionary ideas. The royal governor heard about these liberal discussion groups and decided to arrest the participants, but his crackdown backfired. In a dramatic incident on 6 March 1817, a liberal army officer resisted arrest and, in front of his troops, killed the royal official trying to take him into custody, then raised the cry of revolution.

The troops followed their rebellious officer, a normal procedure. More surprisingly, however, the ruling class of Recife also endorsed the rebellion without delay. The next day, the intellectuals, clergy, military officers, merchants, and plantation owners who had converted to liberalism declared Pernambuco a republic and formed a provisional government. Even the local church hierarchy formally endorsed the republic. The highest royal judge at the time in Pernambuco happened to be Antonio Carlos, brother of José Bonifácio de Andrada. In an April 1817 letter to his brother, who was still in Portugal, Antonio Carlos described how he had joined the government of the new republic of Pernambuco. Henceforth, Pernambucan citizens were to address each other as "patriot," in a revolutionary spirit. Caste distinctions were supposedly erased, although no move was made to abolish slavery. After all, slave-powered cotton plantations formed the basis of Pernambuco's new prosperity. The contagion spread rapidly. The port cities of two neighboring captaincies soon declared themselves independent republics as well.

Popular support for the new republics proved unreliable, however. The common people appreciated lower taxes on meat and approved of higher pay for soldiers, two concessions of the new republican government. They also approved of the new government's pronounced pro-americano bias. Brazilian cane liquor replaced Portuguese wine on patriotic tables, at least for a while. Portuguese merchants became lightning rods for popular resentment. Here was an issue on which all the native-born, rich and poor, could easily come together in Brazil, just as had occurred elsewhere. América for americanos! Down with the europeos! Eager to maintain the goodwill of Recife's merchant community, the provisional government took measures to protect it from unruly crowds.

Unfortunately for the patriots, their adversary João VI was not helplessly imprisoned, as Fernando had been. He was not even far away across the Atlantic Ocean, and he reacted quickly to this blatant challenge to his kingship. José Bonifácio's head was still spinning from Antonio Carlos's letter when, only a few weeks later, news reached him in Portugal that royal troops had suffocated the Pernambucan rebellion and imprisoned hundreds of its protagonists, including his brother. Antonio Carlos would languish in a Bahian dungeon for four years, during which many prisoners were tried and executed for treason against the king.

The 1817 rebellion seemed to vindicate João's decision to stay in Brazil, guarding it against the contagion of liberal ideas. It also steeled José Bonifácio's determination to return home. Finally, permission to return was granted.

Bolívar's Big Comeback

Simón Bolívar did not use the alias "Comeback Kid," but it fit. On 18 July 1817, when his small army occupied Angostura, a strategically important town on the Orinoco River, Bolívar effectively began to turn the Spanish royalist flank in northern South America, just as San Martín had begun to do in the south earlier that year.

Bolívar had, in fact, made not one but several comebacks since his Jamaican exile. He had been given arms by Haitian president Alexandre Pétion in return for a promise to free slaves in Venezuela. Bolívar had again joined forces with his old ally Santiago Mariño and other eastern leaders of Venezuela's failed Second Republic, who gathered to make common cause with him in Haiti. These leaders had something Bolívar did not—an army, or at least the men to make one—and they had a toehold on the continent at Güiria, near the mouth of the Orinoco River. Assuming command, Bolívar used the arms and the army to attempt an extremely ill-considered amphibious assault on central Venezuela, with predictable results. Once again, as he had done at nearby Puerto Cabello years before, the blushing Liberator evacuated by boat, leaving arms and army to their fate. Bolívar spent several weeks sailing around the Caribbean before returning, finally, to Güiria, where he was no longer welcome. Surely the Liberator's least dignified moment occurred when one of his erstwhile allies chased him down a pier at swordpoint and back onto his boat, which carried him once more to Haiti. Nevertheless, after several months Bolívar got a call to return to Venezuela, where only he, it seemed, could unite the fractious patriots.

Manuel Piar, the eastern leader who called Bolívar back, surely regretted it later. Piar had excellent revolutionary credentials. His mother, Isabel Gómez, a parda midwife, had been involved in the same 1797 "French" conspiracy that sent Bolívar's tutor, Simón Rodríguez, fleeing from Venezuela under the name Samuel Robinson. From his mother, Piar had inherited a tradition of pardo radicalism inspired in the example of the Haitian Revolution. He had served under Miranda in the first republic and under Mariño in the second, and by early 1817 he had made himself the winningest patriot general in Venezuela. Piar's great achievement was to create an army of patriot llaneros. The death of Boves had scattered his unstoppable followers, and Piar recruited some of them for the cause of América. Then Piar began to operate on the eastern Orinoco plains. In April, Piar's army won a major victory—the most important in years—over recently reinforced Spanish forces on the south side of the Orinoco river, bringing rich resources to the cause. Furthermore, Piar's triumph undercut the Spanish bases at Guayana and Angostura, leading eventually to their abandonment.

Bolívar congratulated Piar, then relieved him of his command. Dismayed, Piar withdrew from Bolívar's army and accused Bolívar of discriminating against him as a pardo. The accusation was a sensitive one in the Llanos, where pardos predominated. So Bolívar quickly ordered Piar arrested and, after a summary court-martial in October 1817, had his own most victorious general shot by a firing squad in the Angostura town square—a highly unusual procedure, to say the least. The next day Bolívar harangued his pardo troops, explaining that racial discrimination was a thing of the past and announcing the distribution of bonus pay.

Within weeks of the execution of Manuel Piar, Bolívar's dream of British aid finally came true. Five ships carrying eight hundred British volunteers set sail for Venezuela. Rather than an official British force, these were mercenaries assembled by Bolívar's representative in London from among the thirty thousand British troops being demobilized after the Napoleonic Wars. Bolívar hoped that the Europeans would provide modern training for his ragged llaneros, who fought mostly with lances. Fitted with surplus equipment and colorful uniforms, the British Legion, for their part, hoped to win glory, make money, visit an exotic location, and found a republic or two. One of their five ships sank in the Atlantic with all its occupants, however. And even before the rest disembarked in Angostura, they faced the tropical sun and mosquitoes the size of European sparrows, with no pay in sight. Their illusions began to evaporate and the desertions began. Most of the disappointed mercenaries departed before they ever saw action. Gradually, the remaining members of the British Legion were integrated into other units as officers. Daniel O'Leary, a young Irishman who learned Spanish quickly, became Bolívar's personal secretary.

The arrival of the British Legion did not get Bolívar very far. Piar's idea, to recruit llaneros, had proved the right one. Bolívar now contacted another group of patriot rebels operating several hundred miles west in the Arauca and Apure regions of the upper Orinoco plains, under the command of an imposing llanero named José Antonio Páez. Páez had a rapport with his llanero followers like that between Artigas and his gauchos. Páez was a centaur, a military athlete who carried a gigantic lance, led charges personally at a full gallop, and occasionally went into a Viking-style battle frenzy that culminated with something like an epileptic seizure, leaving him unconscious on the field. Páez was socially white in Venezuela, but, slandered by wagging tongues, his father had needed to defend the family's "purity of blood" in the colonial courts. Whatever Bolívar thought of Páez, he needed him, especially in the absence of Piar, as Páez controlled a large part of the Orinoco plains. Bolívar wrote to arrange a meeting and in January 1818 marched west to meet him. The Caracas aristocrat and the rude llanero studied each other for a few seconds, then embraced with a laugh. The independence of a continent came a little closer.

Policarpa and Gertrudis

In Bogotá, now "pacified" under a new viceroy, acts of official brutality discredited royal rule as elsewhere in América. Among the most famous was the public execution of a woman, Policarpa Salavarrieta, accused of aiding the cause of América. Policarpa was guilty as charged. As a young seamstress boarding with relatives in Bogotá during the first years of the revolution, she had admired Nariño and proudly sent her young suitor, Alejo Sabaraín, with Nariño on his failed campaign to subdue Pasto. Alejo returned to Bogotá as a prisoner of war after Morillo's reconquest of New Granada, and Policarpa joined a patriot resistance group operating around the prison. The prison did not supply the prisoners' food, which Policarpa helped provide in her visits to Alejo—concealing a steady stream of communications. When Alejo was finally released, he and others headed immediately for the Llanos with the intention of joining Bolívar, whose whereabouts were known thanks to the communications network maintained by people such as Policarpa. Unfortunately, one message fell into the hands of royal authorities, who recaptured Alejo and began to search for Policarpa. She could have avoided capture easily by getting out of Bogotá, but she refused to abandon Alejo, who was again imprisoned there. Eventually, the authorities located the house where Policarpa was hiding and detained her. They quickly found her guilty of treason against Fernando

VII, which her own proudly defiant declarations left hardly in doubt. Perhaps because of Policarpa's uppity demeanor, the viceroy took the unusual step of making her execution public. At the peril of her immortal soul, Policarpa refused to accept Catholic last rites from the hand of a europeo priest. She and Alejo faced a firing squad together in the main square of Bogotá only a few weeks after Manuel Piar died at Angostura.

Almost at the same time, Gertrudis Bocanegra, another patriot americana, was executed on similar charges in New Spain. Like Juana Azurduy, Gertrudis had grown up with a special affinity for indigenous people and became involved in the cause of América along with her husband. In fact, she reportedly recruited her husband for the cause after insisting, as a condition of their marriage, that he resign from Spanish royal service. Her son, too, joined the cause because of her influence. When both were killed, Gertrudis participated in the struggle directly, with famous disregard for her life. Like Policarpa Salavarrieta, she aided the patriots through secret supply and communications work, which is how she was captured. Like Policarpa, Gertrudis refused to give any names of her patriot collaborators. Like Policarpa, she used the moments before her execution to make a dramatic display of defiance, tearing off her blindfold and crying to the crowd, "The day of liberty will come!"[1]

Enter Guerrero

Gertrudis died at a moment when New Spain appeared a securely reconquered colony. Following the capture and execution of Morelos, New Spain's independence movement had gradually disintegrated. Centralized command had faltered, then ceased. Highland rebel strongholds in western New Spain had succumbed one by one. The National Junta created by López Rayón finally disappeared, as did the congress created by Morelos. A new viceroy reigned, goods moved, and royal authorities governed all the cities of New Spain. Leona Vicario and Andrés Quintana Roo had withdrawn into the mountainous countryside of the south, staying away from towns for months at a time. Leona gave birth to their first child in a cave. Eventually, royalist forces caught up with them and captured Leona. To rejoin her, Andrés negotiated his own surrender. Other guerrillas held out locally, many turning to banditry to survive, but most patriots of New Spain had already given up.

So Vicente Guerrero's 6 March 1818 capture of the town of Jaujilla was a notable, if temporary, accomplishment. Soon enough, Guerrero was scrambling away down the brush-covered mountainsides with royalists in hot pursuit, but he always persevered, and a string of small victories in September 1818 led to the reconstitution of a symbolic patriot government under the constitution of Apatzingán. Like Manuel Piar, and for that matter like Morelos himself, Guerrero was a light-skinned pardo who could pass for white but chose not to. He had been a muleteer and spoke several Indian languages, as muleteers commonly did in New Spain. Guerrero's followers, in turn, were almost all dark-skinned. They were pardos from the hot lands of the Balsas River valley and the Pacific coast, indigenous people from the remote mountainous south—Morelos country. Morelos had personally named Guerrero commander of the south, so the pardo general represented the direct continuation of the Morelos movement.

Meanwhile, a patriot force made up of whites and light mestizos and led by a Spanish liberal, Javier Mina, organized in New Orleans and then launched a fleeting and unsuccessful debut on the Gulf coast around Tampico, never joining forces with Guerrero. The lack of connection between the two patriot groups symbolizes the historical division within the americano cause in New Spain. The heirs of Morelos continued to rely on talent promoted from below, rather than on aristocratic leaders such as Bolívar or international liberals such as Mina. Guerrero installed the patriots' only Indian general, for example: Pedro Ascencio Alquisiras of the village of Tlahuitlan.

Still, if Guerrero's guerrilla war could smolder indefinitely in the hardscrabble mountainous south and the Balsas River valley, smoldering was all it could do. It needed larger connections, the breezes of broader horizons that the Mina expedition might have provided.

Bolívar Wins at Boyacá Bridge

Meanwhile, in the Llanos, Bolívar had exactly the connections and horizons that Páez didn't. Páez recognized as much and accepted Bolívar's leadership. In early 1819, Bolívar left his cavalry under Páez's command in Apure and returned to the town of Angostura to greet more arriving British volunteers and organize the sort of patriot government that had not existed in Venezuela for years.

The government that Bolívar now envisioned would also include New Granada, whose cause he had served more than once. Calling a constituent assembly to meet at Angostura and draft a constitution, Bolívar invited delegates from both New Granada and Venezuela. Of course, most of New Granada and Venezuela remained under Spanish control, so only twenty-six delegates gathered to hear Bolívar's almost interminable address to them on 15 February 1819, recommending principles for the new republic's constitution. These included a president with quasi-monarchical powers and a hereditary senate along the lines of the British House of Lords. "Unity, unity, unity" was Bolívar's creed. He warned against federalism as practiced in the United States, maintaining that the diverse populations of Venezuela and New Granada, long deprived of the experience of self-rule by Spanish tyranny, needed strong, stable authority. He believed in popular sovereignty and even stressed that people of all colors must be equal before the law, but Bolívar was not enthusiastic about democracy. América was not ready for it, in his view. After concluding his speech, Bolívar turned over his marshal's baton, the emblem of command, to the president of the congress. The next day, however, when the Congress of Angostura designated the first president of the new republic, it turned out to be (to nobody's surprise) Simon Bolívar. Within a few days, President Bolívar was on his way back to Apure to resume command of the army.

Together, Bolívar and Páez dominated the Llanos, trouncing Spanish forces there in March and April 1819, but they were not strong enough, even together, to challenge the forces that the Spanish reconqueror Morillo arrayed against them in the Venezuelan highlands. As the rainy season approached in May, bringing the prospect of many months of forced inactivity and rampant desertion, Bolívar advanced a risky but brilliant plan, one that would parallel and complement San Martín's trans-Andean attack on Chile two years earlier. To see the unexpectedness of Bolívar's plan, one must know three things. First, the Llanos extend beyond Apure, into Casanare, New Granada—though neither Páez nor Bolívar had ever operated there. Second, the rainy season creates pervasive flooding on these plains as rivers flow over their banks and cover the fields with vast sheets of water for weeks and months. Third, Bogotá, the capital of New Granada, where a Spanish viceroy had resumed control during the last three years, stood at the edge of the Llanos, though high above them. So far from the sea, the interior plains of New Granada were the remotest of all its regions. This rear approach to Bogotá was almost unguarded. So, reasoned

Bolívar, an army that appeared there during the rainy season would have the advantage of surprise.

Bolívar floated the idea at a war council in May 1819 and started out almost immediately. Bolívar's secretary O'Leary wrote that, on one occasion, the army walked through waist-high water for a week. It was hard to get any sleep, even harder to keep the army's precious supply of gunpowder dry. Fortunately, an army of llaneros could endure this experience better than almost anyone else. Many of them wore only a loincloth and fiber sandals, anyway. In Casanare, a young man from New Granada, Francisco de Paula Santander, met them and led the way west. On 22 June, they began to climb up and up and up. These were the Andes, after all, and not the tail end of them, as in Venezuela, but the towering, volcano-studded main range, similar to what San Martín's army had traversed on the way to Chile. Unlike San Martín's army, however, Bolívar's was beginning the climb already physically extenuated from traversing the flooded plains. There had been no methodical preparations, no careful caching of supplies along the route. Day after day, the climb steepened and the temperature dropped. The scant clothing and flimsy sandals of the llaneros served them poorly on the rocky mountainside. Horses that had never left the plains slipped on the slick stones and fell; hundreds collapsed along the route and refused to budge. Still, Bolívar's army climbed, the men themselves beginning to fall behind because of exhaustion, countless numbers dying from exposure, others deserting. But then they crossed through the last pass and emerged onto the high Andean plateau.

Immediately, the local people helped them. Bolívar's shivering army had a few days to recover its strength before facing its enemies. Then they fought two battles and won them both. At the second and most decisive of these, Boyacá Bridge, 7 August 1819, the Spanish forces were completely shattered and sixteen hundred taken prisoner. Bolívar rode into Bogotá and dismounted in front of the viceroy's palace only three days later, but the viceroy had already fled in the direction of Cartagena along with all the judges of the royal audiencia, never to return. Just as in Chile, the heavy-handed Spanish reconquest had prepared the way for the patriots' comeback. Morillo's reconquering army had been an army of europeos, not an army of americanos loyal to Fernando. In all, about twenty-seven thousand Spanish troops had been sent to América since Napoleon's defeat, and every blow these troops struck defined their americano adversaries as patriots. Therefore, the people of Bogotá welcomed Bolívar's soldiers as heroes, and spontaneous patriot uprisings all over interior New Granada greeted the news of the viceroy's abrupt departure.

The Portuguese Again Invade the Eastern Shore

José Artigas, meanwhile, had lost the roll of history's dice. It was not Buenos Aires that got him in the end but rather his old nemesis, the Portuguese. Shortly after the defeat of Napoleon, João VI had decided to use the turmoil created by Artigas and the Federal League as an opportunity to stake a claim, once again, to the Eastern Shore province of the Río de la Plata. By doing so, he simultaneously accomplished a longtime Portuguese geopolitical objective and found a way of dealing with post-Napoleonic demobilization in Portugal. Like England and Spain, Portugal had a surplus of men in uniform, and so five thousand Portuguese veterans promptly deployed to Brazil and, from there, marched against Montevideo.

Artigas had continued to gain strength against Buenos Aires, but his loyal bands of indigenous and gaucho lancers could not halt the relentless advance of João's well-equipped, well-supplied army. That army pushed Artigas west out of the Eastern Shore, into the other Federal League provinces of Entre Ríos, Corrientes, and Misiones. Artigas felt at home in this milieu of Guaraní-speaking rural camps, but he knew that the end of his political career had come. On 19 October 1819, at a camp called Mandisoví, Artigas wrote to his son, Juan Manuel, putting him in charge of the family members who remained behind along with their possessions, poor relations, and slaves. It is interesting that a leader who counted freed slaves among his first recruits had never abolished, or even seriously criticized, slavery as an institution.

His land occupied, his forces decimated, his personal energies spent, the erstwhile Protector of Free Peoples went into exile—though not, as so many other independence leaders did, in Europe. Instead, Artigas chose Paraguay, which had maintained its independence since 1811 under the perpetual presidency of Gaspar Rodríguez de Francia. Francia had broken Paraguay out of the orbit of Buenos Aires by isolating Paraguay altogether from the rest of the world. Francia was not particularly eager to allow a popular leader such as Artigas into his country, but he decided that having Artigas under his watchful eye (as everything in Paraguay seemed to be) was better than having him on the loose nearby.

Fernando VII took the same approach to post-Napoleonic demobilization as did his absent neighbor, João VI. To winnow down the army of 150,000 that had saved his throne in Spain, Fernando planned to send 14,000 more soldiers to punish his disobedient subjects in América. Fernando's main approach to americano rebelliousness had always been, first and foremost, military reprisal. Like the veteran soldiers of Morillo's previous army of reconquest, these had an experienced general—none other than the ever-victorious former viceroy of New Spain, Félix María Calleja. Calleja promised his troops that, once in América, they would outdo the glories of legendary Spanish conquistadors such as Cortés and Pizarro. But, as preparations dragged on, the thousands of soldiers waiting to board the transport fleet at Cádiz became discontented with their low pay and shabby treatment. Gradually, the formerly Desired One's vengeful persecution of liberal patriots who had resisted the French led to a revival of the constitutionalist spirit among Spanish army officers.

On New Year's Day 1820, the revival of the constitutionalist spirit became a revolt among Spanish troops assembled for Calleja's expedition. The revolt spread, and on 7 March 1820 Fernando was forced to announce from the balcony of his palace in Madrid that he relinquished absolute power and accepted the reinstatement of the liberal Cádiz constitution. Similar conditions in Portugal—compounded by the humiliation of a large, ongoing British military presence in that country—led to a copycat uprising among military officers there. Portuguese veterans had a different reason for feeling angry at their king: his continued residence in Rio de Janeiro. So, on 25 August 1820, when the garrison of Porto, Portugal's second most important city, declared itself in rebellion, it immediately demanded João's return to Lisbon. It also demanded the meeting of a cortes to write a constitution.

Spain had sneezed, and Portugal had caught cold. What would this mean in América?

San Martín Sails for Peru

In Chile, San Martín was about to find out. The fleet that carried his amphibious invasion force, so many years in planning and preparation, raised anchor on 20 August 1820 and set sail for Peru. Just before it did so, San Martín climbed into a small boat and reviewed his forces in the harbor of Valparaíso, amid the cheering of ships' crews, soldiers already embarked (forty-one hundred of them, with eight hundred horses, thirty-five cannons, and fifteen thousand muskets), and crowds along the waterfront.

The three and a half years since the liberation of Santiago had been arduous ones for San Martín. Royalists still in control of southern Chile had fought hard against the patriot comeback. Receiving reinforcements from Peru, the royalists had advanced north and beaten the patriots in one battle before finally succumbing to San Martín's and O'Higgins's forces in a second one. San Martín repeatedly traveled back and forth across the Andes to Mendoza and Buenos Aires, trying to keep his strategic plan on track, but complications multiplied. In Buenos Aires, Lautaro lodge members sympathetic to San Martín's project still held sway. Buenos Aires had many pressing problems, however, including the Portuguese invasion of the Eastern Shore (which Buenos Aires still claimed) as well as the new expedition of reconquest gathering at Cádiz. Even more pressingly, two Federal League provinces contiguous to Buenos Aires—Santa Fe and Entre Ríos—were growing strong enough to threaten Buenos Aires. San Martín therefore found it understandably difficult to raise money in Buenos Aires for his Pacific invasion fleet. Meanwhile, raising money in Chile, now governed by O'Higgins, proved no easier. A proliferation of taxes and forced loans made both O'Higgins and San Martín unpopular. Still, one by one ships were acquired—captured from the Spanish or bought from Britain or the United States.

Because commanding a warship was a nonexistent skill in Chile, San Martín's navy sought experienced naval officers on the international market. A number of demobilized British naval officers hired on, including a renegade Scottish lord, Thomas Alexander Cochrane, as admiral. Cochrane was arrogant and greedy, but also intrepid and resourceful, and he soon showed his worth. He made several initial forays to Lima during the last months of preparation for the expedition, and while unable to do anything much against its heavily fortified harbor, Cochrane also made a spectacularly successful raid on a Spanish naval installation at Talcahuano, in southern Chile, permanently neutralizing the southern royalists and allowing San Martín's expedition to sail north without fear of attack from the rear.

As news of Spain's constitutionalist revolution made its way across the Atlantic and San Martín prepared to sail, however, the United Provinces of the Río de la Plata began to unravel totally. Combined forces of Santa Fe and Entre Rios, gaucho hordes much like those former commanded by Artigas, shattered the army of Buenos Aires, leading to the dissolution of its revolutionary junta and the Tucumán congress. For the next two generations, the city of Buenos Aires would rule only the province of Buenos Aires. Ironically, the Federal League had triumphed against Buenos Aires just as the Portuguese finished crushing the political life out of Artigas. San Martín, for his part, had repeatedly failed to respond to requests to abandon his strategic plan and lead his Army of the Andes back to rescue Buenos Aires from its many perils. He had written to Artigas and other Federal League commanders pleading with them to reject federalism, and he sent an anti-federalist proclamation to his countrymen before sailing from Valparaíso. But San Martín refused to abandon his assault on Peru, finally under way.

Three weeks after leaving Valparaíso, the fleet landed in southern Peru, and representatives of the viceroy appeared with talking points. As a newly minted constitutional monarch, Fernando VII offered his rebellious subjects the benefits of enlightened liberal legislation. Recent events in Europe tinged the negotiations at the seaside village of Miraflores, today a neighborhood of Lima, with an atmosphere of vacillation and ambivalence. Spanish officials in Peru still included absolutist hard-liners as well as liberal constitutionalists, who now regarded one another with suspicion. The americanos insisted on recognition of their independence from Spain as the precondition of anything else. San Martín signaled the possibility of common ground with the constitutionalists, given his own monarchist leanings. Perhaps Peru could become an independent monarchy ruled by some certifiably blue-blooded European prince. But the talks got nowhere.

So, after several weeks spent provisioning on shore and launching a diversionary expedition into the highlands, San Martín's army rowed out to its small fleet of transports and reembarked. It sailed past Lima and executed a phony landing just north of it, to create panic in the city, then withdrew to a comfortable distance and finally disembarked on 9 November 1820. San Martín knew that his forty-one hundred men might be able to take Lima, but they could never subdue the massive Andean highlands that rise into the clouds immediately behind Lima. Peru could only be won by winning hearts and minds, and the moment seemed propitious for that, given the changes afoot in Spain. Strategy, caution, and preparation—not the hell-bent impetuosity of Bolívar's backdoor assault on Bogotá—were the hallmarks of San Martín. This was going to be a long campaign.

Meanwhile in New Spain, Vicente Guerrero, the pardo general who proudly wore the mantle of Morelos, and Agustín de Iturbide, a leading royalist, had reached an agreement. Now based at Iguala, a hot-country town in the Balsas River basin, Iturbide had been sent by the new viceroy to defeat Guerrero, but Spain's constitutionalist revolution had given Iturbide a different idea. Political turmoil in Spain was once again making life difficult for servants of the crown in New Spain. Fernando, no longer the Desired One, had lost his royal mystique. The arrogance of New Spain's europeos rankled more than ever among its americanos. If liberal constitutionalism prevailed after all, who needed Fernando and his gachupín favorites? New Spain could have its own constitutional monarch. At least, so Iturbide reasoned.

Since 1810, the light-skinned ruling class of New Spain had kept its distance from the brown-skinned cause of América led by Hidalgo, then Morelos, and finally Guerrero. All other things being equal, New Spain's españoles americanos inclined toward América as much as did their counterparts elsewhere. They could live with liberal constitutionalism, too. What distanced New Spain's españoles americanos from the cause of Guerrero was all that brown skin, the specter of Hidalgo's rampaging hordes that had defined the cause of América in New Spain early on. Brown-skinned people were not so scary, though, as long as they had light-skinned people leading them. And that was the opportunity Iturbide saw. Guerrero's fighters were formidable, a force to be reckoned with, but militarily, they had been contained on their home turf in the Sierra Madre del Sur. Morally, on the other hand, they carried the banner of América for all of New Spain. Iturbide, for his part, had what Guerrero's people did not—military and political connections in Mexico City and all over New Spain. Together, they might have a winning combination.

Events in Spain had suggested new possibilities of negotiation to Guerrero as well. When Iturbide contacted him in early 1821, Guerrero responded receptively. Iturbide proposed an independent monarchy for New Spain, following the basic provisions of the Cádiz constitution. Had he thought more about it, Iturbide might have noticed that the Cádiz constitution disfranchised pardos—and that the bulk of the patriot army of the south, including Guerrero himself, was made up of pardos. Perhaps Iturbide believed that Guerrero would be content simply to pass for white, accept honors for himself, and not worry about his followers. Guerrero, however, made enfranchisement of pardos his sticking point. Iturbide complied with Guerrero's demands and, on 24 February 1821, presented his Plan de Iguala—an accord designed to achieve independence by rallying diverse constituencies around three basic points of agreement, called "guarantees."[2] The first guarantee was separation from the Spanish monarchy. The second guarantee was devotion to Catholicism as the official creed. The third guarantee was equality for all the inhabitants of the new country. The third guarantee had something for everyone. White americanos were guaranteed their longtime goal, full parity with europeos. Españoles europeos were guaranteed that an independent government would protect their lives and property. And people of indigenous and African descent were guaranteed citizenship.

When the Plan of Iguala was worded to Guerrero's satisfaction, he put himself under Iturbide's command.

João VI Returns to Portugal

Then something just as momentous happened in Brazil. An uprising of Portuguese army officers in Rio de Janeiro forced João VI to swear allegiance to an as-yet-unwritten Portuguese constitution. Twenty-two-year-old Prince Pedro took a leading role in political events that day for the first time. The liberal contagion appeared to have infected even the heir to the throne.

Ripples from the constitutionalist revolution in Porto had been washing Brazilian beaches for several months. More specifically, news of Porto was brought to Rio de Janeiro by the commander of British forces in Portugal, General Beresford, who had led the 1806 rogue British invasion of the Río de la Plata. Beresford had spent many of the intervening years in Portugal, but the constitutionalist government wanted Beresford's troops out. João had disappointed Beresford by responding with characteristic indecisiveness. Perhaps some reforms might be required. Perhaps he would send Prince Pedro to Portugal in his place, and so on. Meanwhile, the Portuguese constitutionalists appealed directly for support in each port up and down the Brazilian coast. Pará, at the entrance to the Amazon basin, and Salvador, Bahia, Brazil's second most important city, established home rule juntas in precisely the same spirit as had their Spanish-speaking neighbors a decade before. Once again, European events had called higher authority into question. Should the various captaincies of Portuguese América obey João or the constitutionalist revolutionaries, Rio or Lisbon? Eventually, each captaincy formed a provisional junta.

Shortly after news of Bahia's provisional junta arrived in Rio de Janeiro (and two days after the Plan of Iguala was announced in New Spain), troops gathered before dawn in the Rossio, a commons area frequented by Rio's general population. Their officers announced the advent of the Portuguese constitutionalist revolution, demanding that the king swear publicly his intention to accept and obey whatever constitution the newly called Portuguese cortes might write. These demands came from João's own army, and the timid king submitted gently. João swore in writing what the rebels demanded and sent eager Prince Pedro back to the commons carrying his written oath to the people. Pedro, whose father had never involved him in affairs of state before now, was ecstatic. The prince prided himself on his advanced political ideas, and to be young and cosmopolitan in 1820s Brazil was to be a liberal.

Pedro rode right into the gathering of rebellious troops at the Rossio, unafraid. Not only did he feel somewhat affiliated with their cause, but Pedro was also a royal with the common touch, who felt at ease talking about horses with common soldiers. When he climbed the steps of a nearby theater to read his father's written statement to the crowd, however, the rebellious officers refused to accept the document's formal indirectness. They asked that Pedro bring his father to the Rossio personally. They wanted to see and hear their king say, "I swear I will obey the constitution." So Pedro galloped back to the palace and returned to the Rossio with the king in his heavy, ornate carriage. The humiliated monarch, feeling royally jerked around, publicly forswore his absolutist ways to the delight of almost everybody. Joyful people unhitched the horses and pulled the royal carriage (and its helpless occupant) around the streets with glee.

João decreed freedom of the press a few days later and, soon after that, announced elections for Brazilian representatives to the cortes. He also gave news of his departure for Lisbon—in obedience, though he did not say so, to the wishes of Lisbon's constitutionalist government. On 21 April 1821, elected representatives from Rio's various districts were called to formalize the transfer of authority whereby, after João's departure, Pedro would govern in Rio as his father's regent.

The meeting was held in the city's Merchant Exchange, and liberals quickly took control of it, demanding constitutional rule immediately. Until the Cortes of Lisbon wrote a Portuguese constitution, they called for temporary adoption of the Cádiz constitution as a model of liberal legislation. The leaders of the meeting communicated this demand to the palace in the middle of the night. They also issued orders that no ships sail from Rio until further notice. Young radicals led the meeting, but all Rio's key public figures participated. Many were Portuguese and barred João's exit not because they wanted him to stay in Brazil but because of rumors that João and his attendant courtiers planned to abscond with half the gold in the treasury. Under pressure, João agreed to put Pedro's regency under the Spanish constitution, but Pedro, always more liberal in theory than in practice, sent troops to clear the building. Soldiers "restored order" to the Merchant Exchange, wounding and killing several in the process, and the next day João revoked his acceptance of the Spanish constitution.

João finalized his preparations for sailing four days later, sad to say goodbye to Rio, doubtless forever. Even Rio's deafening tropical thunderstorms did not bother him anymore. Carlota Joaquina, on the other hand, almost danced for joy. But she detested the "new" Portugal, as she found out when no one kneeled in the mud to greet her arrival. The liberal contagion had ruined everything, in her opinion. Her husband was more resigned to the new order. On the very eve of boarding the vessel that would take him back to Lisbon, João took his son aside and spoke prescient words: "Pedro, if Brazil goes its separate way, let it be for you. I know that you, unlike some upstart, will always respect me."[3]

Bolívar and Morillo Become Acquainted

After Bolívar's victory at Boyacá Bridge, General Pablo Morillo had watched in dismay as his five-year labor of reconquest and pacification in New Granada rapidly came apart. Within months, major royalist holdouts remained only at Cartagena (where the fleeing viceroy Sámano took refuge, before fleeing even further, to Panama) and around Pasto. In the rest of New Granada, royal control had simply melted away. A decisive shift in public sentiment favored the cause of América. Morillo, the patriot hero of Spain's own independence war against Napoleon, had never liked the role of reconqueror, and now he renounced it. After news of Spain's constitutionalist revolution reached Morillo's headquarters in Caracas, the Spanish commander gladly followed instructions to offer Bolívar an olive branch. In November 1820, Morillo and Bolívar met to parlay in western Venezuela. First their negotiators agreed to a six-month truce, and a few days later, on 27 November, the two generals met to ratify the agreement personally. When they came face-to-face, Morillo and Bolívar dismounted, embraced, and had their soldiers roll a boulder to the spot so that a monument could be erected there in the future. The two men toasted each other's bravery, declared eternal friendship, and slept under the same roof. By ironic coincidence, they were celebrating the end of War to the Death in the very same house where Bolívar had declared it seven years earlier.

The truce did not hold. Before it expired, Bolívar and Páez attacked Morillo's forces to decide matters once and for all. So it was that the llanero lancers of Páez won an utter triumph at the battle of Cara-bobo, fought on 24 June 1821, completely demoralizing the royalists, who managed to save less than a tenth of their army. For all practical purposes, Carabobo decided Venezuela's permanent independence from Spain. José Antonio Páez emerged as a hero, but it was Simón Bolívar for whom the crowds cheered loudest when the victorious patriots made their triumphal entry into Caracas shortly thereafter. No one snickered anymore at the title of Liberator, given him years earlier.

Central America Declares Independence, Too

A crash of falling dominoes resounded metaphorically through América in mid-1821. On 15 September 1821, excited crowds gathered in the main square of Guatemala City, many of them carrying copies of a newspaper called the *Genius of Liberty*. Spain's liberal revolution had freed the press, which published news of Iturbide's Plan of Iguala and, in quick succession, news of a series of his triumphs, as the royalists of New Spain gave up almost without a fight. Iturbide's Army of the Three Guarantees had marched from Iguala to the rich Bajío region, his movement snowballing as local militias switched sides en masse. Guanajuato, Querétaro, and Valladolid put up little resistance. Guada-lajara, Veracruz, and Puebla followed. By August 1821, every major city in central New Spain had accepted the Plan of Iguala. The 15 September issue of the *Genius of Liberty* announced these americano triumphs for Guatemalan readers. Moreover, it announced that Chiapas, a province of the Kingdom of Guatemala bordering on New Spain, had accepted the Plan of Iguala, too. "Long live the Sovereign Guatemalan People! Long live their Liberty and Independence!"

trumpeted the paper in large letters, and the people of Guatemala City filled the streets to affirm their approval.[4]

Then, as had so often happened before, a capital city's cabildo abierto spoke tentatively for an entire nation, endorsing large street demonstrations. There was no opposition. Spain's liberal revolution of 1820 had installed a liberal Spanish governor in Guatemala City, one who willingly accepted the popular desire for independence under the Plan of Iguala. Subsequent voting confirmed that the entire Kingdom of Guatemala (including the provinces of El Salvador, Honduras, Nicaragua, and Costa Rica) wanted to follow Iturbide. The independence of Central America was therefore achieved without bloodshed, and nobody was better pleased than the old leader of the americano caucus at Cádiz, Father Antonio de Larrazábal, now back in Guatemala. Larrazábal was venerated in his homeland, where the population had felt significantly empowered by the Cádiz constitution. So when the liberal star rose again in 1820, Larrazábal became rector of Guatemala's distinguished University of San Carlos. The cabildo hung his picture in their council room. On 15 September 1821, Larrazábal naturally played a leading role in the cabildo abierto's declaration of independence. The Cádiz constitution, which he had helped write, would become the law of the land, according to the Plan of Iguala.

Central America had achieved independence without a single battle.

Iturbide Proposes a Mexican Empire

Before the end of the month, Iturbide's triumphant army marched into what was by far the greatest Spanish administrative capital in América—Mexico City, a city that no insurgent force had threatened since Hidalgo's had done so momentarily a decade earlier. During that decade, whatever province might present problems, from time to time, because of troublesome rebels, successive viceroys had ruled securely from Mexico City. But on 27 September 1821, Iturbide led his Army of the Three Guarantees into Mexico City and beneath a triumphal arch that had been erected across a main street for the occasion. Behind him were finely uniformed militia units who had never fought a battle for the patriot cause, and behind them were a thousand or so brown-skinned men dressed in rags who had fought dozens of battles but never set foot in a city: General Guerrero's men.

Awaiting him was a new viceroy—O'Donojú, a second Spanish viceroy of Irish extraction, like Ambrosio O'Higgins before him—recently arrived from Spain. O'Donojú had decided that Iturbide's armed victory tour could not be halted, so he mounted no opposition. He reported to Fernando VII that an independent Mexican Empire had become inevitable. O'Donojú therefore presented Iturbide with the keys to Mexico City, and together the two men heard mass sung by the archbishop of Mexico.

The Plan of Iguala called for the new imperial Mexican crown to be offered to a European prince willing to occupy a throne in América. To assuage pangs of remorse for their act of disloyalty, the eleventh-hour patriots who created the Mexican Empire offered the crown to Fernando himself. Because Fernando seemed unlikely to leave Spain to come to Mexico, there was a list of backup candidates, beginning with Fernando's brothers. Iturbide established a regency to govern while Fernando made up his mind, and the regency, in turn, put almost total control in the hands of Iturbide. Bolívar wrote his Mexican counterpart a letter of congratulation. Let "Colombia and Mexico appear before all the world hand in hand and, what is more, one at heart," wrote Bolívar to Iturbide, trying out the names of their two newly independent nations.[5]

Pedro Says *Fico*

A few weeks after Mexico moved toward becoming an independent monarchy, Brazil did, too. On 9 January 1822, Prince Pedro announced from the balcony of the royal palace to an excited crowd that he intended to defy instructions lately sent by the Portuguese cortes, demanding that he return to Lisbon as his father had done. The word *fico*, meaning "I'll stay," was what the crowd wanted to hear, and so Pedro's declaration is known to history by that name. But why did the crowd love to hear the prince proclaim his disobedience to the will of a cortes that included their own elected representatives? After all, the Cortes of Lisbon was writing the constitution that, less than a year ago, mutinous Portuguese troops and the people of Rio had together obliged the humiliated João to publicly swear he would obey. What new had been added? An interesting part of the answer is José Bonifácio de Andrada.

José Bonifácio had, at last, returned to Brazil. Or rather, he had returned to his beloved Santos, chief port of his native São Paulo captaincy, where he embraced his aged mother. He also embraced his brother Martim Francisco, with whom he shared many interests, but not his brother Antonio Carlos, who was still imprisoned in Bahia. Immediately, José Bonifácio threw himself into the work he had dreamed about for so many years—fomenting the development of the São Paulo captaincy. Soon after his arrival, he and Martim Francisco began a five-week horseback tour of the province, surveying its agriculture and resources, a trip during which José Bonifácio crystallized his strongest and most controversial recommendation for the progress of Brazil as a whole: the abolition of slavery. Within a few months José Bonifácio had assumed a leading role in the provincial administration of São Paulo. These were exciting times for him to lead São Paulo. Provincial delegates were being elected to attend the Lisbon cortes. His brother Antonio Carlos was released from prison following Portugal's constitutionalist revolution and became one of those delegates. José Bonifácio had an opportunity to put his developmental vision on paper when he wrote the official instructions that São Paulo delegates carried to Lisbon. This wish list of improvements included, in addition to the abolition of slavery, a better distribution of land and the creation of a new capital city in the interior of the country.

But José Bonifácio quickly learned that visionaries such as he could expect little from the new cortes. Like the americano delegates in Cádiz before them, the Brazilian delegates to the Cortes of Lisbon were greatly outnumbered by representatives from tiny Portugal. They got themselves noticed, certainly. The outspoken, sharp-tongued Antonio Carlos, informal leader of the Brazilian delegation, was soon embroiled in conflict. Another delegate, Cipriano Barata, a flamboyant republican from Bahia, wore his revolutionary credentials on his sleeve. A veteran conspirator and occasional political prisoner, Barata walked around Lisbon like an advertisement for Brazil, wearing a characteristically Brazilian wide-brimmed straw hat and clothes of Pernambuco cotton, speaking with an exaggerated Brazilian accent. But the majority of Portuguese delegates remained unamused, unpersuaded, and undeterred from their basic goal, which was to regain primacy over Brazil. The loss of their monopoly on Brazilian trade had been devastating to Portuguese merchants. In addition, though they might be good constitutionalists, most Portuguese delegates to the cortes regarded Brazilians as vulgar colonials. To obliterate forever the idea of the United Kingdom ruled from Rio, the cortes vetoed the idea of a separate Brazilian kingdom. They wanted no throne, and no prince regent, in Rio. Instead, they thought that each Brazilian captaincy should take orders directly from Lisbon.

On the other hand, practically every inhabitant of Rio wanted the city to be a royal court. Thus, during the year 1821, the people of Rio had broken ranks with Portugal's constitutionalist revolution and rallied around Prince Pedro. Pedro proclaimed his intent to stay in Rio shortly after reading a message urging him to make Brazil independent, a message sent to him from São Paulo by José Bonifácio. A week after the fico, the twenty-three-year-old prince named the aging scholar, now sixty, his chief minister. Pedro obviously wanted and needed a wise, fatherly advisor by his side, and José Bonifácio was more than ready to play the part.

The first challenge that the two faced together was the threat of an uprising by the city's Portuguese garrison. Pedro and José Bonifácio mobilized the city's populace in an impressive display of wide support, facing down the Portuguese military commander, who withdrew his troops to the other side of Rio's Guanabara Bay. The Portuguese troops embarked for Portugal a few weeks afterward. Then, for the first time in his life, Pedro traveled into the interior of Brazil, visiting the province of Minas Gerais to widen his political base geographically by displaying his royal personage in the backlands. And because Pedro's royal personage was winsome and athletic, the people of Minas Gerais were generally delighted. So, as the recolonizing intent of the Lisbon cortes became clear in the early months of 1822, Brazilians began to perceive Pedro in a new light. Even for liberals who might, ideally, prefer a republic rather than a monarchy, Prince Pedro now symbolized Brazil's equality with Portugal, its right to remain a separate kingdom rather than simply a collection of overseas Portuguese colonies dependent on Lisbon. When Pedro and José Bonifácio refused to implement any further laws emanating from the Lisbon cortes, the Rio city council ceremoniously offered him— and Pedro happily accepted—the title of "Perpetual Defender of Brazil."

Mexico City Acclaims Agustín I

Fernando VII did not wish to cross the Atlantic, and the Spanish cortes denied the request for one of Fernando's princely siblings to grace the throne of the new Mexican Empire. Who sent soldiers into the streets of Mexico City, after the news arrived, and who sent officers into to the city's crowded theater shouting "Long live Agustín I"? Was it Agustín Iturbide himself? Probably. Yet although the acclamation of Agustín Iturbide as Mexico's emperor was partly staged, it was partly genuine, too. Iturbide's sudden, overwhelming rise made him Fortune's favored son. The crowds that cheered for Agustín I and surged through the streets to his house on that day were real enough. Iturbide accepted the verdict of the vox populi from his balcony. Bonfires and artillery salvos greeted the news. Ardent patriots pulled down statues of various members of Fernando's ousted dynasty. Even Vicente Guerrero accepted the idea, at least officially. So on 21 July 1822, Agustín I was crowned emperor in the cathedral of Mexico City.

Bolívar and San Martín Meet at Guayaquil

Five days later, in what is today Ecuador, the two greatest liberators of América stood face-to-face, Bolívar nervous and wiry, San Martín large and phlegmatic, each having fought for years and traveled thousands of miles across the South American continent to meet, finally, at Guayaquil, formerly an important Spanish naval base and shipbuilding center. The last two years had been kind indeed to the cause of América, as Spanish resistance more or less evaporated over much of the continent. Only the Andean highlands of Peru and Upper Peru remained under the control of Fernando VII by mid-1822. Unfortunately for the americano cause, however, Bolívar and San Martín could not work together, as both immediately recognized.

San Martín did nothing without painstaking preparation, and San Martín–style groundwork for an assault on the Andean highlands, which had now become the last royalist stronghold in América, had proved expensive and time-consuming. In the meantime, San Martín's army had still not fought a meaningful battle in Peru. The methodical general did have something to show, having occupied Lima, the viceregal capital, after all. But he had done so only when the Spanish viceroy La Serna withdrew from Lima into the Andes.

In Lima, San Martín had declared Peruvian independence, with himself as its temporary military protector, keeping the possibility of a monarchy on the table. He had expelled europeos and confiscated their goods. From now on, San Martín declared, Peru's majority Indian inhabitants would no longer pay tribute. Instead, they would be members of the nation, Peruvians like everyone else. San Martín did not abolish slavery, but he did proclaim that the children of enslaved mothers would be born free in independent Peru. On the other hand, his control was limited and his reforms did not extend outside of Lima.

After abandoning Lima, La Serna had established himself at Cuzco, the old Inca capital in the central Andean highlands. The high Andes had beaten back repeated patriot assaults from the Río de la Plata since 1810. Although royalist sympathies remained strong in the highlands, the Spanish had done the cause of Fernando great harm as they callously "pacified" the region. Still, San Martín did not feel ready to scale the highlands, and simply to garrison and govern Lima in San Martín's judicious, detail-oriented way sapped his energy. In the meantime, the people of Lima complained that San Martín's idle army had become restless and ill-behaved. The long-unpaid Admiral Cochrane, more than restless, had become mutinous and sailed away to serve liberty elsewhere, taking the Chilean navy with him. Cochrane was a dazzling fighter, but his commitment to América was strictly business.

San Martín thus arrived in Guayaquil in a position of weakness. His troops were from Chile and the defunct United Provinces of the Río de la Plata, and once in Peru, his army had received few resources and no reinforcements from home. On the other hand, Bolívar arrived at Guayaquil stronger than ever. Pasto had finally surrendered to Bolívar after bloody fighting. Moreover, Bolívar had sent a thousand troops ahead of him to Guayaquil by sea under his new right-hand man, Antonio José de Sucre, a twenty-six-year-old veteran commander from Cumaná. During the past year Sucre had reinforced a spontaneous patriot uprising in Guayaquil, then scaled the Andes and captured Quito with help from a division of San Martín's army. Sucre's victory at the battle of Pichincha, fought on the side of the volcano so named, was the first example of cooperation between Bolívar's and San Martín's forces. It was also the last.

Guayaquil had been contested territory between Colombia and Peru, something San Martín planned to discuss at the meeting with Bolívar. But on 26 July 1822, when San Martín landed at Guayaquil, Bolívar had already occupied Guayaquil and effectively annexed it to Colombia. Playing host as president of Colombia, Bolívar greeted the taciturn liberator of the south and ushered him to a house especially prepared for their confidential negotiations. Although there are conflicting reports of their conversation, no doubt exists concerning the basic outlines. San Martín did not even raise the issue of Guayaquil. Instead, he asked for Bolívar's help in assaulting the highlands of Peru and Upper Peru. Bolívar readily offered troops, but not nearly the number that San Martín needed. Desperate to see his great project completed, San Martín offered to put himself under Bolívar's command, but Bolívar declined. Finally, San Martín expressed his desire to see Peru become an independent monarchy like Mexico. On that point Bolívar, a sincere republican, was adamant, refusing even to discuss a monarchical Peru. After their talks, Bolívar invited San Martín to celebrate at a dance in his honor. But San Martín sat glumly all evening, left early, and went directly to his ship, setting sail for Lima at dawn. The late-rising celebrants of the night before awoke to find him gone. In Lima, he resigned as protector and embarked again, via Santiago, for Europe, his active participation in the cause of América definitively ended.

Bolívar, meanwhile, had met the greatest love of a life rich in loves—Manuela Sáenz. Now twenty-five years old, Manuela had laid eyes on Bolívar during his triumphal entrance into Quito in 1822. They met and danced together during the patriotic festivities, and soon fell secretly into each other's arms. By that time, Manuela's family had married her to a British merchant, James Thorne, and she now lived in Lima, having recently returned to Quito with her father on a visit. Manuela's love affair with Bolívar lasted for the rest of her life, which was considerably longer than his. Manuela Sáenz had been a patriot sympathizer since adolescence. As a teenager, she had escaped from a convent school to run away with a dashing officer, marking her as a rebel. Manuela had lived in Lima during San Martín's protectorate over the city and been decorated by him for her patriotism. Like Sucre, with whom she got along well, Manuela Sáenz had come of age in the cause of América.

Manuela wanted all she could get of Simón Bolívar, and, at least for a while, she could get most of him. After San Martín's departure from Guayaquil, Manuela met Bolívar there and the two spent an idyllic few days frolicking at a country estate before Bolívar had to swing into action again. Pasto, royalist to the death, absolutely refused to toe a patriot line. Not once but twice more within a year, the indomitably loyal Pastuzos raised the tattered banner of Fernando VII and had to be put to the sword to stop them from waving it.

Pedro I was acclaimed emperor of an independent Brazil on his twenty-fourth birthday, 12 October 1822. Rather than being pseudo-spontaneous, like the acclamation of Agustín I, Pedro's acclamation was totally staged, a bit of political theater. In two ways, though, it was entirely authentic: Pedro had undeniably royal blood, and he certainly was Brazil's consensus candidate.

By this time, Pedro and José Bonifácio had clearly opted for independence from Portugal. For Pedro, clarity came on 7 September 1822, when he learned that the Portuguese cortes had demoted him from the status of regent and invalidated his authority. News of his demotion reached him by emergency dispatch rider near the Ipiranga River while Pedro was on his second trip to the interior of Brazil, this time to São Paulo. Defiantly, Pedro ground the order of the cortes under his boot heel and shouted what was to become known as the Cry of Ipiranga, "Independence or death." Back in Rio, liberals on the city council, not theoretically friendly to the idea of monarchy, nevertheless saw an opportunity to advance their own agenda. As long as Pedro's power came from the sovereign people, embodied in a constitution written by their elected national assembly, they would accept a monarchy. The Rio city council had already prevailed on Pedro to call elections for a national assembly. Two days after the Cry of Ipiranga, a joint meeting of Rio's three political lodges agreed that Pedro should be acclaimed a specifically *constitutional* emperor.

Prince Pedro had no objection to being acclaimed constitutional emperor, but José Bonifácio wanted no mention of the constitution in the acclamation, and he got his way. A national assembly elected in each of Brazil's far-flung provinces would be difficult to control, and José Bonifácio de Andrada liked being in control—a family trait, as anyone around Antonio Carlos and Martim Francisco found out as well. All three Andrada brothers had a tendency to make enemies, and that would be their downfall.

Overall, support for Pedro was strongest in Rio de Janeiro and nearby Minas Gerais and São Paulo. More distant captaincies (all of them currently ruled by provisional juntas) demonstrated less sympathy for a Rio-centric imperial project. Local leaders in northeastern Brazil, especially, approved of Pedro's call for an elected national assembly. Still, the challenge of provincial autonomy had scarcely been addressed by the time of Pedro's coronation on 1 December 1822 as monarch of the independent Brazilian Empire.

Mexico Becomes a Republic

Ironically, the very next day was the beginning of the end for the independent Mexican Empire. Conflicts with the national assembly had bedeviled Agustín I even before his coronation. Perhaps the most vexatious problems came from the dissenting intellectual Father Servando Teresa de Mier, whom we last saw in Cádiz. After leaving Cádiz, Mier had spent years in European and U.S. exile, then joined the Mina expedition to Mexico in 1817, which failed, landing him in a Veracruz prison. Mier emerged when the Spanish accepted Mexican independence, and he then led the republican opposition in Mexico's new national assembly until, accused of plotting to overthrow the emperor, he returned to prison. Mier continued to publish from his cell, and Agustín I had little patience with him or with the assembly's lack of cooperation. The irate emperor eventually closed the national assembly. One month after that, on 2 December 1822, a revolution to overturn the empire began in Veracruz.

The leader of that revolution was Antonio López de Santa Anna, of later fame in the separation of Texas from Mexico. Santa Anna, like Iturbide, had joined the cause of América, after years of fighting against it, at the last minute. Santa Anna had secured Veracruz for the Plan de Iguala and received high honors from Agustín I. But when Santa Anna sought to marry Agustín's sister, the ambitious young man was spurned, and so he became a republican. Santa Anna's rebellion quickly attracted adherents among men such as Vicente Guerrero and Guadalupe Victoria, who had never really liked the idea of a Mexican Empire. Political lodges in Mexico City now played a leading role that they had played earlier in Buenos Aires, Rio, and elsewhere. Their chief contribution in Mexico was to promote federalism—the political doctrine so criticized by Bolívar, San Martín, and José Bonifácio. Those who aspired to shape new nations from the top naturally opposed federalist limits to centralized control. But many provincial leaders, eager to escape centralized control, preferred federalism. Therefore, Mexico's federalist Plan of Casa Mata, formulated by the rebels, quickly developed strong support around the country, forcing the improvised emperor to step down. Furthermore, the rebellion against Agustín I changed not only the ruler but also the form of government, creating a federal Mexican Republic. Agustín Iturbide sailed away to European exile in May 1823.

The Pendulum Swings Toward Absolutism in Europe

In May 1823, just as the crisis in Mexico wound down, one began in Spain, where a French army was occupying the country again, without resistance. The invaders this time acted in accord with Metternich's reactionary league of European monarchs, the Holy Alliance. Their mission was to save Fernando VII from his liberal tormenters and restore his traditional privileges and prerogatives. Fernando, pleased to accept the favor, canceled the constitution again and reassumed absolute power.

Spain had sneezed once more, and Portugal once more caught cold. As the rapid French occupation of Spain became a fact, conservative officers in the Portuguese army stationed outside Lisbon announced their own coup d'état restoring absolute power to João VI. João had no particular use for absolute power, though, since he lacked the desire to take any drastic measures. João allowed nothing like the retribution unleashed in Spain by the ever vindictive Fernando, who had tens of thousands of liberals imprisoned or exiled. Carlota Joaquina's mood was more like her brother's than her husband's.

One thing was for certain: the rapid and violent political oscillations of Spain and Portugal impeded their recovery of former colonies slipping away in América.

Brazilians Fight a Miniature War of Independence

The year 1823 saw the entire Brazilian war of independence, a miniature of what had wracked Spanish America. By early 1823, most Brazilian captaincies, now "provinces," had followed Rio's example and acclaimed Pedro emperor. Resistance came from the remote north— Ceará, Piauí, Maranhão, and Pará—as well as, most importantly, from Salvador, Bahia. In Salvador, a strong garrison of regular Portuguese troops had been under siege for months. On the land side of Bahia, the besiegers were local Brazilian militias. On the sea side, the indomitable Scottish seadog Admiral Cochrane, recently of the Chilean navy, blockaded the city with a small Brazilian fleet cobbled together by José

Bonifácio. On 2 July 1823, however, the Portuguese garrison gave up the siege, boarded their ships, and sailed away, allowing the multicolored militias of Bahia into the city to celebrate a patriotic triumph still annually commemorated in Salvador on that day. The small Brazilian navy did some damage to the retreating Portuguese convoy, then sailed up the coast to the last two holdout provinces, Maranhão and Pará, which Cochrane bluffed into surrender by pretending to have a complete battle fleet just over the horizon. By that time, Portuguese forces in Ceará and Piauí had been defeated by local patriots. The last Portuguese troops in América, those still occupying Montevideo, were evacuated in November.

Ironically, the successful conclusion of this miniature war for independence toppled José Bonifácio, who had done so much to engineer the victory. The political battle lines had formed at the time of Pedro's acclamation. Soon thereafter, José Bonifácio arrested and exiled many of those who had insisted Pedro swear an oath to the constitution. The overbearing chief minister thus angered many during his stormy tenure. Pedro himself now wanted less of José Bonifácio's advice, too. When news of the capture of Bahia reached Rio, Pedro fired both José Bonifácio and Martim Francisco, who was minister of finance.

Meanwhile, the third Andrada brother, Antonio Carlos, had returned from the Lisbon cortes to participate with his siblings in the first Brazilian national assembly. This was no ordinary national assembly but a *constituent* assembly, empowered to write a constitution for the new Brazilian Empire. Soon the Andrada brothers were leading a faction known for Portuguese-bashing. The earlier power struggle between Pedro and the cortes had loosely followed the lines of birthplace, Brazil versus Portugal, but there had been little scapegoating of europeos so far, nothing like what patriots had done elsewhere in América. Pedro himself had been born in Portugal, after all. Men of Portuguese birth, now Brazilian citizens, predominated in many sectors of the infant empire's commerce, civil administration, and ecclesiastical hierarchy. Portuguese-bashing, which pried these men out of their favored positions, now became a popular political tactic throughout urban Brazil. News of the recent absolutist military coup in Portugal added ardor and urgency to the Andradas' nativism. Then a small incident brought events to a head, when Portuguese officers of Rio's military garrison beat a Rio man for offending their honor. The Andradas' faction in the assembly made the affair a political issue. Brazilian honor, too, was now at stake. Incensed at the assembly's behavior and particularly furious with José Bonifácio, Pedro sent troops to close the constituent assembly and arrest the Andrada brothers.

Bolívar Almost Falters

In Peru, Bolívar was beginning to feel the toll of a decade of continuous campaigning. On New Year's Day 1824, he was aboard ship and had to be carried ashore at a place called Pativilca because of a first attack, apparently, of the tuberculosis that would eventually kill him. Tuberculosis was common in the nineteenth century, yet it is still striking that both Bolívar and San Martín suffered from it. A visitor who saw the emaciated Bolívar slumped on a bench at Pativilca believed that the Liberator could not long survive. With trepidation, he inquired what Bolívar intended to do now. Bolívar looked up at him incredulously with sunken eyes. "Triumph" was his firm answer.[6]

It seemed an impossible task. Three years after San Martín first entered Lima, and more than a year after he gave up in despair, Peru was as much a quagmire as ever. Fernando VII's forces—now numbering something like twelve thousand, under experienced command—continued to hold the highlands, and they seemed able to reenter Lima at will. Lima's patriot movement, on the other hand, was extremely divided, its leadership hesitant and its military forces heterogeneous, having been brought by Bolívar and San Martín from opposite ends of América. San Martín's troops—sans San Martín, and also without supplies, funding, or reinforcements—were on the verge of mutiny. After a few months in Lima, Bolívar had withdrawn to Trujillo, in northern Peru, where he could pull his army together and, by ascending the Andes there, accustom it to the lofty altitudes at which it would have to fight. He was still supposedly president of Colombia but was getting scant cooperation from his vice president in Bogotá. Vice president Francisco de Paula Santander, who had helped guide Bolívar's army from the Orinoco plains into the mountainous rear approach to Bogotá in 1819, had become the Liberator's chief rival. Sucre and Manuela, on the other hand, were both still at his side, and recent events in Spain had helped matters a bit, too, by renewing tension between absolutists and constitutionalists within the Spanish ranks. By June 1824, Bolívar's health was improving and his army was finally ready to begin its march south through the Andes toward Cuzco, where the last viceroy in América awaited.

On the other side of the continent, the independent Brazilian empire began to crumble in 1824, or so it seemed. The political earthquake was again in the northeastern provinces, and the epicenter was, again, Pernambuco. The local leaders of Pernambuco had refused to accept the provincial governor designated by Pedro, whom they accused of illegally closing the national assembly. On 2 July 1824, the anniversary of Bahia's liberation from Portuguese forces, they announced the creation of a new nation, a republic, to be called the Confederation of the Equator. The name fit because the provinces likely to join the new republican confederation lay in the equatorial zone along Brazil's northern coast, a region only loosely linked to Rio.

Here, obviously, was the same centrifugal force that encouraged federalism in Argentina and Mexico. But it was also a principled resistance to the emperor's high-handedness. The voice of Pernambuco's political conscience was a radical priest whose given name, Joaquim do Amor Divino, contrasted amusingly with his nickname, Caneca, "bottle." (Bottles were used to dispense tannic acid at his father's tannery.) Friar Caneca was a scholar who led a quiet life amid his books until the political excitement of Brazilian independence lured him into journalism. His writings abounded with references to classical history and citations in Latin, more suitable for impressing cloistered students than inspiring a crowd in the street. Still, Friar Caneca's new periodical hammered at a central point. Pedro had written a constitution himself, with the help of few advisors, and imposed it on Brazil. Only a national assembly that embodied the sovereignty of the Brazilian people could create a valid constitution for the new empire, argued Friar Caneca. If Pedro ruled without a constitution written by elected representatives, his rule was arbitrary, absolutist, and illegal.

Unfortunately for Friar Caneca and his lofty principles, Pedro now had considerable armed force at his disposal, and he was in no mood for theoretical discourse. The Confederation of the Equator turned out to be a larger replay of Recife's 1817 rebellion, spreading a little further, lasting a few weeks longer, and collapsing with a louder crash. The treacherous Friar Caneca, sentenced to die for his treasonous writings, had to be executed by firing squad because Recife's royal executioner refused to hang a man he considered saintly and innocent. Another martyred hero of the confederation was an international liberal revolutionary named João Guilherme Ratcliff, who had offered his services as commander of the Confederation of the Equator's one-ship navy. Captured and imprisoned, Ratcliff made an impassioned speech before his execution. Apparently his liberal activities had deeply offended Pedro's mother, Carlota Joaquina, at some earlier juncture, and so, as a conciliatory gesture within the royal family, Ratcliff's pickled head was sent to Lisbon for her viewing pleasure.

By the end of 1824, with Pernambuco pacified and Pedro's constitution in place, the Brazilian empire had weathered its greatest test so far.

Spain Surrenders at the Battle of Ayacucho

Also by the end of the year, Bolívar's army had entered the Andean stronghold of the last Spanish viceroy and, on 9 December 1824, won the final victory for the cause of América.

Actually, there were two battles. The first one, Junín, occurred in early August 1824, when Bolivar's forces had had more than a month to get used to the altitude and Bolívar's horsemen were able to operate as lancers. Swords and lances were the primary weapons used in the fighting. The results were inconclusive and the casualties light. Ayacucho, the more decisive battle, occurred months later, after weeks of intensive maneuvering at over ten thousand feet above sea level. Sucre commanded the patriot forces at Ayacucho because Bolívar and Manuela had returned to Lima. Across the field was the viceroy La Serna, with the entire royalist army of Peru. As the two armies faced one another before the battle, various Peruvian soldiers stepped out of the ranks on each side to shout farewells to relatives on the other side.

The battle of Ayacucho itself was anticlimactic. It ended quickly and definitively when the patriots captured La Serna himself. The viceroy's surrender at Ayacucho constituted a total capitulation of remaining Spanish claims in América. Riders galloped in every direction carrying the news. After fifteen years of hard fighting, the struggle for independence was really over.

Why had the tide of Spanish reconquest ebbed so dramatically? Battlefield triumphs tell only part of the story. The victories won at Boyacá Bridge, Carabobo, Chacabuco, Pichincha, and Ayacucho were significant, but battles of a few thousand soldiers on each side defined control of vast territories only indirectly. Ultimately, the reaction to such victories in a hundred surrounding cities and towns made all the difference. And throughout América, beginning in 1820 with the constitutionalist revolutions in Spain and Portugal, the reaction was more and more unanimous. After Ayacucho, a few renegade Spanish commanders held out in Upper Peru for a few weeks, but no groundswell of support gathered around them. When the last Spanish soldiers withdrew from América, resistance to the americano cause ended absolutely. The most unbending royalists throughout the continent accepted Ayacucho as the verdict of history. No royalist guerrillas fought on for years; no stubborn partisans lurked, ready to reemerge at a moment of crisis. In coming decades, only the most reactionary fringe elements would propose a return to colonial status. Everyone else considered the matter settled. América was independent.

Six

NATION BUILDING BEGINS

1825–1840

A LONG-TERM SHIFT in public sentiment underlay the military victories of the 1820s. The independence of América was clinched, but not really decided, at Ayacucho. Rather, it had been decided gradually in people's hearts during the entire period of debate, fighting, and "pacification" since 1808.

The decision began to take shape in the highly unanimous assertions of an identity unique to América during the initial debate about how to respond to Napoleon. But then civil wars wreaked havoc in the region, eclipsing that unanimity in remembrance of old neighborhood grudges, pitting cities, provinces, and occasionally social classes against one another. While they confused and temporarily thwarted the emerging cause of América, the not-so-civil wars ultimately intensified and broadened the crucial opposition between americanos and europeos. That simple binary distinction became the persistent public explanation for fighting whose causes were really more complicated. Whatever their complicated personal motives, there was no denying that Hidalgo and Morelos had died for América. And in the grim tallies of retribution—no matter which side did the tabulation—mestizos, pardos, and Indians all counted as americanos. The revolutionaries strategically proclaimed this new meaning, but it was bloodshed, not proclamations, that drove the semantic change.

Thus did the cause of América become more poignant in defeat, even as the cause of Fernando VII lost attractiveness in victory. Spanish reconquerors, an invasion of europeos arriving from post-Napoleonic Spain, proved time and time again to be the worst enemies of reconciliation, alienating the people they were sent to pacify. And the return of Fernando himself had been a major disappointment. Petty and vengeful, the former Desired One had seized absolute power and used it to persecute the liberal patriots who had fought the French in his name. Cornered by a mutiny in his own army, Fernando had accepted a constitution only to renounce it later when rescued by nothing less than another French invasion. Such disarray in Spain coincided exactly with San Martín's and Bolívar's great transcontinental campaigns of 1817–24.

The winning armies of these two greatest patriot generals were relatively small, many of their soldiers seasoned veterans. These were nothing like earlier mass uprisings from below. While men of color filled the patriot ranks, their officers tended to be white, reproducing the social hierarchy and winning support from liberal (or conservative) españoles americanos. These liberators displayed little cultural radicalism to alienate conservatives, rich or poor. Even republicanism did not seem as outlandish to the average person as it had fifteen years earlier. The English-speaking republic of North America, so admired by Miranda and others, had won its second war of independence (the War of 1812) against Britain, no less, and entered a phase of rapid growth. Meanwhile, Fernando VII's formerly awesome mystique evaporated, and the Spanish reconquest reminded everyone why they had never liked gachupines in the first place. Fernando lost América, so to speak, more than anyone won it.

So it was that after a decade of ruthless, unfaltering royal control in New Spain, Iturbide's Army of the Three Guarantees marched into Mexico City in 1821 without having to fight a single significant battle. So it was that the Kingdom of Guatemala declared independence without even forming a patriot army. The Brazilian case, finally, offers a third example of independence asserted off the battlefield, through a consensual assertion of the rights of popular sovereignty.

By 1825, popular sovereignty, founded in a vague idea of nation, undergirded all the new American governments. But in the wake of independence, regional and local identities mattered more than national ones. Regional and local identities tended to encode cultural variations and contrasting lifestyles. Economic activities, and thus economic interests, were organized more locally and regionally than nationally. The same old centrifugal tendencies that had splintered the former viceroyalties of New Granada and the Río de la Plata, denying primacy to the juntas of Bogotá and Buenos Aires, expressed themselves powerfully in the newly independent nations. Their vehicle was the federal republic, the idea that would-be state makers such as San Martín and Bolívar so abhorred. The struggle between centralists and federalists wracked virtually all the new nations. Effective republican institutions took decades to emerge. In the meantime, things began to fall apart very fast.

Alexander von Humboldt, fifty-six years old in 1825, celebrated the proliferation of American republics. He had retained his faith in the basic principles of the French Revolution but gave them a bit of flexibility in practice. While Napoleon was invading all of Europe, including Humboldt's native Prussia, the famous scientist had made his residence in Paris, Napoleon's glittering capital. Unquestionably, for one of Europe's most famous intellectuals no place in Europe could be more stimulating than Paris. There Humboldt began to publish the original thirty-volume French edition of his *Personal Narrative*, which was ponderous and rambling but full of new information and romantic descriptions of nature that greatly appealed to readers of the mid-1800s. By 1825, however, Humboldt wanted to get out of Paris, and if possible out of Europe. He had a special interest in exploring Central Asia, where Tibet, particularly, beckoned. Exploration of the Himalayas would be a fitting follow-up to his exploration of the Andes.

Humboldt's former companion Aimé de Bonpland had returned to América some years previously, an alternative plan that Humboldt also considered. Humboldt was quite receptive when a group of French investors began to mention the possibility of retaining his services as a paid consultant for operations that they intended to undertake in newly independent Mexico. What better guide than he, after all, to the potential wealth of Mexican silver mines? Humboldt's hopes were dashed, however, when he received a letter from a minister of the Mexican government, an intelligent young man named Lucas Alamán whose family's wealth came from the mines of Guanajuato. Humboldt had met Alamán in Paris while Alamán was in Europe finishing his education. Alas, Alamán's letter said not a word about Humboldt's potential consulting position. That was quite possibly because Alamán in fact endorsed a competing group of investors, British rather than French, which he also did not mention in the letter. At that point, Humboldt turned his mind away from Mexico.

It was better for Humboldt, in fact, that he not follow Bonpland's example. Bonpland had set out to explore the southern regions of América that he and Humboldt had not visited during their earlier expedition. Unfortunately, Bonpland strayed too close to Doctor Francia's Paraguay and ended up a prisoner there, along with José Artigas. Francia, who continued to rule Paraguay as perpetual president, kept Bonpland under house arrest for the entire decade of the 1820s. Humboldt's plan was to go to Mexico, not Paraguay. And he intended not to collect scientific specimens but instead to help European capital profitably invest in the Mexican economy. Had he gone, surely he would have worked with Lucas Alamán. Although a conservative with monarchist tendencies, Alamán had ambitious visions of economic development and public education for Mexico, along with the kind of competence that Humboldt respected.

Alamán exemplifies the spirit of Mexican conservatives in the new republic. Conservatives basically endorsed the political and social values of the colonial "good old days," but under their own benevolent control. Alamán was the son of a successful europeo businessman in Guanajuato. Alamán's mother had actually socialized with Miguel Hidalgo, and Hidalgo sent a soldier to protect the Alamán house during the pillage of Guanajuato in 1810. Even so, some of Hidalgo's followers threatened to kill the young man, taking him for a gachupín, until family servants convinced his assailants that Alamán was an americano. Alamán had been elected to the Spanish cortes called in 1820, so he was in Spain when the Plan of Iguala ended Spanish rule in Mexico. On his return, Alamán's education and ability got him a job as a minister in Mexico's post-Iturbide government—first under a transition team that included Vicente Guerrero and then under the first elected president, another of Morelos's former lieutenants, Guadalupe Victoria. These veteran leaders of the dark-skinned patriot armies of the south suited Alamán not at all. They tended to represent the views of Mexico's nonwhite majority and also tended to exploit the continuing popular anger against europeos resident in Mexico. The pro-Spanish Alamán, who came from Iturbide's eleventh-hour wing of the independence movement that broke with Fernando VII only in 1821, resigned in disgust from Victoria's government.

Humboldt moved to Berlin instead of Mexico City. Gradually he assumed some official responsibilities in Prussia, and he began to concentrate on a Central Asia trip, which he eventually did make, overland through Russia. At the age of sixty, Humboldt could still walk ten miles a day. Some of his most influential work still lay ahead of him. But he would never again visit América.

Bolívar Writes a Constitution

Simón Bolívar reached the high point of his life in 1826. After Ayacucho, his trusted protégé Sucre had defeated all Spanish resistance in Upper Peru and, with a nod from Bolívar, declared Upper Peru independent from Lima and Buenos Aires as well as from Madrid. Henceforth, Upper Peru would be the Republic of Bolívar, later shortened to Bolivia. Bolívar was eager to make the long climb from Lima through the highlands to Cuzco, La Paz, and Potosí, which, with its great mountain of silver, stood as a symbol of Spain's extraction of wealth from América and its mistreatment of the Indian miners, newly minted as americanos. Enthusiastic crowds gathered to cheer Bolívar's entrance into each town along the way. Bolívar traveled in the company of his old tutor, Simón Rodríguez, with whom he had made his walking tour of Europe years before. Climbing Potosi's mountain of silver to plant the flags of four newly independent nations, the Liberator was thrilled to be with the man in whose presence, during their visit to Rome twenty years before, the young Bolívar had sworn on his knees to liberate América. Bolívar's party then descended from Potosí to nearby Chuquisaca, where Sucre would govern as Bolivia's first president.

Now in his mid-fifties, Rodríguez had spent the last twenty-six years wandering around Europe. He was brilliant but quirky and exasperating even to his most devoted friends. Simón Bolívar, it has been said, was the only important man who ever took him seriously. Nothing could be more to Simón Bolívar's credit. His old tutor hated hierarchy and believed in the potential of América's common people, the pardos and Africans, the mestizos and Indians—as long as they passed through one of his schools. The Rodríguez method of primary education, which he developed as a young schoolmaster in Caracas during the 1790s, was to educate all children, rich and poor, boys and girls, in the same classroom, where, he believed, even the wealthy should learn trades. Rodríguez argued that América had undergone a political revolution but needed another, socioeconomic revolution. He argued that as long as Indians, blacks, and mixed castes remained an uneducated and exploited lower class, the newly created republics would never function as intended. Bolívar made his old teacher, whom he insisted jocularly on calling Robinson, Bolivia's first minister of education.

Bolívar now poured his personal inspiration into a constitution for newly invented Bolivia, and the result was an unmitigated disaster. Bolívar did not exactly institute a constitutional monarchy, but he might as well have done so, to judge by his charter's authoritarianism. Bolívar's constitution was an original creation, inspired by his voracious but erratic reading. It featured a lifetime presidency, with each president to name his successor, and a lifetime, *hereditary* vice presidency. Totally indirect elections offered little role to the common people. Bolívar believed that his constitution responded to the need for stability, above all, and he considered it a masterwork. He wanted to see it adopted in Peru, where that did happen, briefly, and in Colombia, where it didn't.

At the same time, Bolívar outlined a geopolitical vision that, more than any other aspect of his legacy, has inspired later generations of americanos. Essentially, Bolívar thought big, keeping all of América—not just Venezuela or Colombia, Peru or Bolivia—in his frame of reference. And his first thought was the need for a defensive alliance. Even before Ayacucho, he had written to the heads of several already independent American states convoking a diplomatic meeting in Panama. The choice of Panama was not accidental. Both Miranda and Bolívar had assigned it a special place in their visions of an independent América. As a diplomatic gesture, Bolívar also invited the United States to the Panama meeting, though, like Lucas Alamán, he believed that the main threats to the sovereignty of América would come, in fact, from the United States.

In addition, Bolívar imagined an Andean Federation that would have as its backbone the countries liberated by his own armies. At his most speculative he spoke of uniting everything from Mexico to Chile and Argentina. The temptation to start such a project must have been great. In addition to being president of Colombia (which included Venezuela and Ecuador at this point), Bolívar had been named dictator of Peru by the country's new national assembly, and his ever-loyal Sucre was now president of Bolivia. When Bolívar returned to Lima in early 1826, there was talk of offering him a crown, but he refused it without a moment's hesitation. Bolívar's dream of an Andean Federation was a republican dream—or at least not a monarchical one. No student of Simón Rodríguez could be a monarchist and escape a thrashing at the hands of the old schoolmaster. Bolívar had been among the first patriot leaders to cast off the mask of Fernando. He had waved the banner of republicanism all his adult life, and he was not about to betray it now.

The euphoric moment passed quickly, however. By mid-1826 problems demanded Bolívar's personal attention in Colombia. A rift between Santander and Páez threatened to break that country apart. Bolívar set out for Bogotá in September, leaving his army in Lima. But Bolívar's army of soldiers from all over the continent was beginning to wear out its welcome in postwar Peru. The army would follow him home soon enough. Nor would Sucre last long as president of Bolivia. Bolívar's vision of an Andean Federation receded further with every step of his two-month journey north.

Fragmentation Continues in the South

Political unity receded in the far south, too. In 1826, the old Río de la Plata viceroyalty lay divided into half a dozen nations or would-be nations. The former United Provinces had lost all semblance of unity when the federalists had marched into Buenos Aires, reducing it to one independent state among many in a loose federation. Meanwhile, Pedro I had formally annexed the Eastern Shore into the Brazilian Empire, while Bolivia and Paraguay, both subject to rule by Buenos Aires in colonial days, had gone their separate ways forever.

José Artigas (whom many regarded as the chief architect of this disunity) seemed destined to spend the rest of his life under house arrest in Paraguay. Doctor Francia offered Artigas a small stipend, allowing him to farm, raise some livestock, and live unmolested in a hut that he built for himself in the Paraguayan countryside. The former Protector of Free Peoples showed no eagerness to escape and return to the Eastern Shore even after a patriot uprising against Brazilian domination began there. In tranquil Paraguay, Artigas received periodic news of dramatic events in his homeland, but he had been cured permanently of the desire to be in the thick of them.

The 1825–28 uprising on the Eastern Shore responded, in part, to news of the definitive Spanish defeat at Ayacucho. The fighting gauchos of Artigas were back, without Artigas, but led by several of his old lieutenants. A last bit of América not yet liberated! Even the chronically fragmented United Provinces of the Río de la Plata managed to put together an army to help. Britain began to intervene diplomatically because of its strong interest in both Brazil and the Río de la Plata region. Negotiations dragged on for two years. Meanwhile, Pedro I traveled to the southern edge of Brazil to command Brazilian forces personally. Against him, the United Provinces fielded none other than San Martín's former friend Carlos de Alvear and, more to the point, a stronger army.

Foreign wars can inspire unity, of course, and efforts to unify the United Provinces made some headway during the conflict with Brazil. Interestingly, the main promoter of these efforts was Bernardino Rivadavia, the earnest republican secretary of the early Buenos Aires junta and associate of Mariquita Sánchez, recently returned from exile.

In 1826, Rivadavia became the first president of a new attempt to integrate the United Provinces.

Rivadavia was the wrong man for the job. Nobody better exemplifies the cadre of ideologically driven leaders who guided América to a republican future, despite the conservatism of most people. These men wanted to transform their society and economy according to the advice of British and French experts. Rivadavia opened Buenos Aires to maximum British commercial influence, which flooded in. He showed interest in European immigration—something that would one day characterize Argentina, though few immigrants arrived in the 1820s. In the meantime, Rivadavia opened public land to ranchers and used harsh measures to discipline the gaucho workforce of the pampas, aiming to make them more docile and productive. Rivadavia also promoted public primary education, something very Argentine, and founded the University of Buenos Aires. He also tackled the church, a powerful symbol of the old regime in the eyes of doctrinaire liberals, but never a popular issue among the common people in early independent América. Overall, Rivadavia's program of transformation, like so many in these years, focused on European—especially English and French—models. To impose his program of transformation, this good son of the May Revolution wanted power centralized in Buenos Aires. The rough federalist heirs of Artigas refused to accept Rivadavia's liberal, unifying policies and overthrew him.

In 1828, British mediation created an independent buffer state, the Republic of Uruguay, from what had been the Eastern Shore province. In Paraguay, Bonpland went to visit Artigas, taking him a copy of the new Uruguayan constitution, which the old warrior pressed fervently to his lips. Then Artigas went back to his peaceful rural life. Ten years later, after Francia's death, Artigas was invited to return, a hero, to Montevideo, but he declined ever to leave Paraguay, a country that, it must be said, does seem to grow on its long-term visitors.

Back in the United Provinces, the semblance of a unified national government disappeared totally in the 1830s and 1840s. The federalists ruled even Buenos Aires, in the person of the flamboyant dictator Juan Manuel de Rosas. Rosas drew on the imagery of republicanism and titled himself the "Illustrious Americano." His populist gestures garnered favor with the poor populace of Buenos Aires, while his economic policies kept the ranching elite on board. A rancher and former manufacturer of jerked beef himself, Rosas identified with dominant economic interests. And when all else failed—or perhaps even before—Rosas applied physical violence to his opponents, the much vilified "unitarians," as centralists were called because they favored a unitary, rather than federal, constitution.

San Martin, now living in Belgium, had seen this sort of thing coming. In 1829 he even tried to return to Buenos Aires, arriving off its shore in a European vessel just as tension between federalists and unitarians reached a high point. Like Artigas, San Martín wanted peace and quiet above all. He did not even go ashore in Buenos Aires, but instead landed at Montevideo and stayed there for a few weeks until he became certain that he could not escape involvement in the struggle between federalists and unitarians. San Martín predicted that disorder would lead to dictatorship as vested interests demanded protection of their property, which is exactly what did happen in many young republics. Fearing that he might be made dictator himself, San Martín returned to Belgium and never again set foot in América.

Bolívar's Time Comes to Die

Bolívar's time had not yet come on a chilly Bogotá night in September 1828, when a group of officers tried to assassinate him. Bolívar was with Manuela when the men entered the presidential palace. She had read him to sleep but woke him when she heard the attackers in the hall. Bolívar leaped from a window while Manuela stalled the would-be assassins for a few minutes. He hid under a bridge in the dark, cold water, then made his way to a barracks, where his soldiers protected him.

Things had gone totally awry for the Liberator since his return to Colombia. Bolívar had never lived in Bogotá for long and had stayed away south in Ecuador, Peru, and Bolivia for five years. In his absence, Vice President Santander had gained the upper hand politically. Santander did not share Bolívar's vision of an Andean Federation and rejected Bolívar's constitution. As vice president, Santander had terrible conflicts with Bolívar's old Venezuelan ally, José Antonio Páez, leading Páez to declare Venezuelan independence from Colombia. That was what finally brought Bolívar back from Peru to a lackluster public reception in Bogotá. Bolívar reassumed the presidency of Colombia and dealt directly with the crisis by going to Venezuela himself. Face-to-face with Bolívar, Páez soon accepted reconciliation, but Bolívar spent many months in Venezuela before returning to Bogotá. Perhaps he dreaded his increasing unpopularity and proliferating enemies in Bogotá.

Bolívar's obsession now was a national assembly that could consider his constitution and his Andean Federation project. An assembly met, but Santander's supporters dominated it, and Bolívar got nothing he wanted. At that point, he assumed dictatorial power unconstitutionally. The attempt to assassinate him must be understood in that context. Still, it shook Bolívar deeply. Several men were executed because of it—though not Santander, who faced exile instead. Bolívar pardoned many of those involved. Nothing mattered more to him than public esteem—"his glory," as he put it. He very much wanted to be loved. His great political projects, the culmination of his life's work, crumbled before his eyes in the coming months, and his tuberculosis advanced rapidly, making him look sixty rather than forty-five. Manuela Sáenz cared for him loyally, and Bolívar adored her, but she added some complications to his life as well.

Manuela's unconventional behavior, such as riding around on horseback in men's clothes, infuriated the straitlaced society of Bogotá. Manuela did it very much on purpose, too. She had put aside social conventions when she left her English merchant husband to follow Bolívar. Manuela had scandalized even the much less straitlaced society of Lima when she took up residence with Bolívar in the former viceroy's summer house, while her husband lived not far away. Bolívar preferred to travel without Manuela, but she always followed. A staunch patriot, she was above all a Bolívar loyalist. She had stayed behind in Lima at first when Bolívar returned to Bogotá, and when the Colombian army in Lima soon mutinied, Manuela went personally to change their minds with a pistol and a fistful of gold coins. Once in Bogotá, with President Bolívar and Vice President Santander now sworn enemies, Manuela amused her dinner guests one evening by staging a mock execution of the vice president. Some of Bolívar's officers liked Manuela, but others thought she needlessly discredited Bolívar.

During 1829, rebellions against Bolívar's rule sprouted in various parts of Colombia. Still eager for Venezuelan independence, Páez declared it again. Ecuador also separated from Colombia. Outside of the army, Bolívar had lost all political support in Bogotá. By early 1830, he lacked the physical and emotional stamina to continue as dictator. In May he said goodbye to Manuela in Bogotá and took a boat down the Magdalena River to Cartagena, intending to leave the country, though bound for where, he wasn't sure. In Cartagena, Bolívar received the worst possible news: his most trusted general and chosen successor, the man he counted on above all to redeem his political vision, Antonio José de Sucre, had been murdered at the age of thirty-five, apparently at the hands of Bolívar's enemies.

Poor Sucre. Bolivia's former capital, Chuquisaca, was renamed Sucre because he had declared Bolivian independence. Ecuador's peso was called the sucre in tribute to Sucre's generalship at Pichincha. But his life makes depressing reading because his honesty, competence, and self-sacrifice won him fame but not personal happiness. Betrothed to a woman in Quito, Sucre did not seek to become Bolivia's first president and accepted reluctantly out of loyalty to Bolívar. Two years later, when the Bolivians decided to rule themselves, Sucre survived an assassination attempt and, characteristically, declined to execute the captured assassin, instead setting him free with two hundred pesos. Wounded in the arm trying to put down a subsequent army mutiny, Sucre finally resigned the presidency and went to Quito to get married. Marital bliss eluded him. Almost immediately, Bolívar ordered him away from Quito to counter a Peruvian attempt to reincorporate the port of Guayaquil, which Sucre did brilliantly. Then Bolívar, the reins of power slipping from his fingers, called Sucre to Bogotá to take over his political legacy in Colombia. Sucre had no ambition to be president of Colombia, but that did not save him from Bolívar's enemies. After his death, Sucre's only child mysteriously died at the hands (it was whispered in Quito) of her stepfather, abruptly ending the posterity of this admirable americano.

After learning of Sucre's assassination, Bolívar, now deathly ill, proposed to travel to his hometown, Caracas. But independence-minded Venezuela, in the throes of an anti-Bolivarian reaction, would not receive him. Bolívar got only as far as nearby Santa Marta. The moribund Liberator was despondent, believing that his efforts had been useless, that he had, in his famous phrase, "plowed the sea."[1] He must have felt at home on the sugar plantation where he was invited to stay, just outside of town, and where tuberculosis killed him in December 1830. Bolívar died destitute, having consumed and given away his entire fortune during his two decades of struggle. His baggage did not even include a shirt appropriate for his funeral, and one had to be provided.

Guerrero Becomes President for a Year

Vicente Guerrero, the successor to Morelos, who represented the revolution of the south and the color-equality guarantee of the Plan de Iguala, became president of Mexico in 1829, riding a wave of popular support.

The disputed election of 1828 had been settled, ultimately, by a great riot called the Acordada, a wake-up call that unmistakably signaled the sentiments of the people of Mexico City. The target of the Acordada riot was an exclusive shopping area on the city's central square, the Parián market, where Spanish merchants offered the best in luxury consumer goods imported from Europe. The Plan of Iguala had guaranteed the rights of Mexico's resident españoles europeos, who began life in independent Mexico with the same social and economic privileges they had claimed over the previous three centuries. They strolled through the Parián market like the owners of Mexico, which, in many ways, they still were. The ghosts of Hidalgo and Morelos objected, of course, and their voices sounded in a grassroots village government movement in the south powered by pardos, mestizos, and Indians, many of whom were veterans of the struggle for independence. The Acordada riot, which left the Parián market a smoking ruin, formed part of a countrywide agitation to force all remaining españoles europeos out of the country and take away their property. That agitation boosted Guerrero into the presidential palace just in time to face Fernando VII's one real, if not very formidable, attempt to engineer his own comeback in América.

Spurred by the expropriation and expulsion from Mexico of Spanish citizens, a small fleet of ships unloaded an invasion force of several thousand Spanish soldiers near Tampico in July 1829. Unfortunately for the invaders, the coastal lowlands of Mexico's Gulf shore, like the Pacific lowlands on the other side of the country, had been a hotbed of patriot guerrilla activity during the war of independence. The rural pardo population of the coast, proud americanos, were quick to take up arms against invading europeos, and effective in using them. A Mexican army mobilized to meet the threat within a month, but it hardly seemed necessary. The local patriot resistance was so fierce that the invaders never got beyond their beachhead. President Guerrero received news of the destruction of this last-gasp Spanish invasion while in a theater box watching a play, and he immediately stood and announced the victory to a wave of applause. Just four days earlier, he had abolished slavery. Like Páez, who had become the first president of Venezuela's new republic, Guerrero captained a political movement in which pardo veterans of independence exercised strong influence.

Mexico's conservative establishment was stronger than Venezuela's, however. The expulsion of thousands of europeo merchants from

Mexico, the liberals' hot-button issue of the late 1820s, had divided families and fractured Mexican commerce. Conservative reaction came quickly. Guerrero retired to his home base in the south, and a new government formed in Mexico City. Its figurehead was one of Iturbide's last-minute patriot generals, and its driving force was chief minister Lucas Alamán, who admired Spain, recalled the "good old days" of New Spain, and hated Vicente Guerrero. The tough veterans of the Pacific coast rose up against the conservative government in what became known as the War of the South, a war that the South more or less won. Guerrero's liberal party returned to the presidency. But they would have to govern without Guerrero. In early 1830, the conservative government had Guerrero abducted, enlisting the aid of an Italian ship's captain to invite Guerrero to dinner aboard ship, overpower him, and deliver him into the hands of official executioners, who put him before a firing squad in an obscure location after a fig-leaf trial. Alamán never completely escaped the stigma of complicity in the treacherous assassination.

América was dividing into two political parties in the 1830s and 1840s, usually called simply liberals and conservatives. Liberals generally represented the ideological legacy of the independence movements, as did Guerrero, whereas the conservatives generally represented a reaction to that legacy, as did Alamán. Liberals were, above all, innovators. They wanted a new system of government for new nations. Very often, they were Europhiles—but oriented toward France or England, never toward Spain. Liberals viewed Spanish traditions of close association between church and state as holdovers from Europe's Middle Ages. In some cases, liberals championed the extension of effective citizenship to pardos, mestizos, and Indians. Most of all, however, liberals extended the claim of popular sovereignty, the right to self-rule, to the provincial level, usually demanding a weak central government under a federalist constitution.

Conservatives such as Alamán were on the opposite side of all these issues. Not eager for innovation, they expressed nostalgia for the old system. Alamán made an imprint on Mexican history, not only as a government minister but also, and principally, as a historian. He considered himself a guardian of Spanish heritage and gladly served as the administrator of the estate that had belonged to the famous conquistador Hernán Cortés. At one point in the 1830s, he hid Cortés's bones to keep them safe from potential vandalism by gachupín-hating liberals. Alamán studied the history of the Spanish monarchy and especially admired Fernando and Isabel, the proudly titled "Catholic Monarchs" who had completed the Christian reconquest of Spain in 1492 just as they launched Columbus on his famous voyage. Alamán considered the Catholic Church to be an essential part of the political order in the Spanish tradition. Conservatism naturally attracted Mexico's elite families, who had so many resources and privileges to conserve. But it also attracted poor but pious people who responded to conservative defense of the Church. The Church issue became the conservatives' ticket to national power in Mexico by the mid-1830s.

A Child Becomes Emperor of Brazil

Liberals forced the abdication of Pedro I on 7 April 1831 when, in the wee hours of the morning, elements of his army began to join with a large and unruly crowd of his subjects who demanded personnel changes in his government. Pedro angrily declared that he would do "anything *for* his subjects, but nothing *because of* them," that is, nothing they forced him to do.[2]

The somewhat dissipated Pedro had tired of being a constitutional monarch. Brazil's continuity between colony and empire had put him in control of the strongest state apparatus in early independent América. Yet a string of blunders had made the years since his royal fist metaphorically smashed the Confederation of the Equator unhappy ones for the impulsive monarch. Martyrs such as Friar Caneca had become potent symbols of the opposition and stains on the imperial reputation. The death of Empress Leopoldina was another stain. Leopoldina, bold and bright and adaptable, had made herself well loved in Rio, and she was widely believed to have died because of Pedro's scandalous emotional mistreatment of her. Pedro had made his well-known mistress one of Leopoldina's ladies-in-waiting and had publicly recognized his paternity of their illegitimate daughter, to whom he also granted a title of nobility. He gave two titles of nobility to the mistress herself. The people of Rio emphatically disapproved.

Pedro had no better luck in affairs of state during the 1820s. He had returned to Rio from the southern war zone to attend Leopoldina's funeral, when she died, and he had lost the war partly as a result. To make matters worse, mercenary troops brought from Germany for the war had mutinied in Rio, terrorizing the populace. An 1827 treaty with Britain limiting the slave trade had antagonized powerful interests in a country still driven by plantation agriculture. For various reasons, the Brazilian economy sputtered and inflation spiked. Worst of all, though, in terms of its negative impact on Pedro's popularity, was his ongoing involvement in Portuguese politics. Pedro's father, João VI, had died a few years after returning to Lisbon. Pedro had abdicated his claim to the Portuguese throne in favor of his seven-year-old legitimate daughter, Maria da Glória, but when Pedro's brother Miguel challenged her, Pedro became his daughter's chief advocate. That kept him perpetually embroiled in Portuguese affairs.

Brazilian liberalism gained adherents with each of Pedro's missteps in the 1820s. The liberals' most popular issue was agitation against the Portuguese-born who continued to occupy Brazilian government and military positions. Liberals tended to identify their cause symbolically with the mixed-race native population and to identify their enemies with the specter of Portuguese recolonization of Brazil. And there was Pedro, surrounded by Portuguese-born ministers and each day more immersed in Portuguese affairs, while simultaneously demonstrating incompetence at governing Brazil. Brazilian liberals expressed themselves particularly in the new press that mushroomed in the late 1820s. During the first years of independence, Brazilians were finally getting the level of exposure to new political thinking that Spanish Americans had gotten earlier. The cumulative result of all this was a mass protest in Rio that led Pedro I to abdicate the throne of the Brazilian Empire in favor of his son, the future Pedro II, then only five and a half years old. Once again a Prince Pedro stayed behind in Rio while his father sailed back to Portugal.

Regents wielded the power of the Brazilian monarchy through the 1830s, until the prince came of age. The young prince also had a tutor and personal guardian: none other than José Bonifácio de Andrada. José Bonifácio had spent six years in French exile before being pardoned and returning to Rio before the dramatic events of 7 April 1831. Authoritarian though he might be, and nearly seventy, the arrogant but kindly old minister was as brilliant an intellectual as Brazil possessed. His supervision of Prince Pedro was the beginning of the boy's truly superior education, an education that would make him a bookish ruler entirely unlike Pedro I. As feisty as ever, though, José Bonifácio clashed with the regents, who represented the liberal forces that had overthrown Pedro I, and soon returned to retirement.

The regency was one of the most dramatic periods in Brazilian history. Without eliminating the monarchy, the liberals aimed to subordinate the emperor to the national assembly and generally decentralize power in Brazil. Loosening the bonds of the centralized monarchy, however, gave freer play to the forces of Brazilian regionalism. During the 1830s and 1840s a string of regional revolts rocked Brazil, from the Amazonian north of the country to its southern border with the new Uruguayan republic. Liberals in Pernambuco revolted once again, too. So did those of Bahia, Minas Gerais, and São Paulo. Several breakaway republics briefly formed, or threatened to. In Rio, the liberal reformers learned their lesson and reversed course; a number switched to the conservative side. They even allowed Pedro II to assume power early, in 1840, because they so needed the stabilizing power of the monarchy against ongoing regional rebellions. By 1850, the recentralization of power had succeeded. Pedro II would rule as a constitutional monarch for almost forty more years.

A Generation Passes

The generation that won independence did not govern long after independence arrived. At least, that can be said of the principal leaders. There are some exceptions. José Antonio Páez, who had become one of Venezuela's great landowners, would remain a political mover and shaker until the middle of the century, by which time all the other great leaders of independence had vanished from the scene. He sometimes championed the cause of Venezuela's pardo majority, but his main goal, in most cases, was the triumph of his own family and friends. In that, Páez represents the rude war captains called *caudillos* who emerged from the wars of independence to partially fill the void left by the withdrawal of colonial rule. Caudillos embodied both military and political power. In Venezuela, and throughout much of América, they controlled regions and localities through the 1800s. Sometimes, like Páez, they became presidents of entire nations. More often, presidents had university degrees, as did Doctor Francia, who finally relinquished the presidency of Paraguay in 1840—apparently the only way he ever intended to, by dying.

We should also finish the story of poor Bernardo O'Higgins, who died in 1842 after a long and humiliating exile. O'Higgins's story is especially poignant. He was a reformer who hated aristocracy and sincerely wanted to make Chile a better place, but he offended the country's powerful vested interests and behaved dictatorially. An uprising in Concepción, in Chile's perpetually oppositional south (ironically, O'Higgins's own home ground), overthrew him even before Ayacucho. O'Higgins left Chile and joined Bolívar in Peru, though he saw no military action there. Still persona non grata in

Chile after Bolívar's final victories and withdrawal from Peru, O'Higgins remained the rest of his life in exile, living alternately in Lima and on a rural estate nearby, while Chile became one of the most stable and prosperous countries on the continent. Fortunately for O'Higgins, his memory has been rehabilitated since his death. He now figures as Chile's great hero of independence, overshadowing the clan of Javiera Carrera.

Something similar happened to both Artigas and San Martín, both of whom died in exile and whose bodies were later repatriated. Today, both lie in patriotic shrines on either side of the Río de la Plata. Bolívar's statue presides at several such shrines in Venezuela, Colombia, Ecuador, and Bolivia. His body was eventually returned to Caracas and now lies in Venezuela's national pantheon. The cult of Bolívar has somewhat overshadowed that of other Colombian independence heroes, who at least got to die at home. Antonio Nariño died early, in 1823, under close watch by his rival, Santander, but under his own roof in the Colombian highlands. Santander's turn came in 1840, also at home, after having been president of Colombia in the 1830s. Despite his conflict with Bolívar, Santander is recognized as a founding father of the Colombian republic.

And what of the founding mothers? Few have appeared in this book because few appear in the annals of independence. During those years, women seldom assumed the sort of public role that gets people into history books. Still, there are a few whose names do appear. Policarpa Salavarrieta and Gertrudis Bocanegra, of course, had no subsequent lives to report. There is more to tell about Leona Vicario. Her husband, Andrés Quintana Roo, broke early with Iturbide and became an important political player in the early Mexican republic. Taken prisoner by the same ruthless government that summarily executed Guerrero in 1831, Quintana Roo was fortunate to have Leona keeping his case in the public eye by sparring in the press with Lucas Alamán. Vicario died in 1842.

Then there is Juana Azurduy, who trained the Indian battalion to help Manuel Belgrano fight Spanish rule in what eventually became Bolivia. Juana, her husband, Manuel Ascencio Padilla, and other Bolivian guerrillas fought on after Belgrano retreated, but they gradually lost ground. All four of Juana's children died in the conflict, and so did Manuel Ascencio. The Spanish were so proud to have killed Juana's husband that they displayed his head on a pike until her men recaptured it to give it burial. Eventually, Juana withdrew south to Salta, where she lived under the protection of patriot general Martín Güemes.

After Ayacucho, however, she returned to her beloved Chuquisaca, where Bolívar visited her and awarded her a pension for her patriotic services. Not much attention was paid her after that, nor was the pension paid for many years. Juana Azurduy died alone, ignored, and impoverished at the age of eighty-two.

Mariquita Sánchez also lived to be eighty-two, and her postrevolutionary life happily contrasts with Juana Azurduy's. Mariquita's first husband died in 1819 while returning from a diplomatic mission to the United States. Her second husband was a French diplomat, and she spent the rest of her life as Madame Mendeville. Mariquita's fascination with the world beyond Buenos Aires was symptomatic of her political liberalism. When her old liberal friend Bernardino Rivadavia took the helm of the Buenos Aires revolution in the 1820s, Mariquita helped him institute public education for girls. During the 1830s and 1840s, she lived periodically in Montevideo, where Buenos Aires liberals fled to escape the persecution of the Rosas dictatorship in Buenos Aires. In Montevideo, Mariquita became a sort of "den mother" for young political radicals and Romantic poets in exile. When liberals finally overthrew and replaced Rosas in the 1850s, Mariquita figured prominently in the public ceremonies of the liberal regime. In her sixties, she had become a living symbol of the May 1810 Revolution.

Manuela Sáenz died in Peru. Why she did not accompany Bolívar on his final journey seems a mystery. Eventually driven out of Bogotá by Santander, Manuela left Colombia in 1833, but she could not go back to her native Ecuador at that time because Bolívar's enemies dominated it. So Manuela spent a year in Jamaica and finally took up residence in Paita, a small town on the Peruvian coast, near Ecuador. Manuela's British husband still lived in Lima and still wanted her back, but she refused to go. Nor did she return to Quito, the city of her birth, when the Ecuadorian government finally gave her permission to do so. Instead, she spent the next twenty-five years living quietly in Paita, where she supported herself by making and selling sweets, lace, and embroidery. She maintained a political correspondence with several old Bolivarians, and she named her dogs for Bolívar's enemies, which she thought was a good joke. Manuela received a number of distinguished visitors in Paita, among them Giuseppe Garibaldi, the Italian national hero, who stopped by to meet her as he sailed up the South American coast after fighting for liberal causes in Brazil and Uruguay.

Another of her visitors was not distinguished at all. Simón Rodríguez darkened Manuela's door in Paita around 1840, with his wire-rimmed spectacles pushed up on his forehead and wearing a shirt that appeared to have been chewed by burros. Bolívar's old tutor had spent the last twenty-five years roaming the length of the Andes from Concepción in southern Chile to an Ecuadorian town called Latacunga, setting up house with a string of Indian women, starting candle factories at various locations, writing impassioned defenses of Bolívar's reputation, and everywhere founding primary schools that closed soon after he continued his journey. Now in his seventies, Rodríguez had lasted only a couple of years as Bolivia's first director and inspector general of public instruction back in 1825–26. The radical schoolmaster's attempts to educate boys and girls, rich and poor, whites and Indians in the same classrooms were unacceptable to Bolivia's dominant social groups. Also unacceptable were his notions that all students, even the well-to-do, should learn practical skills such as carpentry and weaving, or that Quechua was preferable to Latin as a second language. Nor did Rodríguez get support from President Sucre, who was desperately trying not to antagonize anyone. In a gesture that is pure Rodríguez, the disgruntled soon-to-be former director and inspector general of public instruction invited Sucre and other distinguished personages of Chuquisaca to a banquet and served them their food in chamber pots (the porcelain repositories of what was then called "night soil"), a token of his esteem. Then he resigned and left Bolivia, via Peru, for a stay in Chile.

While in Chile, Rodríguez met with Andrés Bello, who had accompanied Bolívar on the 1810 mission to London and stayed, never returning to Caracas. By the 1830s, when Rodríguez visited, Bello had entered Chilean diplomatic service and then traveled to Santiago to preside over Chile's national university, becoming América's leading man of letters. Rodríguez's chamber pot story made the academic Bello laugh until he could not catch his breath. He agreed with Rodríguez about the importance of education, but Bello's interest was higher education—the training of an intellectual elite—whereas Rodríguez wanted to transform and empower the common people.

Spanish and Portuguese colonization had steeped América in hierarchy, argued Rodríguez. The caste system, the labor drafts of Indians, and African slavery had been the very worst formational experiences that a society could have. A political revolution, carried out by an ideologically driven minority, had ended colonization, but it had not erased the colonial legacy of servitude and exploitation, with its inevitable correlates ignorance and poverty. Slavery, for example, disappeared only gradually in the 1830s and 1840s from the new republics. (It would linger much longer in Brazil, as well as in Cuba, which remained a Spanish colony.) Until that poisonous legacy was eliminated, the republics created by the political revolution would not be real because they would not truly embody the sovereignty of a free, enlightened people. This mad genius had devised a plan for universal public primary education, which he described urgently and at length to anyone who would listen. He also wrote about it and published his writings at his own expense in dense and almost unreadable tracts that he later saw being used to wrap vegetables at the market. But he always persevered and never prospered materially from his efforts. How could he? To make money from education, he declared, was the lowest thing imaginable.

But public education cost money, and good public education cost a lot. Bolívar had supposedly created an endowment of fifteen million pesos to set up public education in Bolivia, after which, according to these plans, Rodríguez would supposedly follow Bolívar to Colombia to establish a public school system there. None of this got beyond the talking stage, however. Many liberals suggested ambitious schemes of public education, as did even some conservatives, such as Alamán. Generally, they expressed interest in the Lancastrian ("each one teach one") system in which advanced students teach others up to their own level. The Lancastrian system had obvious advantages in countries with few trained teachers, but it encouraged a sort of rote repetition that made Rodríguez fume: that was not what Rousseau had had in mind. In the end, pedagogical theory mattered little, however. What most distinguished primary education in newly independent América was its scarcity. Public primary education constituted a low priority for weak, underresourced governments, perpetually fighting for their survival and staffed almost exclusively by a social elite whose children already enjoyed access to education themselves.

We have no idea what was said when Simón Rodríguez visited Manuela Sáenz at her sandy-floored house in Paita around 1840, except that, without question, they talked about Bolívar. Rodríguez always carried with him the last letter that Bolívar had written him. He refused to recognize, it seems, how much his great pupil had lacked deeply democratic sentiments. A few years later, a French traveler to Lake Titicaca found an old man who he assumed, hearing his fluent French, was a fellow countryman. The old man was living in very humble circumstances with an Indian woman, making candles. It was Rodríguez, of course, who finally died, still a teacher and a reformer, in Peru. Today his remains rest near Bolívar's in the national pantheon of Venezuela. As for Manuela, she outlived her old friend by only a few years, dying in 1856. She ended up in a common grave, today lost. The letters from Bolívar that Manuela had kept in a coffer until the end of her life were burned, apparently, along with the other poor furnishings of her house, to prevent contagion in the diphtheria epidemic that killed her.

Alexander von Humboldt died the same year as Manuela Sáenz. He had written his masterwork, a synthetic overview of natural science called *Cosmos*, but, as an official of the Prussian government, he had become increasingly engrossed in affairs of state. Perhaps that is why the older Humboldt seemed most concerned, when the subject turned to América, with the railroads and telegraph lines that he wanted to see span the continent or with the canal he wanted to see built according to the route he had charted half a century earlier. Europe's expansive energies were creating a new era of global imperialism in the mid-1800s. Britain dominated the international trade of América, or rather, it dominated south of Cuba and Mexico, which gravitated into the commercial orbit of the United States. The French, runners-up in the race for political hegemony in América, began popularizing the new name "Latin America" to stake a claim to cultural affinity with the region—because the French language, like Spanish and Portuguese, descends from Latin.

At the end of his life Humboldt took a dim view, it appears, of Latin American governments that had suffered chronic instability and proved unable to develop the natural resources that Humboldt had enumerated and surveyed in thousands of published pages. Although he maintained his old opposition to slavery, that wasn't enough to make Humboldt withdraw his instinctive approval of U.S. aggression toward Mexico in the 1840s, which paved the way for an expansion of the southern U.S. slave system. Humboldt privately approved of the United States' acquisition of half of Mexico's territorial claims—the means by which the victorious republic of the north compensated itself for the expense and trouble of subjugating its sister republic of the south. He seems to have accepted the U.S. rhetoric of a "Manifest Destiny" for English-speaking people to expand across the continent at the expense of "less competitive races." What had become of the idealistic young man who clambered ashore in Cumaná in 1799? Humboldt's transformation into a curmudgeonly imperialist by the 1840s suggests, at least in part, his disappointment in the outcome of Latin America's struggles for independence. Here Humboldt is no longer a good guide, except as an indicator of ideas common to his age.

He remained, after all, Europe's great expert on América, intensively consulted by explorers, scientists, entrepreneurs, crackpots, and heads of state.

A few weeks before his death, Humboldt posted a notice in several German newspapers asking to receive by mail no further news, inquiries, or requests for his opinion; also, no further unsolicited specimens of anything by parcel post. Being Humboldt, he supplied abundant supporting data. An average of sixteen hundred to two thousand letters and packages had arrived at his house each year in the 1850s, and none of this was junk mail that could be casually discarded unopened. Humboldt's passing was the end of an era. Fortunately for his memory in América, his later imperialist sentiments never became well known.

EPILOGUE: THE LEGACY ENDURES

U PON HEARING OF Humboldt's death in 1859, Mexican president Benito Juárez planned to erect a statue in his honor. Ironically, however, a French intervention in Mexico forced Juárez out of office before he could commission the bronze. The French intervention established an imperial throne in the 1860s and briefly put an Austrian archduke on it. This was one of several notable European interventions in mid-nineteenth-century Latin America. The United States, for its part, expanded its own territory militarily at the expense of Mexico, as we have seen. Meanwhile, the harbors of Latin America bristled with the masts of British, French, and U.S. trading ships, a commercial invasion of major proportions. In view of all this, not a few observers have said, in effect, paraphrasing Gandhi's quip about Western civilization: "Latin American independence? It would be a good idea!"

And not only have hegemonic powers often infringed sovereignties from the outside. The Sovereign People often have been unable to exercise their citizenship at home because of authoritarian governments representing the interests of an entrenched ruling class. It is time for a full assessment of América's independence struggles. For starters, they did not soon result in stable national states with liberal institutions to foment economic development, as occurred in the

United States. That seems to have been Humboldt's disappointment. Such a critique appears shortsighted in light of later experience around the world, but it is understandable and was shared by many in the 1850s, including, apparently, Simón Rodríguez.

Long before the 1850s, Bolívar's tutor was concerned not so much about meddling outsiders as about the failure of independence to transform América socially and economically. A social and economic revolution needed to accompany the political one, and it had not. At midcentury, when Rodríguez made his farewell visit to Manuela Sáenz, he saw around him in the Andean republics very few social and economic transformations of the sort he believed necessary to make liberal republics work.

In Buenos Aires, Mariquita Sánchez de Mendeville took a rosier view. When asked, shortly before her death, to write a memoir of her early life, she described "three chains" that had bound colonial América to Spain: "terror, ignorance, and Catholicism."[1] By terror, she meant a government without popular support that imposed its will through acts of violence such as the spectacularly terrifying execution of Tupac Amaru, pulled apart by four horses, back in the 1780s. She evoked ignorance by recalling the refusal of colonial parents to educate girls for fear that they would correspond secretly with lovers. Finally, there was the religious justification of all this, exemplified by the Inquisition's list of banned books. The May 1810 revolution in Buenos Aires—in which she was, after all, a participant—had broken those three chains, at least in the estimation of Madame Mendeville. Strictly in terms of formal political institutions, a major transformation—a positive one—had indeed occurred.

The two old revolutionaries both had valid points. Social and economic revolutions would still be needed in the twentieth century. A general consensus eventually endorsed that idea. Also undeniably, powerful outsiders would occasionally infringe Latin American sovereignties after independence. A postcolonial or quasi-colonial or neocolonial relationship remained, but direct colonial rule of América had, for the most part, definitively ended. In addition, liberal political structures—including elections, representative legislatures, limited-term presidencies, and guarantees of civil rights—had been established everywhere. Even the Brazilian empire was a strictly constitutional monarchy. Admittedly, some of the gains were illusory: many liberal institutions functioned poorly through the 1800s.

Who could be surprised? Latin America's struggles for independence were not liberal revolutions at the outset. The almost unanimous surge of loyalty expressed toward the "kidnapped" Fernando VII in 1808 and the consistency with which the few republican ideologues had to wear the mask of Fernando thereafter show beyond question that republics lacked majority support in the first years of struggle. Liberal ideology in all its forms spread rapidly in these years as printing presses produced political tracts and news sheets by the hundreds, yet the print revolution encountered inherent limits in societies that were nine-tenths illiterate. The leadership of América's independence movements went republican not because republics had wide popular appeal at home but because republicanism was prestigious internationally. French and English political philosophy had inspired their dissidence (or at least helped them justify it), and the U.S. Constitution provided a much-imitated model. When the time came to establish governments, in the absence of a prince suitable for a constitutional monarchy, most intellectual authors of independence regarded a republic, with an elected president and legislature, as the only option for progressive, modern people. But they were kidding themselves.

Overall, América was not a very liberal place in the wake of independence. Most people seem to have maintained very traditional understandings of the political order. It is worth remembering that in 1822, Mexico and Brazil, the two largest countries, saw waves of popular enthusiasm install emperors who wore crowns. Indian villagers and rural populations, especially, showed strong conservative tendencies, as did the owners of great estates, who everywhere dominated the countryside. Most americanos still organized their lives by social rules that were slow to change. They presumed religious truths to be unchallengeable and social hierarchy to be the natural way of the world.

The new political ideal of equal citizenship, inherent in the republican model, contrasted with the colonial emphasis on hierarchy and authority. Large populations of subjugated Indian "citizens" made these societies different from the young United States, where most Indians and people of color were conveniently excluded from citizenship. Spanish tyranny, argued Bolívar and many others, had deprived the common people of a civic education by forbidding them self-government. The republican model implied a totally new set of political institutions. Constitutions, elections, and legislative assemblies had played no part in the Spanish and Portuguese colonial governance of América—in contrast to the colonial experience of the United States, where charters, elections, and assemblies had been the norm. The U.S. Constitution and the institutions that it created were relatively homegrown. They stemmed from the historical experience of the English colonists. In contrast, the new republican constitutions of América seemed a bit like exotic plants on Colombian or Chilean soil—remote indeed from the historical experience of the people. Learning the new procedures took only a little while, but investing them with awe-inspiring authority took a long time. América's "airy republics" obviously would not work well if divorced from realities on the ground.

In that regard, imperial Brazil offers an instructive comparison and contrast to the early Spanish-speaking republics. In a nutshell, Brazil's more conservative political institutions meshed better with the inequality and exploitation of its colonial legacy. Its constitutional monarchy was more stable, but also more frankly hierarchical, than the Spanish American republics. Consequently, Brazil suffered less from the mismatch between political institutions and traditions that worried Alamán in Mexico. As Mexico lurched from one civil war to another in the mid-1800s, the sprawling archipelago of former Portuguese captaincies held together remarkably well, increasing its export production decade by decade. Imperial Brazil retained and multiplied its titled nobility, and slavery continued to drive the production of Brazilian plantations long after it disappeared from the Spanish-speaking republics.

Cohesive, inclusive nations, the foundation of popular sovereignty and republican government, took a century to build after the declarations of independence resounded through the hemisphere. Identity politics, América for americanos, had made independence possible, but identity politics soon became an obstacle. To be an americano was no distinction once everybody had become one. To be a *mexicano, guatemalteco, colombiano, peruano, boliviano, chileno, paraguayo,* or *argentino* had relatively little meaning in daily life. The new nations lacked much national identity. Who really belonged? The participation of Indians and blacks, while undeniable, remained problematic for the elite. Gradually artists, educators, and politicians would craft serviceable national identities in dialogue with their audiences. Shared experience would congeal in national narratives that eventually featured the idea of racial mixture as the genesis of distinctive ethnicities. Those processes had hardly begun, however, in 1825. Indeed, they would not gain momentum for two generations. Here is a lesson—strongly exemplified in the Latin American experience—that would-be nation builders and state makers around the world should take to heart in the twenty-first century.

Another lesson is this: despite the difficulties of creating inclusive nations and political institutions that truly embody popular sovereignty, nothing else will do in the long run. The sovereignty of the people was neither uniquely an Enlightenment concept nor peculiarly French. No doubt the French version caught on effectively in América because it matched a conviction already in people's minds. After all, the americano juntas of 1810 based their wide appeal squarely on traditional claims to autonomy under the monarchy. América was a separate pillar of the crown. América for americanos—even unwavering monarchists such as San Martín and José Bonifácio responded to that idea. The americano representatives to the Cortes of Cádiz responded to it, too. Hidalgo, Morelos, and Guerrero stood for it; so did Bolívar and Páez and Piar, Belgrano and O'Higgins, Artigas and Azurduy—and so, too, did even Iturbide and Pedro I. Today, it seems clear that the ordinary people of América, men and women, townspeople and country folk, from the frigid mountains and steaming lowlands, artisans and peasants, also responded to notions of popular sovereignty. Self-determination was the most fundamental promise of independence, the promise that could never be taken back.

Seeing this makes the region's subsequent history easier to understand. During the 1800s, liberal institutions often seemed a fiction, especially to outsiders, but one that americanos were curiously determined to maintain. Why did dictatorships that routinely managed electoral outcomes, as was well known, still never neglect to hold those elections? And why might constitutions be frequently violated but never ignored, often removed but always replaced? Why were liberal republican institutions maintained in theory while being abridged in practice? This tenacious insistence on liberal republican institutions in the face of their chronic violation was, in fact, persuasive evidence of their significance. Simply put, elections and constitutions signified the consent of the people. They were the indispensable symbols of popular sovereignty even when they failed to provide its real substance.

The promise of popular sovereignty did not help postwar americanos solve many practical problems of self-governance. Wartime rhetoric in the voice of the Sovereign People had implied a unanimity that never really existed. Unlike wartime rhetoric, practical governance required that the Sovereign People be defined more precisely. Who should be a voting citizen? "Men of virtue, discernment, property, and social distinction," said conservatives, who had in mind themselves, their fathers, and others like them. "Any americano," Morelos would have said had he been alive. Clearly, though, even Morelos would not have suggested that women vote. No longer a simple unifying motif, popular sovereignty had become contested space and a source of conflict.

The great contribution of Latin America's struggle for independence, then, was to establish the sovereignty of the decolonizing world, not as a functioning reality but as an undying aspiration, a basic principle of Western political culture. Postponement became a standard tactic of those who, unable to deny the principle, wished to avoid the consequences of applying it. Thus, in the late 1800s, Pedro II publicly regretted that Brazil needed an emperor and hoped that one day it no longer would. Porfirio Díaz, who ruled Mexico at the time, justified his management of electoral outcomes with similar, possibly sincere, excuses. General Julio Roca, who finally presided over a unified Argentina, was of the same mind, as were authoritarian leaders across Latin America. More democratic systems were desirable, they lamented, but must be postponed. The common people were "not yet ready" for them.

Postponement was the mantra, too, of European imperialists who spoke of "the white man's burden"—the responsibility to train the world's childlike non-European populations, undeniably deserving of self-determination but not yet ready to exercise it. Postponement justified the more limited imperialist adventures of the United States when it seized Puerto Rico and the Philippines from Spain in 1898. Many of those who proposed postponement of real popular sovereignty around 1900 were racists who believed that non-Europeans might never measure up. But if they respected modern Western political values, they could rationalize postponement of popular sovereignty only as a temporary period of well-meaning tutelage. The enshrinement of popular sovereignty in América had made it the first principle of global decolonization by 1945, when that process moved into its sweeping final phase in Africa and Asia.

Today, América stands somewhat ambiguously at the divide between the West and the rest. Americanos are overwhelmingly Western in language, religion, material culture, and political values. Most americanos do not descend purely from Europeans, and their societies have not been shaped exclusively by European traditions, but the strikingly multiracial nations of Latin America rank today among the most durable liberal republics in the world. Making them socially inclusive republics, winning for everyone the full benefits of citizenship, has been an ongoing battle, one that is far from over. Americanos have trod a steep and rocky path in pursuit of liberal ideals. Their struggles for independence constituted a crucial step in the global expansion of Western political values, showing both the revolutionary potential of those values and the challenges they bring when introduced in societies formed by different traditions. The region's constitutional frameworks have been often disrupted but always stubbornly reestablished. Liberalism might have started as an exotic plant in América, but it has sunk deep roots.

NOTES

Prologue

1. Carmen Clemente Travieso, *Mujeres de la independencia: Seis biografías de mujeres venezolanas* (Mexico City: Talleres gráficos de México, 1964), 36–37.

Chapter 1

1. Alexander von Humboldt, *Cartas americanas*, ed. Charles Minguet (Caracas: Biblioteca Ayacucho, 1980), 16.

2. Ibid., 14.

3. Helmut de Terra, *Humboldt: The Life and Times of Alexander von Humboldt, 1769–1859* (New York: Alfred A. Knopf, 1955), 114.

4. Félix de Azara, *Memoria sobre el estado rural del Río de la Plata y otros informes* (Buenos Aires: Editorial Bajel, 1943), 5.

5. Alexander von Humboldt, *The Island of Cuba: A Political Essay*, intro. Luis Martínez-Fernández (Princeton: Markus Wiener Publishers, 2001), 256.

6. Gastón Montiel Villasmil, *La parentela y las relaciones femeninas del Libertador* (Maracaibo: Comisión Ejecutiva del Bicentenario del Libertador, 1985), 34.

7. Salvador de Madariaga, *Bolívar* (Mexico City, Editorial Hermes, 1951), 1:94, 103.

8. Gerard Helferich, *Humboldt's Cosmos: Alexander von Humboldt and the Latin American Journey That Changed the Way We See the World* (New York: Gotham Books, 2004), 262.

9. Terra, *The Life and Times of Alexander von Humboldt*, 196.

10. Octavio Tarquinio de Sousa, *História dos fundadores do Império do Brasil,* vol. 1: *José Bonifácio* (Rio de Janiero: José Olímpio Editora, 1957), 93.

11. Sousa, *História dos fundadores do Império do Brasil,* vol. 9: *Fatos e personagens em tôrno de um regime,* 13.

12. Alexander von Humboldt, *Political Essay on the Kingdom of New Spain,* ed. Mary Maples, trans. John Black (New York: Alfred A. Knopf, 1972), 20.

Chapter 2

1. Karen Racine, *Francisco de Miranda: A Transatlantic Life in the Age of Revolution* (Wilmington, DE: Scholarly Resources, 2003), 163.

2. Ibid., 161.

3. Fernando Assunçao and Wilfredo Pérez, *El jefe de los orientales* (Montevideo: Editorial Próceres, 1982), 212.

4. Octavio Tarquinio de Sousa, *História dos fundadores do Império do Brasil,* vol. 2: *A vida de Pedro I* (Rio de Janiero: José Olímpio Editora, 1957), 13.

5. José Mancisidor, *Hidalgo, Morelos, Guerrero* (Mexico City: Editorial Grijalbo, 1956), 54.

6. Salvador de Madariaga, *Bolívar* (Mexico City, Editorial Hermes, 1951), 1:287.

Chapter 3

1. Matilde Gómez, *La epopeya de la independencia mexicana a través de sus mujeres* (Mexico City: ANHG, 1947), 8.

2. Timothy E. Anna, *Spain and the Loss of America* (Lincoln: University of Nebraska Press, 1983), 68.

3. Thomas Blossom, *Nariño: Hero of Colombian Independence* (Tucson: University of Arizona Press, 1967), 77.

4. Mario Rodríguez, *The Cádiz Experiment in Central America, 1808–1826* (Berkeley: University of California Press, 1978), 67.

5. Rubén Hermesdorf, *Morelos: Hombre fundamental de México* (Mexico City: Editorial Grijalbo, 1958), 93.

6. Ibid., 96. The actual verse reads: "Por un cabo doy dos reales, / Por un sargento, un doblón. / Por mi general Morelos / Doy todo el corazón."

7. Roberto Blanco Moheno, *Historia de dos curas revolucionarios: Hidalgo y Morelos* (Mexico City: Editorial Diana, 1973), 176.

Chapter 4

1. Wilbert H. Timmons, *Morelos: Priest Soldier Statesman of Mexico* (El Paso: Tesas Western College Press, 1963), 77.

2. Rubén Hermesdorf, *Morelos: Hombre fundamental de México* (Mexico City: Editorial Grijalbo, 1958), 111.

3. Salvador de Madariaga, *Bolívar* (Mexico City, Editorial Hermes, 1951), 1:375.

4. Rebecca Earle, *Spain and the Independence of Colombia, 1810–1825* (Exeter: University of Exeter Press, 2000), 53.

5. Walter Rela, *Artigas: Cronología histórica anotada, 1811–1820* (Montevideo: Alfar, 2000), 126

6. *Selected Writings of Bolívar*, ed. Vicente Lecuna and Harold Bierck Jr., trans. Lewis Bertrand (New York: Colonial Press, 1951), 1:105.

Chapter 5

1. Matilde Gómez, *La epopeya de la independencia mexicana a través de sus mujeres* (Mexico City: ANHG, 1947), 22.

2. Theodogre G. Vincent, *The Legacy of Vicente Guerrero, Mexico's First Black Indian President* (Gainesville: University Press of Florida, 2001), 125.

3. Octavio Tarquinio de Sousa, *História dos fundadores do Império do Brasil*, vol. 2: *A vida de Pedro I* (Rio de Janiero: José Olímpio Editora, 1957), 265–66.

4. Mario Rodríguez, *The Cádiz Experiment in Central America, 1808–1826* (Berkeley: University of California Press, 1978), 146.

5. *Selected Writings of Bolívar*, ed. Vicente Lecuna and Harold Bierck Jr., trans. Lewis Bertrand (New York: Colonial Press, 1951), 286.

6. Gerhard Masur, *Simon Bolivar* (Albuquerque: University of New Mexico Press, 1969), 367.

Chapter 6

1. Gerhard Masur, *Simon Bolivar* (Albuquerque: University of New Mexico Press, 1969), 484.

2. Roderick J. Barman, *Brazil: The Forging of a Nation, 1798–1852* (Stanford: Stanford University Press, 1988), 159.

Epilogue

1. María Sáenz Quesada, *Mariquita Sánchez: Vida política y sentimental* (Buenos Aires: Editorial Sudamericana, 1995), 14.

·

GLOSSARY

AMERICANO—in late colonial usage, American-born Spaniard, short for *español americano*.

AUDIENCIA—high court with administrative functions.

CABILDO—city council.

CABILDO ABIERTO—an open meeting of the city council.

CASTE SYSTEM—a social hierarchy based on inherited characteristics.

CREOLE—a translation of Spanish *criollo*, describing people of pure Spanish (or African) descent in América. Synonymous with *americano* in late colonial usage, though unflattering, as in "homegrown." *Criollo* became a badge of pride during the wars of independence.

EUROPEO—European-born Spaniard, short for *español europeo*.

GACHUPÍN (pl. gachupines)—derogatory nickname for europeos, most common in New Spain. The South American equivalent was *chapetón*. These words are used in the text to evoke sentiments of the time.

GAUCHO—cowboy of the Río de la Plata frontier.

JUNTA—a provisional governing committee, formed first in Spain and then in América during the 1808–13 crisis of the monarchy.

LIBERALS—people who espoused liberties such as free trade, freedom of speech, and limited, representative government. Liberals usually wanted a republic, but some accepted the idea of constitutional monarchy.

ROYALIST—loyal partisan of Spain against the cause of América.

MESTIZO—person of mixed (usually European/indigenous) descent.

PARDO—person of mixed (usually European/African) descent.

REGENCY—government that rules in the name of a monarch. Regencies are established when the monarch is disabled or a minor or unable to rule for whatever reason.

REGENT—person who exercises the power of the regency.

TRIBUTE—colonial tax on indigenous people.

VICEROY—ruler of a viceroyalty, representing royal authority.

VICEROYALTIES—the major subdivisions of colonial América.

SOURCES AND READINGS

THE TERM "LATIN AMERICA" generally includes only countries colonized by Spain or Portugal. This book therefore does not cover Haiti, Belize, or Suriname, for example, because they were colonized by France, Britain, and Holland, respectively. The independence of the Dominican Republic, Cuba, El Salvador, Honduras, Nicaragua, Costa Rica, and Panama occurred in a later period, between 1840 and 1903. For a synthetic overview of the region's history, see John Charles Chasteen, *Born in Blood and Fire: A Concise History of Latin America* (New York: Norton, 2006). On Cuban independence, see Ada Ferrer, *Insurgent Cuba: Race, Nation, and Revolution, 1868–1898* (Chapel Hill: University of North Carolina Press, 1999).

On historia patria, see Nikita Harwich Vallenilla, "La historia patria," in François-Xavier Guerra, ed., *Modernidad e independencias: ensayos sobre las revoluciones hispánicas* (Madrid: Editorial MAPFRE, 1992).

Standard accounts of the 1808–1826 period in English include John Lynch, *The Spanish American Revolutions, 1808–1826* (New York: W. W. Norton, 1986); Jay Kinsbruner, *Independence in Spanish America: Civil Wars, Revolutions, and Underdevelopment* (Albuquerque: University of New Mexico Press, 2000); Richard Graham, *Independence in Latin America: A Comparative Approach*, 2nd ed. (New York: McGraw-Hill, 1994); and Leslie Bethell, ed., *The Independence of Latin America* (Cambridge: Cambridge University Press, 1987).

I have been profoundly influenced by the work of John Lynch and Timothy Anna (see titles below); Jaime E. Rodríguez O., *The Independence of Spanish America* (Cambridge: Cambridge University Press, 1998); and the work of Guerra: see, in addition to the work previously cited, his edited collection

Revoluciones hispánicas: Independencias americanas y liberalismo español (Madrid: Editorial Complutense, 1995); and, edited with A. Annino and L. Castro Leiva, *De los imperios a las naciones: Iberoamérica* (Zaragoza: IberCaja, 1994).

The most recent trends in Latin American historiography suggest that the common people embraced the idea of popular sovereignty strongly during the wars of independence and its aftermath. See Sarah C. Chambers, *From Subjects to Citizens: Honor, Gender, and Politics in Arequipa, Peru, 1780–1854* (University Park: Pennsylvania State University Press, 1999); James E. Sanders, *Contentious Republicans: Popular Politics, Race, and Class in Nineteenth-Century Colombia* (Durham, NC: Duke University Press, 2004); Peter F. Guardino, *The Time of Liberty: Popular Political Culture in Oaxaca, 1750–1850* (Durham, NC: Duke University Press, 2005). See also Jeremy Adelman, *Sovereignty and Revolution in the Iberian Atlantic* (Princeton, NJ: Princeton University Press, 2006).

Benedict Anderson's "Creole Pioneers" chapter in *Imagined Communities: Reflections on the Origin and Spread of Nationalism*, 2nd ed. (London: Verso, 1991) is critiqued by François-Xavier Guerra in "Forms of Communication, Political Spaces, and Cultural Identities in the Creation of Spanish American Nations," in Sara Castro-Klarén and John Charles Chasteen, eds., *Beyond Imagined Communities: Reading and Writing the Nation in Nineteenth-Century Latin America* (Washington, DC: Woodrow Wilson Center Press, 2003).

The following bibliographical essay, organized by chapter and section, emphasizes readings in English but provides titles in Spanish or Portuguese when necessary.

Chapter 1

Humboldt and Bonpland Discover America

On Humboldt, I read Gerard Helferich, *Humboldt's Cosmos: Alexander von Humboldt and the Latin American Journey That Changed the Way We See the World* (New York: Gotham Books, 2004); Douglas Botting, *Humboldt and the Cosmos* (New York: Harper and Row, 1973); Helmut de Terra, *The Life and Times of Alexander von Humboldt, 1769–1859* (New York: Alfred Knopf, 1955). Humboldt was "a guy who liked guys" in that "intense and exclusive male friendships" were, unquestionably, a marked feature of his emotional life, in which women played a minor part (Botting, 32). For background, see George L. Mosse, *The Image of Man: The Creation of Modern Masculinity* (Oxford: Oxford University Press, 1996).

Consider a Continent of Frontiers

See Alistair Hennessy, *The Frontier in Latin American History* (Albuquerque: University of New Mexico Press, 1978); David J. Weber and Jane M. Rausch, eds., *Where Cultures Meet: Frontiers in Latin American History* (Wilmington, DE: Scholarly Resources, 1994); and, more specifically on the Río de la Plata frontier, Richard W. Slatta, *Gauchos and the Vanishing Frontier* (Lincoln: University of Nebraska Press, 1983).

The standard biography of Artigas in English is John Street, *Artigas and the Emancipation of Uruguay* (Cambridge: Cambridge University Press, 1959). His early life is better discussed in Nelson Caula, *Artigas ñemoñaré: La vida privada de José G. Artigas* (Montevideo: Rosebud Editions, 2000). Felix de Azara's full 1801 report is in *Memoria sobre el estado rural del Río de la Plata y otros informes* (Buenos Aires: Editorial Bajel, 1943).

Humboldt's Adventure Continues

See Humboldt's *The Island of Cuba: A Political Essay*, intro. Luis Martínez-Fernández (Princeton: Markus Wiener Publishers, 2001); also Anthony McFarlane, *Colombia Before Independence: Economy, Society, and Politics Under Bourbon Rule* (Cambridge: Cambridge University Press, 1993). For an overview of plantation slavery in colonial América, see Philip D. Curtin, *The Rise and Fall of the Plantation Complex: Essays in Atlantic History* (Cambridge: Cambridge University Press, 1998).

Enter Simon Bolívar

The standard Bolívar biography in English has long been Gerhard Masur, *Simon Bolivar* (Albuquerque: University of New Mexico Press, 1969), to which must now be added David Bushnell, *Simón Bolívar: Liberation and Disappointment* (New York: Pearson Longman, 2004); John Lynch, *Simón Bolívar: A Life* (New Haven, CT: Yale University Press, 2006); and Richard W. Slatta and Jane Lucas De Grummond, *Simón Bolívar's Quest for Glory* (College Station: Texas A & M University Press, 2003). A translation of the protest of the City Council of Caracas is available in John Lynch, ed., *Latin American Revolutions, 1808–1826: Old and New World Origins* (Norman: University of Oklahoma Press, 1994).

Enter Father Hidalgo

See Hugh M. Hamill Jr., *The Hidalgo Revolt: Prelude to Mexican Independence* (Westport, CT: Greenwood Press, 1981).

Humboldt Inspects Peru and New Spain

On the mining economy of Peru and New Spain, see Enrique Tandeter, *Coercion and Market: Silver Mining in Colonial Potosí, 1692–1826* (Albuquerque: University of New Mexico Press, 1993) and Edith Boorstein Couturier, *The Silver King: The Remarkable Life of the Count of Regla in Colonial Mexico*

(Albuquerque: University of New Mexico Press, 2003). On Tupac Amaru, see Ward Stavig, *The World of Túpac Amaru: Conflict, Community, and Identity in Colonial Peru* (Lincoln: University of Nebraska Press, 1999).

Considering Liberty and Tyranny

On the (small) role played by U.S. diplomacy in the independence of América, see Arthur Preston Whitaker, *The United States and the Independence of Latin America, 1800–1830* (New York: Norton, 1964). On Simón Rodríguez, about whom little has been written in English, see Alfonso Rumazo González, *Simón Rodríguez, maestro de América: Biografía* (Caracas: Gráficas Armitano, 1976).

José Bonifácio Yearns for Brazil

On Brazil in the period, see Kenneth Maxwell, *Conflicts and Conspiracies: Brazil and Portugal, 1750–1808* (New York: Routledge, 2004). In recounting José Bonifácio's life I have relied substantially on Octavio Tarquinio de Sousa, *História dos fundadores do Império do Brasil*, vol. 1: *José Bonifácio* (Rio de Janiero: José Olímpio Editora, 1957); in English, see Emilia Viotti da Costa, *The Brazilian Empire: Myths and Histories* (Chapel Hill: University of North Carolina Press, 2000).

Humboldt's Famous Travelogue Appears

Humboldt's *Personal Narrative*, trans. Helen Maria Williams (London: Longman, 1818) was quickly translated into English, as was his *Political Essay on the Kingdom of New Spain*, ed. Mary Maples, trans. John Black (New York: Alfred A. Knopf, 1972).

Chapter 2

Miranda Invades América

On Miranda's biography see Karen Racine, *Francisco de Miranda: A Transatlantic Life in the Age of Revolution* (Wilmington, DE: Scholarly Resources, 2003). See also Pablo Viscardo y Guzmán, *Letter to the Spanish Americans*, intro. David Brading (Providence, RI: The John Carter Brown Library, 2002).

British Invasions in the Río de la Plata Also Fail

A standard history that covers this period accessibly is James R Scobie, *Argentina: A City and a Nation* (New York: Oxford University Press, 1971). For biographical detail, see María Sáenz Quesada, *Mariquita Sánchez: Vida política y sentimental* (Buenos Aires: Editorial Sudamericana, 1995). For context on Sáenz's challenge to patriarchal power, see Jeffrey M. Shumway, *The Case of the Ugly Suitor and Other Histories of Love, Gender, and Nation in Buenos Aires, 1776–1870* (Lincoln: University of Nebraska Press, 2005). A number of works explore the creation of colonial militias, see Christon I. Archer, *The Army in Bourbon Mexico, 1760–1810* (Albuquerque: University of New Mexico Press, 1977); and, specifically on Argentina, Gabriel Di Meglio, "Os habéis hecho temibles: La milicia de la ciudad de Buenos Aires y la política entre las invasiones inglesas y el fin del proceso revolucionario, 1806–1820," *Tiempos de América* 13 (2006): 151–166.

Prince Regent João Sails for Brazil

See Roderick Barman, *Brazil: The Forging of a Nation, 1798–1852* (Stanford: Stanford University Press, 1988). There is a more specific recent work by Kirsten Schultz, *Tropical Versailles: Empire, Monarchy, and the Portuguese Royal Court in Rio de Janeiro, 1808–1821* (New York: Routledge, 2001).

Napoleon Invades Spain, Too

See Timothy E. Anna, *Spain and the Loss of America* (Lincoln: University of Nebraska Press, 1983); in Spanish, Ramón Menéndez Pidal, *Historia de España, Vol. XXVI La España de Fernando VII* (Madrid: Espasa-Clape, S.A., 1968). For the life of San Martín I have relied on Patricia Pasquali's extremely thorough and judicious *San Martín: La fuerza de la misión y de la gloria* (Buenos Aires: Editorial Planeta Argentina, 1999).

Americanos Begin to React

Mier's memoir of exile has recently been translated: *The Memoirs of Fray Servando Teresa de Mier*, ed. Susana Rotker, trans. Helen Lane (New York: Oxford University Press, 1998). Also, Genaro García, *Leona Vicario, heroína insurgente* (Mexico City: Editorial Inovación, 1979).

Meet Manuela

On Peru and the Andes, see Timothy Anna, *The Fall of the Royal Government in Peru* (Lincoln: University of Nebraska Press, 1979). On Sáenz, see Alfonso Rumazo González, *Manuela Sáenz: La libertadora del Libertador* (Bogotá: Ediciones Mundial, 1944), and Pamela S. Murray, *For Glory and Bolívar: The Remarkable Life of Manuela Sáenz* (Austin: University of Texas Press, 2008).

Wearing the Mask of Fernando

"The mask of Fernando" is a phrase of Bernardo Monteagudo's. Madariaga's expansive *Bolívar*, 2 vols. (Mexico City, Editorial Hermes, 1951), while it must be read with care, provides a level of detail that other biographies don't.

Buenos Aires Has a Revolution

On the trade issue, see John Robert Fisher, *Commercial Relations Between Spain and Spanish America in the Era of Free Trade, 1778–1796* (Liverpool: Centre for Latin-American Studies, University of Liverpool, 1985), followed by his *Trade, War and Revolution: Exports from Spain to Spanish America, 1797–1820* (Liverpool: Institute of Latin American Studies, University of Liverpool, 1992).

See Manuel Moreno, *Vida y memorias de Mariano Moreno* (Buenos Aires: Editorial Universitaria de Buenos Aires, 1968); and Eduardo O. Dürnhöfer, *Mariano Moreno* (Buenos Aires: Editorial Dunken, 2000).

New Granada Gets Juntas Galore

See Rebecca A. Earle, *Spain and the Independence of Colombia, 1810–1825* (Exeter: University of Exeter Press, 2000). The only biography of Nariño available in English is Thomas Blossom, *Nariño: Hero of Colombian Independence* (Tucson: University of Arizona Press, 1967).

Chile Gets a Junta, Too

See Simon Collier, *Ideas and Politics of Chilean Independence, 1808–1833* (Cambridge: Cambridge University Press, 1967). On O'Higgins, see Jay Kinsbruner, *Bernardo O'Higgins* (New York: Twayne Publishers, 1968).

Chapter 3

A Multitude Rampages Through New Spain

For a more analytical approach, see Brian R. Hamnett, *Roots of Insurgency: Mexican Regions, 1750–1824* (Cambridge: Cambridge University Press, 1986); John Tutino, *From Insurrection to Revolution in Mexico: Social Bases of Agrarian Violence, 1750–1940* (Princeton: Princeton University Press, 1986); and Eric Van Young, *The Other Rebellion: Popular Violence, Ideology, and the Mexican Struggle for Independence* (Stanford, CA: Stanford University Press, 2001). On Hidalgo, see (in addition to sources already mentioned) Roberto Blanco Moheno, *Historia de dos curas revolucionarios: Hidalgo y Morelos* (Mexico City: Editorial Diana, 1973). Hidalgo's modest publication is available in facsimile:

El despertador americano: Primer periódico insurgente (Mexico City: Instituto Nacional de Antropología e Historia, 1964).

The Battle for Upper Peru Begins

The *republiquetas* are described by John Lynch, *Caudillos in Spanish America, 1800–1850* (Oxford: Clarendon Press, 1992). On Azurduy and Padilla, see Pacho O'Donnel, *Juana Azurduy* (Buenos Aires: Editorial Planeta, 1994).

Portuguese Intervention Brings Further Complications

See Street, *Artigas,* and César da Silva, *D. Carlota Joaquina, Chronica episódica* (Lisbon: Torres e Cia, n.d.); and Roberto Etchepareborda, *Política luso-rioplatense, 1810–1812: Fin de las pretensiones de la Infanta Carlota Joaquina a la regencia del Río de la Plata y primera invasión portuguesa a la Banda Oriental* (Buenos Aires: H. Consejo Deliberante, 1961).

On Rio in the period, Mary C. Karasch, *Slave Life in Rio de Janeiro, 1808–1850* (Princeton: Princeton University Press, 1987).

Hidalgo and Allende Meet Their Maker

See Hamill, *The Hidalgo Revolt,* for details on the interrogations, which have been quite glossed over here.

Nariño Becomes President of Cundinamarca

Benedict Anderson's *Imagined Communities* can be credited for awakening new interest in the role that print culture has played in nation building. See Fernando Unzueta, "Periódicos y formación nacional: Bolivia en sus primeros años," *Latin American Research Review* 35.2 (2000): 35–72. Also, Pedro Grases, *Libros y libertad* (Caracas: Ediciones de la Presidencia de la República, 1974).

Artigas Leads an Exodus

A detailed list of the people, free and enslaved, along with their horses, carts, and cattle, has been published: *Exodo del pueblo oriental: Padrón de las familias que acompañaron al Gral. José Artigas en 1811* (Montevideo: Museo Histórico Nacional, 1968).

Enter Morelos

In English, see Wilbert H. Timmons, *Morelos: Priest Soldier Statesman of Mexico* (El Paso: Texas Western College Press, 1963). I have relied mostly on Rubén Hermesdorf, *Morelos: Hombre fundamental de México* (Mexico City: Editorial Grijalbo, 1958). The role of clergy is a special focus of Van Young's *The Other Rebellion.*

For background on the social role of the church, see Martin Austin Nesvig, ed., *Local Religion in Colonial Mexico* (Albuquerque: University of New Mexico, 2006).

The Cortes of Cádiz Writes a Constitution

See Mario Rodríguez, *The Cádiz Experiment in Central America, 1808–1826* (Berkeley: University of California Press, 1978); as well as Anna, *Spain and the Loss of America*.

Chapter 4

The Venezuelan Republic Crumbles

The basic facts about the "capture" of Miranda are not in dispute, but biographers of Bolívar tend to gloss them over. Madariaga's very detailed *Bolívar* is an exception. Madariaga was a Spaniard who thought that Bolívar was excessively glorified by patriotic historians.

Rational Gentlemen Take Over Buenos Aires

The importance of Masonic-style lodges in the independence of América has been more noted than studied. Secret societies, by their nature, leave no documentation of their activities.

Bolívar Declares "War to the Death"

Madariaga, *Bolívar*, shows beyond question that Bolívar's initiative was just that, an initiative intended to reframe the terms of conflict.

Vicario Goes On Trial

The secret Mexico City organization, the Guadalupes, has been well studied by Virginia Guedea, "La sociedad secreta de los Guadalupes: Una nueva forma de organización política," *Siglo XIX: Revista* 11 (1992): 28–45.

Azurduy Creates a "Loyal Battalion"

The role of indigenous people in the wars of independence is an important matter of interpretation. Van Young, *The Other Rebellion*, shows their role in Mexico to have been large in terms of numbers but often short-term, focused close to home, and attendant more on local conflicts than political ideologies. Overall, indigenous people preferred to avoid involvement in the wars. Andean Indians were reputed to have a loyalist preference, yet Pumacahua's

Rebellion, chronicled later in this chapter, shows that the right leader could gather enormous indigenous armies for the cause of América.

Bolívar Meets the Llaneros

In contrast to indigenous people, pardos were everywhere overrepresented among patriot ranks. To see the place of americano independence struggles in the larger history of América's African-descended people, see George Reid Andrews, *Afro-Latin America, 1800–2000* (New York: Oxford University Press, 2004). In addition, his *The Afro-Argentines of Buenos Aires, 1800–1900* (Madison: University of Wisconsin Press, 1980) gives particular attention to the black and pardo troops mobilized by Buenos Aires. The background of this mobilization lies in colonial pardo militias such as those that the city council of Caracas criticized in 1795. See Ben Vinson III, *Bearing Arms for his Majesty: The Free-Colored Militia in Colonial Mexico* (Stanford, CA: Stanford University Press, 2001).

San Martín Hatches a Plan

Güemes gets only cursory treatment in this section, but he is among the most warmly remembered independence heroes in Argentina, particularly in the northwest. See Luis Oscar Colmenares, *Martín Güemes: El héroe mártir* (Buenos Aires: Ediciones Ciudad Argentina, 1998) and, less hagiographically, Roger M. Haigh, *Martín Güemes: Tyrant or Tool? A Study of the Sources of Power of an Argentine Caudillo* (Fort Worth, TX: Christian University Press, 1968).

Abascal Snuffs Out Pumacahua's Rebellion

Independence-era Peru has attracted few historians. See Charles F. Walker, *Smoldering Ashes: Cuzco and the Creation of Republican Peru, 1780–1840* (Durham, NC: Duke University Press, 1999). For the larger Peruvian context, see Anna's *Fall of the Royal Government*. Pumacahua's interrogation and execution are chronicled in Horacio Villanueva Urteaga, *Conspiraciones y rebeliones en el siglo XIX: La revolución del Cuzco de 1814* (Lima: Comisión Nacional del Sesquicentenario de la Independencia del Perú, 1971).

Artigas Builds a Federal League

In Argentine history, which has generally been written from the perspective of Buenos Aires, Artigas appears as a spoiler. An exception is Eduardo Azcuy Ameghino, *Artigas en la historia argentina* (Buenos Aires: Ediciones Corregidor, 1986). Independence-era federalism carried over strongly into the postcolonial period, see Miron Burgin, *The Economic Aspects of Argentine Federalism, 1820–1852* (Cambridge, MA: Harvard University Press, 1946). In Mexico and

Colombia, federalism became synonymous with liberalism; see Helen Delpar, *Red Against Blue: The Liberal Party in Colombian Politics, 1863–1899* (University: University of Alabama Press, 1981); Charles A. Hale, *Mexican Liberalism in the Age of Mora, 1821–1853* (New Haven, CT: Yale University Press, 1968).

Bolívar Writes His Jamaica Letter

Bolívar's production of letters was truly prodigious. A collection of the most important ones is available in English: *Selected Writings of Bolívar*, ed. Vicente Lecuna and Harold Bierck Jr., trans. Lewis Bertrand, 2 vols. (New York: Colonial Press, 1951).

João VI Creates a United Kingdom

In addition to sources already mentioned (especially Barman, *Brazil*), see Luiz Edmundo, *A côrte de D. João no Rio de Janeiro* (Rio de Janeiro: Conquista, 1957) and Luiz Norton, *A côrte de Portugal no Brasil: Notas, documentos diplomáticos, e cartas da imperatriz Leopoldina* (Lisbon: Empresa Nacional de Publicidade, n.d.).

Chapter 5

San Martín Begins to Turn the Tide

Americano monarchists such as San Martín and Belgrano shared with republicans a commitment to constitutional government. Britain, a limited monarchy in which the king "reigned but did not rule," was a much admired political model. If one considers the liberal-monarchical Cádiz constitution, as well as postcolonial monarchist experiments in Mexico and especially Brazil, monarchists in the cause of América seem less odd.

Brazil Catches the Republican Contagion

For Andrada's letter, see Barman, *Brazil*. For a complete narrative of events in Recife, see Muniz Tavares, *História da revolução de Pernambuco de 1817* (Recife: Casa Civil de Pernambuco, 1969).

Bolívar's Big Comeback

Piar is a pivotal and still somewhat mysterious figure. There is, however, a well-documented biography: Asdrúbal González, *Manuel Piar* (Caracas: Vadell Hermanos, 1979).

On Isabel Gómez, see Carmen Clemente Travieso, *Mujeres de la indepen-dencia (Seis biografías de mujeres venezolanas)* (México: Talleres Gráficos de México, 1964). On Páez, there is the old but readable R. B. Cunninghame Graham, *José Antonio Páez* (Philadelphia: Macrae Smith Co., 1929), and Tómas Polanco Alcántara, *José Antonio Páez, fundador de la República* (Caracas: Ediciones GE, 2000).

Policarpa and Gertrudis

Their executions took place on 14 November and 10 October 1817, respec-tively. The lives of ordinary women patriots were relatively undocumented, even when they became martyrs. There are few biographies. See Travieso, *Mujeres de la independencia;* Matilde Gómez, *La epopeya de la Independencia mexicana a través de sus mujeres* (Mexico City: ANHG, 1947); and Vicente Grez, *Las mujeres de la independencia* (Santiago: Editora Zig-Zag, 1966). Yet the inspirational importance of their lives has been large. Policarpa Salavar-rieta is the subject of at least one novel, e.g., Enriqueta Montoya de Unaña, *La criolla: Policarpa Salavarrieta* (Bogotá: Instituto Colombiano de Cultura, 1972), and Gertudis Bocanegra, of a feature-length motion picture.

Enter Guerrero

See Theodore G. Vincent, *The Legacy of Vicente Guerrero, Mexico's First Black Indian President* (Gainesville: University Press of Florida, 2001).

Bolívar Wins at Boyacá Bridge

An English translation of "Address Delivered at the Inauguration of the Second National Congress of Venezuela" can be found in *Selected Writings of Bolívar.*

The Portuguese Again Invade the Eastern Shore

On Artigas's complex relationship with Paraguay, see Ana Ribeiro, *El caudillo y el dictador* (Buenos Aires: Planeta, 2003).

San Martín Sails for Peru

See Pasquali, *San Martín,* for specific data on the invasion force.

Iturbide and Guerrero Agree on Three Guarantees

The negotiation of the third guarantee is covered in Vincent, *The Legacy of Vicente Guerrero.* On the Plan of Iguala, see also Timothy E. Anna, *The Fall of the Royal Government of Mexico City* (Lincoln: University of Nebraska Press, 1978).

João VI Returns to Portugal

On the rise of Prince Pedro, in addition to Souza, *A vida de Pedro I*, see Neill Macaulay, *Dom Pedro: The Struggle for Liberty in Brazil and Portugal, 1798–1834* (Durham, NC: Duke University Press, 1986).

Central America Declares Independence, Too

In addition to Rodríguez, *The Cádiz Experiment*, see Frankin D. Parker, *Cecilio del Valle and the Establishment of the Central American Confederation* (Tegucigalpa: Publications of the University of Honduras, 1954).

Iturbide Proposes a Mexican Empire

On Iturbide's career, see Timothy E. Anna, *The Mexican Empire of Iturbide* (Lincoln: University of Nebraska Press, 1990).

Bolívar and San Martín Meet at Guayaquil

Masur, *Simon Bolivar*, and Madariaga, *Bolívar*, both thoughtfully examine the evidence concerning what was said at the famous meeting.

See also Eduardo L. Colombres, *La entrevista de Guayaquil: Hacia su esclarecimiento* (Buenos Aires: Editorial Universitaria de Buenos Aires, 1972). On the relationship between Sáenz and Bolívar, see Pamela S. Murray, "Of Love and Politics: Reassessing Manuela Sáenz and Simón Bolívar, 1822-1830," *History Compass* 5 (2007), 227–50.

Mexico Becomes a Republic

Richard A. Warren, *Vagrants and Citizens: Politics and the Masses in Mexico City from Colony to Republic* (Wilmington: SR Books, 2001).

Brazilians Fight a Miniature War of Independence

Brazil's top-down independence process has always gotten much less historical attention than Spanish America's long and torturous struggle, because it is both less complex and less patriotically inspiring. Barman, *Brazil*, is the best starting place in English. For a regional close-up, see Hendrik Kraay, *Race, State, and Armed Forces in Independence-Era Brazil: Bahia, 1790s–1840s* (Stanford: Stanford University Press, 2001). In addition, one of the most important early studies was originally written in English: Robert Southey, *History of Brazil* (London: Longman, Hurst, Rees, Orme, and Brown, 1817–22). Finally, Oliveira Lima, *O império brasileiro (1821–1889)* (São Paulo: Editora da Universidade de São Paulo, 1989). There is no good biography of Frei Caneca in any language, but his writings are collected in Evaldo Cabral de Mello, *Frei Joaquim do Amor Divino Caneca* (São Paulo: Editora 34, 2001).

Chapter 6

My explanatory emphasis on Spain's counter-productive reconquest is not original. Timothy Anna makes the argument in many of the books already cited. Rebecca Earle's *Spain and the Independence of Colombia* got me thinking about how "the cause of América" became defined as such in people's minds, despite realities that put americanos on both sides of the conflict. For postcolonial Latin America as a whole, I emphasize low legitimacy, weak states, and economic lassitude, following Tulio Halperín Donghi, *The Contemporary History of Latin America* (Durham, NC: Duke University Press, 1993). Lynch, *Caudillos in Spanish America*, describes the political transition from wars of independence to militarized republics.

The English-language literature on postcolonial Mexico is the most abundant for any country, thanks especially to Jaime E. Rodríguez O. See his collection *Mexico in the Age of Democratic Revolutions, 1750–1850* (Boulder, CO: Lynne Rienner, 1994) and *The Divine Charter: Constitutionalism and Liberalism in Nine-teenth-Century Mexico* (Lanham, MD: Rowman and Littlefield, 2005). In addition, see Harold Dana Sims, *The Expulsion of Mexico's Spaniards, 1821–1836* (Pittsburgh: University of Pittsburgh Press, 1990), then Michael P. Costeloe, *The Central Republic in Mexico, 1835–1846: Hombres de Bien in the Age of Santa Anna* (Cambridge: Cambridge University Press, 1993). See also Will Fowler, *Mexico in the Age of Proposals, 1821–1853* (Westport, CT: Greenwood Press, 1998).

On Argentina, see Mark D. Szuchman, *Order, Family, and Community in Buenos Aires, 1810–1860* (Stanford: Stanford University Press, 1988); Hilda Sabato, *The Many and the Few: Political Participation in Republican Buenos Aires* (Stanford: Stanford University Press, 2001), and Ariel de la Fuente, *Children of Facundo: Caudillo and Gaucho Insurgency During the Argentine State-Formation Process (La Rioja, 1853–1870)* (Durham, NC: Duke University Press, 2000).

On Brazil, Andrew J. Kirkendall, *Class Mates: Male Student Culture and the Making of a Political Class in Nineteenth-Century Brazil* (Lincoln: University of Nebraska Press, 2002); Judy Bieber, *Power, Patronage, and Political Violence: State Building on a Brazilian Frontier, 1822–1889* (Lincoln: University of Nebraska Press, 1999); Jeffrey D. Needell, *The Party of Order: The Conservatives, the State, and Slavery in the Brazilian Monarchy, 1831–1871* (Stanford, CA: Stanford University Press, 2006); and Lilia Moritz Schwarcz, *The Emperor's Beard: Dom Pedro II and the Tropical Monarchy of Brazil*, trans. John Gledson (New York: Hill and Wang, 2004).

On the United States and postcolonial Latin America, see Michael H. Hunt, *Ideology and U.S. Foreign Policy* (New Haven, CT: Yale University Press, 1987); Lars Schoultz, *Beneath the United States: A History of U.S. Policy Toward Latin America* (Cambridge: Harvard University Press, 1998).

INDEX

Note: Page numbers in *italics* indicate maps and photographs.

CPSIA information can be obtained at www.ICGtesting.com
Printed in the USA
LVOW05s1211281114

415995LV00004B/48/P